Strange Boat

Mike Scott & The Waterboys

Ian Abrahams

Strange Boat

MIKE SCOTT & THE WATERBOYS

IAN ABRAHAMS

First published in 2007
by SAF Publishing
First edition.

SAF Publishing Ltd.
149 Wakeman Road, London.
NW10 5BH
ENGLAND

email: info@safpublishing.co.uk
www.safpublishing.co.uk

ISBN 978-0-946719-92-1

A CIP catalogue record for this book is available from the British Library.

Printed in England by the Cromwell Press, Trowbridge, Wiltshire.

This book is in memory of my 'Grampie'

Garnet Harris

1910—1996

'It's alright, Boy'.

CONTENTS

ACKNOWLEDGEMENTS

I must thank the following people who gave generously of their time and memories in support of this project, particularly Colin Blakey, Fran Breen, Lu Edmonds, Roddy Lorimer, Dave Robinson and Anthony Thistlethwaite who all very kindly agreed to interviews and were patient and very kind contributors. Thank you to Michael Johnson for permission to quote from his blog on Mike Scott and Another Pretty Face in the studio. And thanks to Ollie Jennings at Saw Doctors' Headquarters for interview arranging and for my place on the Saw Doctors' Guest List on more than one occasion—nice one!

From the Waterboys' on-line fandom, I greatly appreciated the help given by, amongst others, Jamie Davidson, Derek Hall, Alwies Meuleman, Michael Mönsters, Michael Pickard, Gil Steiner, Gabriele Stollmann and Jack Vervoot. Though it's wrong to single out anybody in particular, Nicky McMillan your support was beyond the call of duty and I owe you!

Mick Mercer kindly contributed photographs to illustrate Mike Scott's time with Another Pretty Face and allowed me access to fanzine articles that he'd written about APF which were of enormous assistance. Mick maintains a website at www.mickmercer.com that features his free to download magazine, *The Mick*, and has an array of writings and photography available for purchase. Give him a visit soon!

Thanks also to Peter Chegwyn and the team at the Eastleigh Festival for their hospitality and guest passes (www.eastleighfestival.co.uk).

From my own band of musical comrades I must mention Scott Abraham, Raymond Altree, Robert Bennetts, Simon Coley, Martin Day, Alan Linsley, Stuart Miller, Richard Pascoe, Tim Stevens, Alan Taylor, Keith Topping and Mark Vinson. The Guinness is on me!

To Janet, Lucas, Morgan and Niall—thanks for your patience and support during the writing of this one! I will find time to draw breath and we will go surfing—honest!

As always, many thanks to Dave Hallbery and Mick Fish of SAF Publishing Ltd.

Over Christmas and New Year 2005, I exchanged a number of e-mails with former Swell Maps musician Nikki Sudden, who had been an early champion and friend of Mike Scott. Though he was a little guarded at the outset, he was amicable and encouraging. He shared some memories and pointed me in the direction of others that he'd posted on his own website. I started to prepare a list of further questions with the intention of following up with him at a future date. That wasn't to be, as Nikki Sudden was shockingly and without warning taken from us on 26th March 2006, after playing a show in New York. There is always less time than you think, sadly.

Ian Abrahams
Celtic Kernow (Cornwall)
www.myspace.com/ianabrahams

INTRODUCTION

Greenock, Scotland, May 2000:

"Where've you been?" shouts a voice from the audience.

"Where've I been? That's a great question and I ask myself that everyday... but I'm still here," responds a bemused Mike Scott.

The riddle is within the question and the singer provides the answer as best he can. Mike Scott is leader of The Waterboys—a group with a truly shifting and evolving membership. True to their name, they remain ever fluid whilst remaining generally subservient to Scott's artistic vision. As a musical wanderer, a travelling minstrel, he has traversed a personal, unique path.

Mike Scott has mostly stood at odds with music industry trends. His musical travelogue started in Edinburgh where he discovered himself in the spit and fury of Punk and in the broad-brushed landscapes of Bruce Springsteen and the giants of Americana whose shoulders The Boss himself stood upon. In the Seaview Studios with early Waterboy Karl Wallinger; he would write, record, re-record into the depths of the night.

As a purveyor of Celtic wall-of-sound anthems, he was compartmentalised with those once described as the exponents of "The Big Music", a description invented to give marketability but which does them all —The Waterboys, The Alarm, Simple Minds, Icicle Works, and most successfully U2—a disservice. Mike Scott however, pulled back from the first moment of measurable commercial success. He refused *Top of the Pops* thereby making chart success for 'The Whole of the Moon' that much harder.

After establishing The Waterboys in the UK, it was in relocating to Ireland that the group's ethos found a synergy with the country's culture and tone. This shift is best symbolised by the gulf between the urgency of the last pre-Ireland Waterboys album *This is the Sea*, its imagery of black winds and rising typhoons, and the raggle-taggle freedom of the second "Irish" album, *Room to Roam*. As a Scotsman adopted and made honorary by the Irish, Scott remains the inspiration for a generation of their bands; The Saw Doctors, The Hothouse Flowers, Lunasa—his work, and his generosity of spirit spurring them on. He became part of the history of Dublin, a city he later found to be full of buskers playing his own songs.

Then, in making the move Stateside to reside in New York and record in San Francisco, he produced an album designated as being of Waterboys origin, but with the feeling that the music was now "Mike Scott".

At the height of his powers Scott found God and has been bold enough to declare this inspiration to the world at large. He rejected the notion that to accept God and to write about it inside the rock genre is to embrace something that doesn't quite fit, or somehow tainted with the squeaky-clean aura of a Cliff Richard in all his painful sincerity.

Seeking spiritual peace in the farthest reaches of the Scottish Isles, and as guest and sometime resident of the Findhorn Foundation he appears perennially outside of the mainstream, remaining neither irrelevant nor embarrassing, always with something to enlighten the listener.

Enigmatic, contradictory, mercurial, ambitious and yet reluctant, predictably when contacted for his possible participation in this book, Scott kept himself at arm's length, reachable only through his manager who, in turn, was polite but discouraging—intent on avoiding any written investigation into Scott's life and works whatever the intent of the writer.

His story had to be unearthed in fragments, from the words of his songs and the autobiographical nature of his works. And, in these songs, we can hear the continual revision of style and of outlook and the constant seeking that characterises Mike Scott and The Waterboys (if, indeed, there can be a meaningful distinction between the two).

It's as though the only thing that he can hold onto is a permanently changing personal revolution—a kaleidoscope of day ones, year zeros that renew him again and again, each new place and new disguise creating its own index of possibilities to explore.

Where've you been, Mike Scott? It's a great question. It's a greater story, in its own way worthy of the words of inspiration that Scott has clung to. These are the works of writers that have impressed their values and affinity with God upon him. George McDonald, the Scottish novelist, poet and preacher, and notably C.S. Lewis, his message urging Scott 'Further Up and Further In', to where personal enlightenment can make its contribution 'Building the City of Light'. In his Irish-phase, Scott suggested that nobody would know where he would 'wander and wonder', but it is in the 'where' he has wandered, and the thoughts that he has wondered, that the enthusiast has to look to discover Mike Scott.

This is his musical journey aboard his very own strange boat.

1

Down In Jungleland

Mike Scott entered the world on 14th December 1958 in Edinburgh, destined to be an only child. His mother was a college lecturer and his father a shadowy, remote figure who has been characterised as having abandoned his family, playing little part in Scott's story until becoming immortalised in the cathartic 'My Dark Side'.

"The dark man of my dreams is my father, who left home when I was very young and I've never seen him since," he recalled. "You know, when I picture my mother I've got a picture in my mind. When I try to picture my father, there's a bit of a blank space." Having believed he had inherited his mother's mind, all he could really acknowledge from his father was an assumed physical resemblance: "My father never stuck around long enough for me to figure out what his characteristics were." In a stark and painful song simply entitled 'Father' and recorded in late 1979 for his band Another Pretty Face he agonised over this long rift. Why and where his father had gone; how there could possibly have been something more pressing or important on his time than his family. He pondered what his father's life was like, a decade on from disappearing—whether he talked about having left behind his son. It's a song raw with disappointment and hurt.

The dislocation and trauma this separation caused took many years to reconcile. It was something that Scott took personally, as though it was his own fault. Alastair McKay of the *Scotsman*, a regular interviewer of Scott, delineated it as "a void," which in turn Scott described as being "so big that I didn't have the measure of it." Mike carried inside himself a typical guilt complex and internalised the blame for his father's disappearance. He felt that "it was not necessarily my fault that my parents split up, but it was my fault that my father wasn't around. I thought, 'Maybe I'm unlovable.'" It was a "shadow question. Never conscious, but in the background of my mind."

On the other hand, his relationship with his mother was always close and protective. "When there was just the two of us, we were great pals," he further explained to McKay. "Obviously I was loveable in that context. I had lots of friends, so this question, 'Am I unlovable?'—it was in the background, but it was only one part of my psyche." To Nikki Sudden, writing for *ZigZag*, he confessed how he "grew up feeling inferior—teachers made me feel ashamed of not conforming to things—grown-ups made me ashamed of not wanting to do the expected things. And I grew up scared of religion, police, school—scared of my mother, because she expected things of me that weren't the things I wanted to give her. The way for me to now overcome that is to prove that what I decided to do in place of all those things that were expected of me was worth doing."

Mike Scott came from ancestors steeped in Scottish heritage, his Grandmother a Gaelic speaker hailing from the Isle of Mull. "When I was growing up, my grandmother would be listening to Gaelic on the radio," he explained, "I never got any Gaelic myself because they don't teach it in Scottish schools. But I understood it as part of my background, almost a lost part of my background." BBC Scotland, through its Gaelic identity Radio Highland—Radio na Gaidhealtachd[1]—had broadcast in the Gaelic language s since 1935, though it didn't have a dedicated service until 1979 (and continues to do so, under the banner of BBC Radio nan Gàidheal). Another time Scott noted how he'd

---

1   Gaidhealtachd is the area of Scotland where the Scottish Gaelic language (Gaidhlig) is spoken, encompassing the Western Isles, the North West Highlands, Skye and Lochalsh and Argylle and Bute. The use of Gaelic in Scotland declined heavily over the 20th Century and these days is used by less than 2% of the population.

"thought traditional Scottish music was uncool. It wasn't until I went to live in Ireland that I got hip to Celtic music."

The family moved to Ayr, probably as part of his mother's career as she taught at the Local College of Higher Education. Mike was twelve. He'd already absorbed some of the things that would ferment into his world outlook and set him on the road to being the Mike Scott of spiritual strength and of musical diversity. He grew up surrounded by books, establishing in him a lifelong passion for the printed page and the wonders it could hold. "I had seventeen bookcases in one room which instilled in me early the value of literature and the beauty of books. I love books. Whenever I go on tour I buy so many books, my case is just full of books." He'd immersed himself in literature that resonated with religious undertones, particularly the Narnian Chronicles of C.S. Lewis, which he'd discovered at the age of seven or eight. He fell in love with the way in which Lewis could move from the mundane to the magical in tales where a simple wardrobe, or more religiously symbolic, a stable door, could provide the entry point into something more fantastical or wonderful. And he loved the romanticism of Pauline Baynes' illustrations, finding them "mythological". He would return regularly to the stories for inspiration and say how they gave him "an early sense of the divine, which has never left me".

He found this elsewhere too. "As a child I always identified with the Indians in the cowboy films. Because they were right!" he told Mat Smith in *Melody Maker*. "In the films they were always portrayed as cold-blooded murders and thieves but there was something more. Something I can't quite put into words." He expressed no particular love of formal education. For a while he had attended the independent George Heriot's School, adjacent to Edinburgh Castle. This imposing school was founded in 1628 and drenched in history, but there is no indication that Scott found it a happy experience. "School? They don't teach you what life is," he exclaimed in an early interview with Chris Heath. "They don't teach you that you can be what you want to be. It requires a massive shift in emphasis in society. We have a society based on having and owning. We need a society based around being and giving."

It was around that time that Scott made a trip down the thoroughfare of Edinburgh's Princes Street and into the record department of the Boots store to buy his first 45rpm single—'Last Night In Soho' in 1968 by Dave Dee, Dozy, Beaky, Mick and Tich. it was a pivotal experience and a starting pointing in his musical education. Journalist Hayley Bartlett related how, "Everyone has to start somewhere and for Scott it was being given a guitar for his tenth birthday." Scott went on to admit that his first strumming was to the tune of Mungo Jerry's 'In the Summertime'.

From there on his record buying became eclectic, as he recalled, "The Sixties were really a wonderful time for music. It was like a crack opened in the sky and this big light came through and everyone thought we'd got there. But we hadn't. We had to go through the Seventies... until Johnny Rotten started spitting." His earliest real enthusiasm was for the Beatles. "It was watching the Beatles doing 'All You Need Is Love' on TV that first showed me that rock music could be a transformative force," he told Jon Wilde in *Uncut*. He particularly identified with George Harrison, perhaps in the process absorbing some of that wistful, melancholic spirituality that Harrison had acquired. He has described George's first solo album, *All Things Must Pass*, as being his "favourite record [ever] since I bought it in 1971. I love the big, full Phil Spector sound and that kitchen sink production. I love the songs. 'All Things Must Pass', 'Awaiting On You' and 'Let It Down'. I love that it's touched by Beatle Magic, the shadow of the Beatles still hanging over it."

On 17th November 1972 Scott travelled to Glasgow for his first taste of a major live band, attending an Emerson, Lake and Palmer show at Green's Playhouse, "sitting way up the back, miles from the stage," as he recalled, "and Keith Emerson hopping around on his Hammond." However, what really impressed him was the train journey to the gig and back, "All these strange looking people with long hair and denim jackets talking about song titles. That impressed me more than the concert—I didn't understand the music and I wasn't even a fan."[2]

---

[2] Questionnaire with *Q* magazine, compiled by Martin Aston.

His musical interests led him to the inevitable round of school bands, then finally aged fifteen to a partnership with John Caldwell, another enthusiastic guitarist who would become Scott's first significant musical comrade-in-arms. They formed a group—Karma—which, writing for *Record Collector*, long-time Scott aficionado Peter Anderson noted as being "a garage band inspired by Scott's chief influences, the Beatles, David Bowie and Bob Dylan."

"This was my first true band—we played in my living room every Saturday," he recalled to Hayley Bartlett, also remembering another band he started which "went under two different names, White Heat and White Light—we were really into Lou Reed at the time." These bands and the initial association with John Caldwell were little more than signposts to the future, while Scott took himself off to Edinburgh University and a degree course in Philosophy and English Literature that he would never complete. Scott had started at University in 1977, one of the most significant years in musical history. Instead of attending lectures, Scott listened to the spit and bile of the Clash and of Patti Smith and got sucked into the exploding storm of Punk.

"With Patti Smith, it was her sense of the transcendent that drew me in," he told Jon Wilde. "It was like there were angels over her shoulder, and she showed that that rock music should be both transcendent and extremely sexual." To Chris Heath, in *Jamming* magazine, he expanded further, "She knew that communication between people on as high a level as possible is one of the highest pursuits that an artist can follow. And she had a fantastic soul that was inspired by wonderful things. She recounted her dreams in songs. She lived on stage—she didn't go and give a show, she went on and lived. And because of that she was real."

His own involvement with Punk was from the sidelines—or from the trenches if you prefer to see Punk as an expansive movement. Writing his own fanzines, firstly *Kingdom Come* (taken, perhaps, from the Arthur Brown band of the same name) and most notably *Jungleland*, its title deriving from the gritty, operatic closing track from Bruce Springsteen's *Born To Run* album. Whilst conceding the bombastic and overwrought side of "The Boss", Scott developed an enduring fascination for Springsteen. In Springsteen's multiple-layered sound, Scott discovered something that resonated with his own huge musical ambitions. 'Jungleland', for example, has been described by Springsteen biographer Christopher Sandford as "switchblade hop… it had the lot, violin, cocktail piano, the guitar solo that virtually gave Boston's Tom Scholz his braggadocio sound and Springsteen's roaring vocal." Not that Scott was uncritical, suggesting to Nick Kelly in the early 80s that Springsteen should steer away from the blue-collar imagery and characters that he was writing and singing about. "If he started exploring the mythology of America, and tying the wisdom that can be gained from that into an exploration of what has to be done to save the Earth ecologically, he'd do it brilliantly." Lofty ideals—and ones that he aspires to himself.

Scott's *Jungleland* fanzine became the focal point for his creative output in the late 1970s, giving him the opportunity to get up close with some of punk's movers and shakers—he interviewed the Damned, the Clash and Patti Smith amongst others. "It was just a fanzine about all sorts of things, just like every other," he recalled. "It was the stuff I liked best at the time that I wrote about, which were Television, Patti Smith and Dylan. I met [Television's] Tom Verlaine and Patti just by hustling. The first person I met was Richard Hell when he was touring with the Clash as Richard Hell and the Voidoids." He finally made a face-to-face encounter with his idol Patti Smith in April 1978 and found her "always really good to all the kids who used to follow her around. I was just one of them." What impressed him was the way in which her stage persona was simply an extension of who she was and how she felt at that moment. "So much life in one person she just had to be admired," he enthused to Nick Kelly. "She went out on stage every night and if she was in a bad mood, it was a bad gig, and if she was in a good mood it was a good gig. I think that's quite justifiable."

The final issue of *Jungleland* was issued in 1980, by which time Scott had established himself as a musician in his own right. "I backtracked and did one extra issue," he explained to Marc Issue in *Beat*. "It was a kind of personal manifesto of where I was at the time, and God, I must have been a pain in the arse! It was so negative! I could hardly believe it could be so depressing to read, but then I recall I was pretty miserable in 1980."

Whilst he was making his first tentative literary mark, and was drifting away from his University education (Anderson, in *Record Collector*, makes note of his assertion that "I was always more interested in what Joe Strummer was saying than William Shakespeare") he was getting involved with a few bands. "DNV was a group that I had in 1978 that only ever did two shows," he recalled. "We did one recording session, twenty-one songs in one night, and from those twenty-one we released a single, 'Death in Venice.'" Others were short associations with groups now long-forgotten, with guitarist Alan McConnel in the Bootlegs and with old friend John Caldwell in the Chaps, though there were other brief flirtations with bands whose legends have endured longer. He made a guest appearance on piano with Edinburgh's TV21, playing on the B-side of their 'Ambition' single ('Ticking Away').

Scott's next band was both more successful and longer-lived than its ad-hoc predecessors. In assembling the line-up for Edinburgh-based Another Pretty Face (APF) he turned again to his Karma band-mate John Caldwell, with Ian Greig (also known as 'Crigg') on drums and Jim Geddes playing bass. The relationship proved to be the real entry point for his into the music business, though it also demonstrated both his affinity for the Punk DIY-ethic and his distaste for many aspects of the industry.

APF formed in late 1978 and by the following May had cut and released their first single 'All the Boys Love Carrie' on a label the band had started called New Pleasures. Scott described the song as being "about a girl, who was great, but never went out with boys,"[3] noting however that "the lyrics aren't personal". Peter Anderson, in his overview of Mike Scott for *Record Collector* summarised the song as having taken "the theme of Dion's 'Runaround Sue' and updated it" and compared APF's sound ("chainsaw guitar... derivative of the fashionable new wave") with The Waterboys ("a million miles [away]"). The *NME* latched on to the record, made it their single of the week, greatly assisting the one thousand initial pressing to sell-out.

3   Interviewed by Mick Mercer for *Panache* fanzine.

Surveying a then burgeoning Scottish music scene, Gary Bushell, writing in *Sounds*, identified that "Scotland currently boasts some of the finest young bands in the country, Mainly (rush out and catch the buggers at the earliest opportunity) the Scars, Trax and Another Pretty Face." Elsewhere in the feature, a round up of up-and-coming Scottish groups, he claimed that "Another Pretty Face were in a different league. Described in *Sounds* as something of a cross between The Clash and Springsteen they loomed large as well as tasty bait. And the description was accurate enough if not quite as earth shattering as that would suggest." Bushell went on to highlight their "impressive single" and claimed that they "proffer a powerful epic rock approach which has got several record companies sniffing and I'm sure will conquer America someday soon." Coincidentally he also profiled the Fakes, whose Mairi Ross (who describes herself at the time as "she of mad, dark hair and much make-up") was then Scott's girlfriend.

In November APF cut a deal with Virgin Records and received the accolade of a *Sounds* cover feature. But they had a tempestuous and short-lived time with the label and, it seems, with each other, probably due to naivety and inexperience. "The band seemed sure that they'd be able to get what they wanted from Virgin without conceding any of their principles in the process," wrote Nikki Sudden on first meeting them, noting his own dubiousness. "Another Pretty Face was really headless chicken time," Scott later explained to *Melody Maker* journalist Mat Smith, though he admitted that most of their problems were due to youthful inexperience. "We were well-intentioned but misguided. It was a democratic group, but the situation deteriorated until by the end I was writing all the songs but not making all the decisions. I realised I needed that degree of total control." It was certainly an uncomfortable position for someone who would later exhibit a need to dominate the bands he worked with; APF had much more of a collective approach than would The Waterboys, with various band members contributing songs. Scott was, however, seen as the principal songwriter, replacement bassist Willie noting that, "He writes better lyrics than me" but going on to say, "We both think you should sing your own lyrics. You can get closer to the meaning, and they should mean something."

Virgin had the band ensconced into London's Britannia Row Studios within a month of signature, working on demos that would include their only single for the label, 'Whatever Happened To The West' (b/w 'Goodbye 1970s', reworked from Mike's previous band DNV). They also laid down versions of 'Let It Loose' and 'A Woman's Place'. In fact, December 1979 would prove both a hectic and productive month, with Scott also returning to Edinburgh and recording a set of piano and vocal demos. 'Linda's Abortion' with its depressing tone of judgement and rejection, the painfully honest and autobiographical 'Father', 'Out Of Control', 'King of London' and 'A Career Girl'. There would also be a gig in Edinburgh, on 8th December at Georges Square, where the band played 'All The Boys Love Carrie' and 'Whatever Happened To The West', and another at Tiffanys on the 7th January.

By the end of February 1980 the band, with the Only Ones' bass-player Alan Mair producing, had once again been at London's Britannia Row Studios, this time recording demos for an album, which one listener described as a "swirling wall of sound rages at humanity." Out of this came a cacophony of disgust, despair and outrage. 'Heart of Darkness', an intense sprawl of guitars and tribal drumming, 'Lightning That Strikes Twice', full band versions of 'Out of Control' and 'Father'. 'Graduation Day', covering some of the same intensity of atmosphere that would characterise early Joy Division and which Willie recalled playing at the Moonlight ("Mike was really dying at the end of the song, just like 'gonna blow them all away, on Graduation Day."). Mick Mercer suggested it was 'a students-get-their-comeuppance song, made personal for the band by Mike and John both having quit university to form APF.' Time would prove Mercer on the money with his observation. Scott would spend considerable amounts of his song-writing currency wearing his heart on his sleeve over people or events on his radar that had caused bad feeling or offence, or, as with the APF song 'Another Pretty Face' railing against "fallen heroes—people who I think have let me down."

Michael Johnson, a tape-operative at Britannia Row, recalls: "Mike, God bless him, was a little bit precious in those days and spent countless hours recording solo piano/vocal pieces, despite the fact it was a group album. Those sessions used more 2" 24-track recording tape than any other in the history of the studio. At £80 a roll, which lasted a mere 15 minutes or so at 30 inches per second, this was a major expense. Taxis delivering chocolate and crisps from London's only all-night shop in Westbourne Grove didn't help. Britannia Row was a fairly basic studio in those days and had no facilities for artists to relax in. The reception doubled as an artist's lounge after the rest of the businesses in the building closed for the night. One evening, a band member popped his head round the control room door and told Mike there was a phone call for him in reception. Off he toddled to take the call. When he came back to the control room his face was a sight to see. It looked like he seen a ghost, witnessed the Second Coming and won the Pools all at the same time. Something big was going off, it was obvious. "You'll never guess who just called! Only Mick Jones! The Clash want us to support them on their tour!"

Mike was elated. He was over the moon. He saw the crescent. Mike was a huge Clash fan, and this was his dream come true. Touring with his heroes. Treading the same boards as them.

Trouble was: a couple of hours later one of Another Pretty Face owned up. He'd made the call himself from an empty office upstairs."

Mercer, interviewing the band at Britannia Row found them already negative about their relationship with Virgin, out of step with the corporate machinery. "Virgin think they know what we should be like, although we have control in the contract over what we put out they can still bring pressure to bear on us over what we do. They want us to sound like… Dire Straits. They didn't want to put out 'West.'"

Various support slots organised by Virgin for APF, including gigs with Classix Nouveau at the Venue and a date opening for Steve Hillage at the Music Machine were refused by the band. They did, however, undertake a tour supporting Ulster punk band Stiff Little Fingers[4], kicking off in Plymouth on 4th March 1980 and running

4   SLF's *Nobody's Heroes* promotional tour.

throughout the month, ending in Glasgow on the 30th. By all accounts, Scott found the lack of variety in the main act's set a disappointment, though noting that "when SLF are good, they're great". The early dates proved a particularly frustrating time. "Liverpool, Bracknell and Birmingham were abysmal," Scott claimed, describing the band was "unrehearsed" and the audiences as "uninterested or gobbing." One SLF fan, recalled the Leicester gig, "This band was not going down very well… covered in spit, disgusting as that sounds… the drummer going nuts with the crowd," and found it "amazing what Mike Scott went on to become". Another Internet commentator recalled their performance as being "good… but [they] got spat at and booed a lot because they didn't look like punks—the audience hadn't quite got the 'punk is about being an individual bit'." Happier were gigs at Bournemouth, Guildford and particularly St. Austell on March 15th at which Mike considered APF had received one of their best ever audience receptions, and where, coincidentally, The Waterboys would also go down a storm many years later.

The recordings for the proposed album (to be called *I'm Sorry That I Beat You, I'm Sorry That I Screamed, But For A Moment There I Really Lost Control* from the lyrics of 'Out of Control') were roundly and immediately rejected by Virgin. By the time the Stiff Little Fingers tour had reached St. Austell, Scott was writing to one fan that "The LP is now complete… I think it's great. Virgin don't agree and so we'll be parting company with them soon." Only six months since the deal was struck APF were out in the cold and reflecting on their experiences with two new songs, 'Kick It Over' and 'Mercenaries'. One was described as being "an anti-record business song" and the other "an aggressive nothing—our message to the world brought on by disillusionment."

"Circumstances weren't very kind to us," Scott remembered. "We had bad luck and we made wrong decisions… but it taught me a lot about the relationship between record companies and groups as well as the folly of worrying about what people think about you." And, in hindsight, he saw that some of the conflict came from his own demanding and uncompromising character. "We never did what anybody told us to do. We were 19, 20, 21 and we weren't listening. We had our own ideas. I was a complete fascist in those days, a terrible man to work with. Many people in London would tell you that." The end result, as he told Jon Wilde in *Uncut*, was that "Suddenly we found ourselves bounced back to Edinburgh without any prospects. It was a sobering lesson all round."

Disheartened by their first brush with the big time, Scott and Caldwell returned to Edinburgh, sharing an Abbeyhill flat with Mairi Ross whilst Scott worked on new outlets for APF's recordings. He recalled to Allan Jones how they started up Chicken Jazz, a label through which they could distribute their own records noting that releasing records proved much simpler than the selling them. "You seem to spend your whole time ringing up these record shops and asking them if they still have enough of your single. I reckon you can either be a musician or a record company boss. I don't think you can be both at the same time." Chicken Jazz issued the next APF single, culled from the abortive Virgin album sessions, 'Heaven Gets Closer' a downbeat anti-war song with an 'Eve of Destruction' theme (b/w 'Only Heroes Live Forever'). The single, though a modest production with a two thousand copy pressing, opened up new avenues for the band.

For starters, it connected them to Nikki Sudden, rock journalist and former guitarist of Swell Maps. Sudden, a Londoner, had been inspired to learn the guitar when he discovered the music of Marc Bolan. During the period 1977 to 1980, Sudden, with his brother, had the even more strangely named Epic Soundtracks, released four singles and two albums under their Swell Maps banner. He encountered the APF duo when they visited the Rough Trade record shop, hoping to supply copies of their single. Sudden, on hearing the record, suggested that he travelled to Edinburgh to interview the pair for *ZigZag* magazine. The visit, which ended-up lasting nearly two weeks, was organised for December 1980, taking place sometime early that month—Sudden recalled being there when the news came through of John Lennon's murder on 8th December.

The liaison was to extend beyond Sudden's write-up of the current state of Another Pretty Face—he spent £125 to get together some studio time with Scott and Caldwell, recalling, "I paid every penny— Mike and John were on the dole back then." With Caldwell on bass and Scott playing drums (which he'd also done with the Chaps). "I played guitar and sang," recalled Sudden. "Amongst other tracks we recorded an effective jungle-style version of [Swell Maps' song] 'Winter Rainbow' and a new song called 'All Right John/Living Dead' in which I voiced my thoughts about the break up of Swell Maps. Both of these turned out pretty well."

The fruits of this session were doomed not to see the light of day, just as APF's aborted album. Indeed, by the time of Sudden's visit to Edinburgh, Scott was already talking about the APF material as though it hailed from a different band in another time and was something that he'd moved on from. "There's about four tracks left over from the album that are fully mixed and current enough to use—the rest of the stuff is either a bit too dated or not relevant." As to their future plans, Scott mused, "At present we're giving ourselves a few months to work out exactly how things are."

It has been said that, "Money is a strange and wonderful thing. Nothing promotes garbage like its presence, and nothing inhibits quality like its absence." For Scott and Caldwell, bunkered down in Cadzow Place, Abbeyhill in the middle of winter, living on Mairi's meagre wages from her job in the Edinburgh Toy Museum and whatever cash they could turnover from the band, success must have seemed a long way away.

2

THE WATERBOYS

The man who would come to the rescue of Scott's creative ambitions was Nigel Grainge of Ensign Records, and the way in which this was to be achieved was via the most classic of routes, the legendary John Peel sessions.

Another Pretty Face cut four songs for Peel in February 1981. 'Lightning That Strikes Twice', a slow studied and downbeat mood piece that explodes into aggressive hectoring. 'I'll Give You Fire' (which Peter Anderson notes as being 'gospel-influenced'), the piano-led 'This Time it's Real' and the song that would prove APF's most significant cut, 'Out of Control'. It was this song that Grainge was to hear whilst driving and listening to Peel's radio show and which he described as sending "shivers up your spine."

In the mid-1970s Grainge was working for Phonogram Records as head of A&R but becoming increasingly disillusioned with the company and looking for a way of establishing his own label. Whilst at Phonogram he had signed Thin Lizzy and Graham Parker & the Rumour and saw in Parker, then viewed as a potential English Springsteen, an opportunity to bring across to this new label Ensign Records[5] an artist he believed to have huge potential. Parker and his

5 Ensign Records operated as an independent subsidiary of Phonogram Records.

manager, Dave Robinson, who was soon to establish Stiff Records with Jake Riviera, had other ideas and this opened the door for the Boomtown Rats to become Ensign's premiere signing and first success.

A contract with Ensign on the table, Scott and Caldwell once again headed down to London. The scale of things in his homeland also had a lot to do with Scott's thinking, believing Edinburgh too insular, too parochial to develop the sort of scene that he wanted to be associated with. "I get very jealous of bands like Echo and the Bunnymen," he claimed. "The power they must get from identifying with a place like Liverpool must be a real advantage to them." And looking to the future of his own work he described a "bigness" to the new Liverpool scene of the Bunnymen, The Teardrop Explodes and Wah! that he found appealing in a kindred way. "I think I share a way of channelling things into the music."

Prior to their relocation to London, Another Pretty Face self-released one more single, 'Soul to Soul' (b/w 'A Woman's Place' and 'God on the Screen'). Caldwell had, however, come across another band (in the States) using the name Another Pretty Face and so, after flirting with the idea of going out as The Noise! The Jazz!, Scott settled on using the title of the Stooges' album, *Fun House*, as APF's new identity.

Funhouse, the album title truncated into one word, would however, prove to be a short-lived affair. Scott and Caldwell, on the advice of Nigel Grainge cut new versions of 'Out of Control' and 'This Could be Hell', songs identified as being the most promising from the APF repertoire. These were released respectively as the 'A' and 'B' sides of the first single of their Ensign contract, to minimal interest. By this time, with the band receiving scant promotional support from the label, there were signs that the long-established working relationship between Mike Scott and John Caldwell was fracturing and that Scott was looking within himself for a new direction for his creativity.

His starting point for this would be a demo session at London's Redshop Studios in December 1981. There, employing a drum machine and otherwise playing all the instruments himself, Scott re-cut a number of APF songs, worked through various new ideas and set the Patti Smith poem 'Dog Dreams' to music. Though they continued to work together in the early months of 1982, this particular demo session must have given Caldwell a signal that the remaining days of APF/Funhouse were likely to be short in number. Though Funhouse performed a number of London gigs in January, by March 1982 Caldwell had returned to Edinburgh, *Record Collector* noting him as forming "the short-lived The Collector" with Scott "remaining in London" and beginning a "search for like-minded musicians to relaunch his career."

It wasn't long before this was underway. A mere month after Caldwell had departed for Scotland, Mike Scott was performing with his latest set of musicians and a new phase in his creative development was underway.

Anthony "Anto" Thistlethwaite wasn't always going to be a professional musician. He was born on 31st August 1955 and after growing up on his father's Leicestershire farm, he went to college and trained to be an engineer. Once qualified, he worked on various projects in and around his native Leicestershire and subsequently spent six months on a petrochemical construction project in Basra, Iraq. But he'd always had a burning desire to play in a band—guitar, bass, saxophone—whatever role he could land himself in, playing with whoever needed his services. The timing of his arrival in the world left him nicely placed and ready for the dizzy heights of Beatlemania when he was seven or eight, perfectly timed to buy 'She Loves You' and 'I Wanna Hold Your Hand'.

"That was a great thrill in my life, to play those records again and again, learn all the words, know every little inflection—every place where they went 'Yeah' or 'Woo'. I had two older brothers and they'd be coming home with Chuck Berry, Bob Dylan—and they were into The Rolling Stones, so I got away from the sweetness of The Beatles and became an avid Stones' fan. A *Desert Island Disc* of mine would be 'Brown Sugar', or *Sticky Fingers*, or *Exile on Main Street*. But I don't love the Stones now—I love what they were. The Mick Taylor era was the quintessential one, where they made their own sound, created something new with a fantastic atmosphere."

Thistlethwaite got his first guitar when he was fifteen learned a few chords so that he could strum along with a Donovan track or a Dylan song, then decided to graduate on to playing bass. "I was into the Groundhogs. A few friends and me would go and see them; one night we waited for them in the car park after the gig and they said, 'If you're coming again, come and say hello.' So another time we went to the dressing room after the show and the bass player had his instrument there and said I could have a go if I wanted to. So I played a couple of lines from their songs and he'd say 'No, that note changes to this note...' and I thought it really kind of him, to first let me play his bass and then to give me a little guidance. He was Pete Cruickshank, a striking looking man and a great bass player!"

Around this time, Anto hooked up with a harmonica player from his local village, "an ardent blues fan," and together they formed a blues band, playing around the village halls. Anto was still refining his bass skills, listening to Muddy Waters and John Mayall and had no particular thoughts of learning saxophone, the instrument he'd later become known for. "I didn't really like saxophone or trumpets when I heard them on Beatles' or Stones' records, but I came around perhaps because of *Exile on Main Street*, Bobby Keys' playing—hearing this fantastic sax solo, like a rocket going off, on 'Rip this Joint'. And I started to hear other things, like Junior Walker's playing on the Tamla Motown records which always had really exciting saxophone playing that drove you mad straight away. So I wanted to investigate this and hired a saxophone for three months and started to find the excitement by listening to the records and copying what was happening on them."

Everything that he learned musically, he describes as being discovered by trial and error. "I was into early Ry Cooder, the bottleneck guitar sound, and I'd sit around the garden with my guitar and a little bit of plumber's tubing on my finger trying to figure out how to get those chords, how to play minor chords. I haven't any musical training.

I can't read music. If you're a sax player people think of you reading the dots, but I can't get on with that stuff to be honest."

Working in Iraq, aged around twenty, Anto continued to practise the saxophone as his preferred instrument. "We lived in these camps in the desert, in Portakabins where you had half a cabin—so I had one half with my saxophone and some poor guy had the other." Returning home (Iraq was "an interesting experience but not very exciting"), he had to decide in which direction his life lay. There were opportunities for engineering work across the globe, Malaysia was one particular destination he considered. Instead, an article in the *Sunday Times* about the buskers of Paris inspired him to go for the long shot and investigate the possibilities of France with no more than his saxophone and the buzz he had gained from reading the article for company.

"Setting out from my parents' farm in Leicestershire with a back-pack and my alto sax I caught the night-train from London. It arrived in Paris early in the morning. After some breakfast at a café outside the Gare du Nord I decided to make my way to the Pompidou Centre, the only building that I knew in Paris apart from the Eiffel Tower. It had been mentioned in the article as being the site of various open-air activities including busking. Once there, I chose myself a vantage-point near the top of the sloping paved area where the action all took place and sat down. It was not long before I saw a woman arrive with a guitar case and begin to open it up. I wandered over to her. "*Bonjour, Madame*," I said, "*Vous allez chanter?*"

"Man, I'm going to sing some blues," she said, and pointing to the sax-case, 'You can join in if you want to!' She started singing Willie Dixon's 'Built for Comfort'. She was a well-built woman and she had a big voice. Soon there was a crowd around us. I blew along with her, taking solos whenever she wanted to give her voice a rest. I could 'read' the chord changes on her guitar so the fact that I did not know all of the songs was not a problem.

After about three-quarters of an hour we packed up and sat down at a café to count the cash that people had thrown into the open guitar case while we were playing. Her name was Marghi Vaughn and she was from Kansas City. She played at Beaubourg most days and had enjoyed my accompaniment. Would I come along and do the same the next day? You bet! We split the money fifty-fifty and I had enough to pay for my lunch and a hotel for the night with some left over.

We played again the next day, and the next, and then the next. Each day we gained another musician until after about a week we had a drummer, a double-bass player and a baritone-sax player. By this stage someone had been employed to actively collect money from, or 'bottle', the crowds that gathered in traffic-free Rue de la Cossonnerie where we now played. I could imagine how pleasant it was for the Parisians and holidaymakers who stumbled upon our 'spectacle' and whiled away half an hour or so listening to our music on a fine afternoon. Occasionally someone sat down and painted us as we played.

My weekend in Paris soon became a month and by then I was living in the Grand Hotel de la Rue St. Denis right next to where we played. Twenty francs a night *and* the landlady let the drummer keep his kit under the stairs! As autumn closed in, and the streets became too cold for our fingers, Marghi and I started playing down in the Metro where it was always warm. We would play two songs in a car and then quickly pass the hat before jumping out at a station and moving into the next one. This was not as pleasant as playing in the fresh air and sunshine but we had fun and made it pay.

By now I was hanging out in the Latin Quarter at the Café Mazet on Rue St. André des Arts where most of the buskers used to go. You could 'phone me there: "Just ask for Tony-le-saxo!" During a typical day I might leave the café two or three times with different singer/guitarists to go down and work the cars in the Metro for an hour or two. There was a period when we would form ad hoc bands in the café and go out to a nearby pitch, often in Rue St. André des Arts itself. These usually consisted of one person who could sing very loud and an assortment of other instrumentalists depending on who was around. The Gendarmes did not appreciate our presence as we could draw big crowds and block the street completely, leading to traffic jams. Concurrent to my activities, which were mainly with Anglophones, I was also rehearsing with a French group, "Les Flambeurs"—we won a

'Battle of the Bands' contest and were described in the press as being *"extremement funky"* but we did not play many gigs.

My weekend in Paris ended up lasting a year. As well as making a living in a most enjoyable way I also made great friends there who I have to this day. In the end it became increasingly apparent that I needed to move to London, the Music Capital, if I wanted to meet like-minded people and create any music of substance. I left Paris a year to the day after I arrived."

Excerpt from website © Anthony Thistlethwaite, used with permission

"I realised that it was all ethereal and that nothing would come of it," Thistlethwaite reflects. "What I needed to do was join a proper band, and to do that I had to move to London, because that was the world centre of rock'n'roll. Of course, I'd been earning my living busking in France, but you wouldn't dream of doing *that* in London, horrible! So I got a job working in an architect's office. In those days, twenty five years ago, you had the *Melody Maker* and its ads for 'musicians wanted', a lot of them just little bands trying to get together—but a lot of them serious as well, signed acts needing someone for a tour and so on. Every Thursday I bought it and rang up all the 'sax' ads and then spend the whole weekend going to auditions. Lots of them were a waste of time, but I joined a band playing around Putney and eventually answered an advert from Robyn Hitchcock who had just split-up the Soft Boys and was going solo. He needed someone who played violin or sax. I met him and we got on and so I did some gigs with him on tour in Holland, and then cut my first record with him—Steve Hillage produced it. It didn't change the world, but for me it was very exciting being in a proper studio and doing something concrete."

Hitchcock was something of an eccentric, "so I was right down his street," Anto enthuses—one gig, for example, involved the band playing in fish masks created by the *Doctor Who* costume team. Concurrently, Thistlethwaite was invited to work at Battersea studios with Nikki Sudden, who had left the Swell Maps. Sudden was recording his first solo album *Waiting on Egypt*, for which Anto had been recruited to provide some sax parts.[6] At the same time, Sudden was a regular visitor to Mike Scott's flat in Notting Hill, seeing himself actually as a "temporary guest" there and working through various songs. These included an early version of Sudden's 'Breaking Lines' entitled 'The Battle of Britain'[7] and 'Road of Broken Dreams', the riff for which earned Scott a co-write credit, a courtesy that Scott would himself later extend to collaborators who chipped-in with ideas or musical bridges. "Mike also put down a piano part and sang backing vocals on 'The Only Boy in Heaven', Sudden recalled. "He got a much deserved co-production credit." What Scott also got was Thistlethwaite, a new collaborator for his own music.

"Nikki was also writing, doing some journalistic things, and had met and interviewed Mike Scott," Anto remembers. "I think Nikki must have gone around to Mike's place with the tapes from Battersea, and Mike heard the sax solo that I did and said, 'I've got to have this on my record.' So I got this telephone call with a funny Scottish voice on the other end."

Mike Scott and Anthony Thistlethwaite met on the afternoon of Thursday, 8th April, 1982—setting in motion the chain of events that would turn Scott away from the path of being a solo artist and onto the creation of The Waterboys. At that point, Scott had been working with a bass player, Steve Fraser who Anto notes, "Used to sleep behind the amps in the rehearsal room because he did not have anywhere to live," and a drummer who he simply remembers as Martin 'Crumpler'. "When I met Mike he had these two guys, a bass player from Scotland and a drummer from London," Anto recalls. "The first time I played with Mike in his rehearsal space it was obvious to me that they weren't very good and that Mike *was*. I immediately thought he should have a good drummer and a good bass player and after a few months the switch was made." Scott was impressed with the "dirty, smoky, New York alley sax" that was Thistlethwaite's stock-in-trade and two more

6   When Sudden came to work on his second solo LP, *Bible Belt*, his intention was to surround himself with what he described as "some of the best musicians available". This was to include both Mike Scott and Anthony Thistlethwaite though they made their contributions separately from each other, Anto recalling driving to make his contribution to these sessions in the company of Kevin Wilkinson

7   Sudden, a huge devotee of British comics such as *Lion*, *Tiger* and *TV21* took the original title from a strip that ran in *Valiant*.

rehearsal sessions took place before they made their first live appearance on Friday 16th April, at West Hampstead's Moonlight Club
under the name The Red And The Black. The name came from a
novel by 19th Century French writer Stendhal, a contemporary portrait of French society during the final days of the Restoration.

A set at the Embassy Club (10th May) and another two days later
at the Hope & Anchor, Islington, meant that by the end of July the
group had performed on nine occasions. Audience recordings of at
least three of these shows are in circulation, the one at the Hope &
Anchor on 15th July 1982 including an early version of 'Red Army
Blues'. A song of epic proportions that, whilst it inhabited some of the
anti-war components of early APF numbers, was clearly the work of
an increasingly confident lyricist comfortable in the art of combining
storytelling with moralising. Scott was now unafraid to present work
that demanded the listener fully inhabit the song rather than a simple
verse/chorus/verse structure. With winding twists and turns, and use
of a train metaphor that was quickly becoming, for Scott, a favourite
allusion for life's journey, the song relates the experiences of a Russian
soldier, young and inexperienced and knowing little of life delivered
to Mother Russia's front-line in World War II. Present at the fall of
Berlin and the raising of the Red Flag over the Reichstag the narrator
discovers, on meeting his first American counterpart, how essentially
alike people are. In so doing, he seals his own fate, abandoned by Stalin
in the Siberian Gulag for being tainted by the contact with the new
enemy, The West, trading the fierce patriotism of the song's opening
verse for an equally burning will to just simply survive.

'Red Army Blues' was to feature on the second Waterboys album
and has obtained almost mythic status in the band's canon. In *Vox*
magazine, Scott described the writing process as being a combination
of two books that had interested him. One was *The Diary of Vikenty
Angarov* by Victor Muravin, a Solzhenitskyn-like Gulag novel about a
Russian sea captain who returns to his homeland only to be swept up
in Stalin's purges. The other he noted as being *The Forgotten Soldier*
and described it as "a war book you can find in railway station book-
shops—a novel." This is probably the supposed autobiographical

WWII memoir by 'Guy Sajer', who claimed to have been drafted into the German Army aged sixteen and which purports to be his experiences on the Eastern Front, though the work is highly controversial and widely regarded to be suspect in its authenticity. "I took elements of both," added Scott. "Put them into a song, added a few bits. The tune itself is a Cossack riding song we [got] taught at school."

Membership of The Red And The Black evolved slowly. The band was already established before the arrival of Thistlethwaite and completed with his recruitment, despite his misgivings about the quality of the musicians that Scott had already surrounded himself with. But a break in gigging between the initial shows in May and the final performances in July saw the line-up regenerated. Although the passage of time has made the actual events a little hazy, Anto recalls the changeover to an ensemble that he was more comfortable with. "We did a few gigs with Mike's mates, and then probably didn't do anything for a couple of months. When he had a few more gigs he probably rang me up and said, 'Do you know anybody who could play?' I knew a really good drummer, Kevin Wilkinson, and a good bass player called Matthew Seligman who'd been playing in the Soft Boys with Robyn Hitchcock and had played with Thomas Dolby. He was a happening guy, and so was Kevin, who in hindsight I always thought was good but realise now was a fantastic drummer. I'd met Kevin in the autumn of 1981 when I was in a band called Boys Will Be Boys. We did a tour supporting the Passions—a very low budget tour because they didn't have a record out or a deal or anything. Kevin was the drummer and I made friends with him then. He'd been playing with Holly Vincent, of Holly & The Italians and had also been on the China Crisis record[8] and played with Robert Fripp. He was very young, but very talented and a really nice bloke as well." Thistlethwaite had also brought Wilkinson into the Nikki Sudden Battersea sessions. "So, The Red And The Black became Mike, Matthew, Kevin and myself, which to me seemed like a supergroup! All the people who I thought were best at what they did!"

8   China Crisis recorded their first single, 'African and White', in 1981 though it was not released until the following year. Wilkinson joined them in time for their debut LP *Difficult Shapes & Passive Rhythms* and their breakthrough single 'Christian' and played on all but one of their albums.

Having split with Mairi sometime before the formation of this latest band, Scott was finding a new sense of liberation and creative energy in his new associations. "It was an interesting time," he told Richard Cook. "A lot of things happened to me that were important. The freedom from Funhouse… and then I split up with my girlfriend who I'd lived with for two years. The two freedoms felt like getting out of jail. Life became an adventure. And the songs I wrote were an explosion." Looking back, he confirmed to Jon Wilde how he was "very dedicated to what I was doing, and intensely driven."

Though The Red And The Black was short-lived, a much more significant pointer to the future was a recording session at Farmyard Studios. On 20th May Scott and Thistlethwaite convened there, along with producer Rupert Hine, to work on a track that Scott had already laid down piano and vocals for—'A Girl Called Johnny'. The song, later described by critic Andrew Collins as "An up-tempo piano-based barroom stomper with prime gut-busting saxophone," was Scott's tribute to Patti Smith. His fascination for her was boundless, at one time he talked of writing her biography and he would seek out musicians who had played with her for various incarnations of his own bands.

"Mike played piano and I did the sax and basically it's just the two of us," notes Anto. "Rupert Hine leapt about enthusiastically when I placed my sax riff over the track and immediately asked me if I was available to play on other people's records." The track had no drummer playing on it so to fill-in Mike and Anto overdubbed their own handclaps, with Anto also providing some additional baritone sax to "fill up the lower end". In some ways it was simply another way-marker, since, as Anto adds, "Ensign waited a whole year to release that," but it was the first track to be recorded that would eventually see the light of day as a Waterboys release.

Summer 1982 drifted into autumn without any more progress being made on what was essentially the embryonic Waterboys, either in the studio or with further live appearances. Thistlethwaite had a number of projects in development with various musicians and Scott was honing his material with his Ensign deal allowing him the opportunity to work on his songs without the constant pressure of recording or gigging. "When I met him he didn't go out and do sociable things," explains Thistlethwaite. "He'd sit at home writing songs on his guitar, smoking lots of dope and listening to music—that was him, dedicated, 'that's what I do.' I'd go round and see him, there was lots of times in the early two years where we weren't doing anything, working or on tour, so Mike might ring me up and say, 'Let's do something,' or I'd go round to his house and sit around and drink beer. There was a whole two years of germination."

One of Thistlethwaite's fledgling associations involved another musician of Celtic stock in the shape of Glaswegian trumpeter Roddy Lorimer. Born 19th May 1953, Lorimer describes his musical background as being "a brass band boy [laughs]. I found out that you got paid if you took up a brass instrument! Someone came into the class and said, 'Can I have Jose Hislop and Alex Beck for the brass band,' and I thought, 'I'm into this!' though I didn't come from a musical background at all. But as soon as I started playing trumpet, I just loved it."

Lorimer worked his way through the ranks, learning the cornet, and became a part-time student at music college, as he didn't actually have the qualifications to study full-time. "I was deputising for the professor when he was on the opera circuit doing professional gigs. So when I wanted to go full-time they couldn't actually say no, I was obviously of a standard to do it. I wasn't on a teacher's diploma though, it was a professional performers diploma that I was looking at."

However, Lorimer found the Royal Scottish Academy of Music and Drama was very focused on classical training, which didn't fit in with his interests or plans. "I hadn't been playing in bands or anything, but it wasn't in my nature to be a classical performer." He stuck it out for a year and then left without completing the course. His introduction to the world of bands and live performances was fortuitous. "One of the other trumpet players [at the Academy] who came from a family of Salvation Army people was asked by a mate to play in a band. But he said, 'No, my folks would never accept me playing that type of music,'—so he asked me if I fancied doing it—and that was my start and I fell in love with rock and pop and blues and everything, it became my life."

Starting off in the exceptionally named Pampas Tramp, Lorimer began to work the local music scene, "a licensed restaurant in a hotel outside Glasgow—weekend gigs. Friday would be Big Band, Saturday would be a Pop night and Sunday would be Rock—the same band having to do three different things." This was an excellent training ground: "Most trumpet players, and saxophone players for that matter as Anto and myself had something similar here, most horn players come from either a classical or a jazz background. But although my training was in classical I never went down the jazz route—nor did Anthony. We fell between these two things; we were unusual in being rock influenced. That's very rare. I really listened to all the soul bands, Stax and Tamla Motown—and Chicago who were probably more along our lines in that they were from a music college background bent to rock and pop."

Although his journey through the Glasgow music scene was developing, playing in a band called Chico and then in Canto with his great friend Davie Taylor, Lorimer was unhappy with the direction his life was taking. "I split up with my wife, I was doing teaching as well as playing in bands and it was almost that David Byrne thing where you wake up one morning—'this is not my beautiful house, this is not my beautiful wife.' What am I doing here, what's this all about? I'm going nowhere. I just had to get out. It was almost an overnight decision. Life changing." It was the start of the 1980s and a new beginning for Lorimer in London. "I got a lift down with a friend and slept on his floor, just like that."

Lorimer totally switched himself off from his previous life, having nothing to do with old friends who had also moved to London and had established themselves in bands or careers. "I wouldn't get together with them, wouldn't talk with them, I wanted to start from scratch again." For the first few years, trying to establish his name and presence on the London scene, Lorimer would play with anyone, in any band, in any style, just to get his face about. To finance his new life he took various jobs, working on a ship (in a band) for six months so that he could raise enough cash to go back to London and further his involvement with the capital's musicians.

In London, Lorimer came into contact with Anto Thistlethwaite. "I was playing in a band called Impulse with Mike Andrews, who became the MD of Papillon Records, and Anto was playing tenor sax. It was a great time, but it ended up being slightly sad as well. Anto was very new to saxophone playing, though he knew guitar and stuff like that, whereas by that time I'd become an experienced trumpet player, I'd worked hard at it since I'd been a kid, seven hours a day, seven days a week. I was single-minded. But at that time, Anto was very inexperienced, unlike our other saxophone player, a guy called Ian Ritchie. Ian was quite arrogant. He wouldn't turn up for sound-checks. I'd had enough of that, so I said to the band that I wanted to start again with the horns section or forget it, because Anto needed to go away and learn more before anything could happen, and Ian was just too arrogant. And they said, 'Do it.' It was an emotionally bad time. Anthony, rightly, was very upset—not angry but hurt and I understood why. But at that time I wasn't there to bring somebody else's playing up to scratch, I'd done the work myself and I was in the situation where I wanted to start with a new player again. Anto said, 'But you're wrong—I am that good and I'll show you.' I said, 'I hope you do' but he ended up in tears, and it was a horrible thing that I felt I had to do at that stage in my career."

Lorimer talks about Anto Thistlethwaite with such affection that it is hard to imagine their friendship having such a rocky start. But however badly Anto took his ejection from Impulse, it seems that the experience left him doubly determined to prove his abilities. "In the ensuing years he'd call me up for sessions," recalls Lorimer, "and we ended up going out as a horn section, called The Little Big Horns or something, doing some fabulous recordings for a whole lot of different people. The Jam had just split up and we got very involved with Bruce Foxton, did an album with him, live gigs and *Top of the Pops*. So, Anto became a much better saxophone player—whether [the Impulse experience] was the spur or whether he'd become that great anyway...

but from that time on he seemed to get a new spirit of belief about him. What an extraordinary person."

By November 1982 Mike Scott was ready to start in earnest on the songs that would eventually comprise both the eponymous debut Waterboys' album and the follow-up *A Pagan Place*. He'd spent a little time in New York, trying some material with Patti Smith's long-time collaborator, guitarist Lenny Kaye. These sessions, compacted into just three days of rehearsals and four recording nights (to take advantage of cheap studio time) came to nothing, Scott later blaming this on his being "a lot less capable studio-wise" but mitigating this with a recollection of "working under very unfavourable conditions."[9]

Work re-commenced at Redshop, initially with Scott simply using Kevin Wilkinson to lay down some drum tracks. From the 19th to the 22nd November, Anthony Thistlethwaite was on-hand to record a large selection of saxophone parts, some multi-tracked with trumpeter and flugelist Barbara Snow. Though at various times in the future Anto would be called upon for his bass playing as well, on these sessions a number of musicians were used to overdub bass parts on an ad-hoc basis—notably Nick Linden of rock band Terraplane.

In fact it is fascinating to see Scott's methods at work over his sessions in both 1982 and 1983 setting up the template in which The Waterboys would effectively be two very different animals. On the on hand, an ad-hoc, pliable arrangement in the studio with a wide variety of artists coming in to deliver their own little bits, and on the other hand, what would become a fairly consistent set of musicians who would form the touring band. The former could be identified as part of the game plan from Scott's earlier studio recordings but is particularly highlighted at Redshop in '82 where the contributors, also included TV Smith (late of seminal punksters the Adverts), violinist Tim Blanthorn, and vocalist Ingrid Schroeder. "I wanted a band that would play the music I was hearing in my head," he explained to Hayley Bartlett. "[Not] fixed like the Beatles, more like the Plastic Ono Band. As my musical preferences evolved, so would the line-up."

9   Interview by Mat Smith, *Melody Maker*.

November 1982 was almost certainly the most productive month of what had already been quite a busy round of sessions. Thistlethwaite noted in his diary the range of songs that he contributed his sax and mandolin playing to. 'All the Things She Gave Me' and, from The Red And The Black, 'Red Army Blues', both of which would be destined for *A Pagan Place*. An early attempt at a 'raggle-taggle' sound that would be a modest way marker for Scott's interest in traditional Celtic arrangements called 'Billy Sparks'. A cover of 'Hound Dog' before the recording of which Anto's tenor sax fell from its stand "which probably explains a rather odd performance, as some of the important high keys were jammed." There was also a version of Nikki Sudden's 'Cathy', which eventually saw the light of day on the remastered release of *A Pagan Place*. 'Going to Paris', which had actually been written several years earlier and which, like 'Billy Sparks' can be heard on the compilation of early Waterboys' out-takes *The Secret Life Of The Waterboys*.

These recordings were straightforward sessions, fresh and exciting for the participants and largely devoid of the demanding approach to studio work that some associates would later attribute to Mike Scott. As Anto reflects with the benefit of years, "I understand the world a bit better now—everyone is dysfunctional. Some people like to make things more complicated than they need to be. So, I don't know why, but sometimes getting a recording done was very arduous—and then again sometimes it was very simple. What I loved about the original 1982 Redshop sessions was that they *were* very simple. Mike had gone in with just Kevin and played the songs. Kevin played very sympathetically with Mike and with a joy and sprightliness. Then I went in and spent a day or so just playing saxophone and did 'Red Army Blues' and 'All the Things She Gave Me', just pouring things out. The interplay between Kevin, Mike and myself just seemed natural and spontaneous—fantastic. There wasn't any effort then, no funny business. The complications occurred later when there was an expectation on the recordings—back then there wasn't any Waterboys, there was no reputation to live up to. When we recorded *Fisherman's Blues* it was completely the opposite—all these articles, 'Are they the new Simple Minds?' or 'Are they the new U2?' and suddenly there was the huge cloud hanging over everything, spending months in the studio doing take after take and of course the spontaneity suffered."

The first public declaration of intent didn't come until the following March, when Ensign finally released 'A Girl Called Johnny' and The Waterboys' name was seen in public for the first time. Derived from those who brought water to labourers on the American chain gangs, Scott had heard the term used in 'Kids' by Lou Reed on his *Berlin* album. "I didn't know what it meant but I liked the sound of it," he explained to Hayley Bartlett. "It seemed like a Waterboy was something fluid and ever-changing and I always want to have a group that could improvise on stage and always be different and grow, because that's what life's like."

Very few players in the rock business have actually achieved the sort of shifting and flowing band of the type that Scott outlines. Fewer still have achieved it without suffering the slings and arrows of disgruntled band members who have felt marginalised or under-valued, badly rewarded or poorly credited. In some instances such an intention has descended into bile and rancour that has characterised many bands to a greater extent than their musical legacy has achieved. Though it would become clear that for some members of The Waterboys over the years the level of subservience the group would have to give to Scott's vision was too constricting, there has actually been very little real complaining. Possibly this was because Scott, though both blessed and cursed at times with tunnel vision, was at least open to input from collaborators and generous with credits. He was able at times to stand back and encourage his fellow musicians to contribute arrangements in the studio or to add to and develop the music on stage. Although The Waterboys might not ever have been a democratic band in the sense of shared decisions and creativity, there are not a host of past members ready to complain about the treatment they have received.

As to whether it is correct to see The Waterboys as a band or a solo-project with regular contributors, Thistlethwaite acknowledges that this is indeed, "A tricky question. Mike was signed to Ensign before I met him. I wasn't signed to Ensign, but I brought a lot of people in and put a lot into it. So, it's Mike's thing, but there's an awful lot of stuff coming in from other people. Can you say it's a band effort or can you say it's a solo artist? I really don't know. A lot of stuff comes down in the end to the fact that Mike is an only child, so it's not being personal, but I've got two brothers and a sister and you grow up in a different world, sharing and compromising. Mike behaves in a different way—but he's a brilliant writer who has great ideas so you have to find a way to try and make it work. Sometimes it's easy, and sometimes it's not easy and you're thinking 'why am I putting up with this?' or 'do I let him get away with that or not?' But if he had siblings perhaps he wouldn't have been such a good writer!"

The first single enjoyed two weeks of significant Radio One airplay but very little in terms of chart success. "Because it was the first single, you couldn't find it in the shops *anywhere.*" Anto recalls. "Nobody could buy it! If that had been the second single it would have done well. That was funny, but it was really good for morale, hearing it on the radio." It was a modest start but it did mean that the ball was now rolling and the investment and time that Nigel Grainge and his business partner Chris Hill had made in Mike Scott's talent was on the way to propelling him as far as he wanted to go. Just how far that would be and in what direction his ambition would drive him was to meander greatly over the following years. But it did mean that The Waterboys had to assemble as a band with at least the semblance of a regular core membership committed to the cause and start to promote themselves as a credible force on the British music scene.

This meant that Thistlethwaite, who had continued to explore many different musical avenues throughout 1982 and well into 1983 had to decide exactly where his loyalties would lie in the forthcoming years. He had his alliance with Roddy Lorimer that had extended beyond their abortive early association in Impulse to their session work with Bruce Foxton. He had also been recruited by Rupert Hine who, following his producing of 'A Girl Called Johnny', had cast Anto as the sax player for another artist he was working with. "Rupert phoned me a couple of months later, he was doing a Chris De Burgh record. I'd never heard of him, but I said, 'yeah—ok' because I was delighted to be asked to play on a proper record by a proper record producer!

Chris hadn't had 'Lady In Red', he wasn't famous, he was just a nice Irish singer and I played on a couple of tracks on his record, *The Getaway*, in 1982. The next year, one of the tracks became a single and I kept hearing myself on the radio. Then a few years later he had the 'Lady in Red' single and his credibility became very dubious! So I don't normally talk about that—or the Mungo Jerry sessions [laughs]! Though, actually, Ray Dorset is great musically and as a character in the musical world—he made great records and was coming from the right place!"

"I'd been playing with lots of other people, because as much as I liked Mike and the things we'd recorded, nothing had happened. I had tapes in my car, 'Red Army Blues', 'Church Not Made With Hands' and I thought it was all great, but I had loads of tapes of stuff I'd done with other groups as well and nothing ever did happen with them. I was in London and as single-minded as Mike. But he had to be himself, and I had to be a sax player playing with lots of people. He didn't have the joy of doing that. I'd be out nearly every night, playing at the Golden Lion in Fulham or wherever, playing in Impulse or with Bruce Foxton—we went on *Top of the Pops* because his first single charted.[10] But all through doing other things, I was secretly hoping that something would happen with Mike, because it just felt right, with Kevin on the drums—there was something there which I found particularly pleasing, strong, something that touched me. Eventually there came a point where I had to choose between dabbling with all the other people... I had to say to Bruce, 'Sorry, I can't do this—I've got to drop out.' I wasn't meant to be a session man, reading music and doing parts. Roddy's gone on to excel at that, but that's not me. I was a bit of an oddball sax player, and sometimes that's great, sometimes not great, because I've got my own way of doing things."

Roddy Lorimer: "Anto said, 'The Waterboys is the thing for me.' And that was fine."

The lack of an official Waterboys line-up soon proved something of a dilemma. Ensign's promotional department secured the band an appearance on the BBC's *Old Grey Whistle Test* in May, by which

10   To promote Foxton's single, 'Freak', on 4th August 1983.

time the core membership had once again withered down to Scott and Thistlethwaite. Kevin Wilkinson wasn't available for the recording, being replaced by session man (and former Atomic Rooster drummer) Preston Hayman. "Mike rang up and said, 'We've got to do *Whistle Test*'; but we didn't have a band," Anto recalls. "Kevin was off doing something else. So we went to a rehearsal studio and had a jam with Preston."

An advert was placed in *Melody Maker* looking for a guitarist for the band. "Mike was really looking to get another person in the band. Karl Wallinger answered the advert even though he wasn't a guitarist but was actually a piano player."

Karl Wallinger was born on 19th October 1957 in Prestatyn, the most easterly of the North Wales coastal resorts, surrounded by older brothers and sisters in a house, as he described to *Q* magazine's Mat Snow, "always full of records." His sisters frequented the Cavern, only some sixteen or seventeen miles away in Liverpool, and listened to "Junior Walker, the Supremes and mainstream, *Top of the Pops*, fodder." He also recalled "Singing along with the Turtles or the Boxtops. The Love album *Forever Changes* came into the house, and my sister bought the *Sgt. Pepper* album as soon as it was out."

But it was in his sister's reactions to the records that they brought home that Karl found his own identity and calling. "They used to push the chairs back and shake and shimmy in the front room," he told Snow. "I thought it was all very exciting—these little bits of plastic do this to people!" To Sylvie Simmons, in *Rolling Stone*, he mused that, "I had this innocent notion that you got growing up in the 60s and this fantasy of a world run by the Beatles and the Beach Boys and Bob Dylan. 'All You Need Is Love': cherry cakes and soda for everyone in the world." Interviewed by Gerry Galipault he expanded on this: "People were crazy then, and I don't think anyone has really captured that eccentricity and looniness in music since. Everyone's so blasé about the Beach Boys, that they don't have any depth, but they were so far out you couldn't even see them. People would say, 'Oh that's just the Beach Boys. They wear striped shirts and sing surf songs.' But they were so much more than that; they did an awful lot to change things, the way albums are recorded."

As his talents developed, his writing never strayed far from these roots—the lineage back to his love for the work of Lennon and McCartney has resonated as a touchstone throughout his solo work. As he once commented: "I've used the language of '60s pop the same way jazz musicians use jazz. I'm basically updating the lyrical content in some way." One, possibly apocryphal, story had him buying every Beatles' book he could lay his hands on that contained pictures of Abbey Road Studios and trying to set his own studio up in the same way.

His first musical association was, appropriately enough, alongside another son of Prestatyn, Mike Peters. Peters, a couple of years younger than Wallinger, would one day be cited alongside Mike Scott as an exponent of the Big Music when his band the Alarm achieved chart success with '68 Guns' and 'Where Were You Hiding When The Storm Broke'. But in the mid-seventies, the principal movers of the Alarm were known as Quasimodo and playing "note for note" run-throughs of The Who's *Live At Leeds*. Karl's opportunity came when their guitarist, Dave Sharp, departed to undertake a Seaman's Certificate, Wallinger offered his services as a keyboardist replacement. "We did a couple of gigs where the audience was pressed up against the back wall as far away from us as they could get," he told Mat Snow. "We were so loud and so bad, and the songs were about half an hour long."

Fame and fortune did not beckon and so Wallinger moved to London and a position at music publishers ATV Northern Songs, whose catalogue, appropriately enough given Karl's passion for the band, included the Beatles. He was a royalties analyst clerk, reading contracts in the nine-to-five and honing his keyboard skills during his lunch breaks. Discovered by an "alcoholic musical director" he found himself with an opportunity to demo his songs and understand the workings of the studio, though the environment of middle-of-the-road Eurovision mulch failed to inspire him.

He departed for a house-share in King's Cross ("Getting wrecked and playing and recording on anything I had to hand") and subsequently a job at the Comedy Theatre in London's West End as the musical director of *The Rocky Horror Picture Show*.[11] "It's a strange old business, the theatre," he told Tim Hibbert. "I like the archetypal Hollywood films where they're sitting in the stalls with no lights on and the actors come on and audition. That's what I was doing—sitting in the stalls eating a Burger King trying to decide who was the best." By his own admission the role was not one that he particularly aspired to, though he had another bite of the cherry as the musical arranger of the 1994 film *Reality Bites*, a moderately well received Winona Ryder vehicle. After working on *Rocky Horror* he took time out to travel around Europe, returning to London and playing in Zero Zero (later the Invisible Body Club) and then, with Alix Sharkey, in white funk outfit Out. "I was singing the soulful, ballady stuff," Wallinger explained to Mat Snow, "because Alix wasn't a singer… everybody was very together, doing Shalamar stuff."

It was whilst Wallinger was still a member of Out that he responded to Mike Scott's advertisement in *Sounds* for a guitarist "into Iggy Pop and Van Morrison." Scott was looking to round up a full band for the *Whistle Test* appearance, the BBC's seminal rock music show. "I phoned the guy up," Karl recalled, "and got a great letter back saying only phone again if I liked the tape enclosed." Clearly Wallinger found some empathy with the creative direction of fellow Beatles' enthusiast Scott, because by the time The Waterboys made their first television appearance, on the 27th May 1983 edition of *Whistle Test*, he was firmly in place on keyboards. In fact, this was an indication of Scott's willingness to be open-minded and flexible in structuring his band given that the vacancy was for a guitar player.

"We met up with Preston Hayman at Nomis Studios, by Olympia," says Thistlethwaite. "I was playing bass, because there was no bass player yet again, and Karl walked in. Mike brought another friend from Scotland down [Norman Rodger] to take over on bass—and then we were on the *Whistle Test*. So it was a really quickly put

11   It was at the end of the show's seven-year run, and with Tracey Ullman—soon to be famous as a member of the BBC television show *Three of a Kind*—as Janet.

together outfit; Mike and I were the only people who really knew each other [as musicians]. I was as nervous as hell! It was the first time I'd been on TV. Back in the seventies I used to watch the *Whistle Test* religiously—John Lennon, the Stones, Bob Marley. So my heart was in my mouth—fantastic!"

They played 'The Three Day Man' and 'I Will Not Follow', both of which Scott and Thistlethwaite, along with Hayman, had also recorded at the BBC's Maida Vale studios when The Waterboys cut their first radio session for the corporation. This was a three track affair, also including a version of 'A Girl Called Johnny', broadcast on the *Peter Powell Show* of 3rd May. The urgent and highly aggressive rendition of 'The Three Day Man', a song that Scott once described as being about someone fucked up by too much speed, can be heard on *The Secret Life Of The Waterboys*. Unlike the recordings at Redshop and Farmyard studios earlier in the year, the BBC tracks were laid down between Scott on piano and guitars and Thistlethwaite on both bass and saxophone. Despite this, all three tracks are stronger on the Powell session than in their "official" incarnation as part of the self-titled premiere Waterboys' album.

Ensign released the eponymous first Waterboys' album in July 1983, a muted and demo-like collection of under-produced songs on the one hand, and a confident, assured and romanticised statement of intent on the other. The years haven't been especially kind to the record, overshadowed by the band's subsequent work and sounding rough and unprepared, with an almost bootleg quality to it. But it certainly repays revisiting in its pointers to Scott's peculiar, perhaps even singular, talent. It opens with 'December', written way back in 1981 in Ayr, tumultuous, raging, optimistic and intense though, as one critic identified, also verging on the side of melodrama. 'December' has a unique lexicography far removed from both the broad-brush swathe of Springsteen and the ferocity of punk and marks Scott out as a literate and considered lyricist. In some ways the tone and use of imagery is still underdeveloped, somewhat 'sixth form' and heavy handed, but it still remains a startling and impressive and brave first track. It's followed up by 'A Girl Called Johnny' (Scott's exultation of Patti Smith) and by songs that delineate the themes that would become the regular emotional fuel of much of his work. 'The Three Day Man', where the keynote is independence and removal and a refusal to be tied to relationships. 'Gala', a mystical and mournful anti-fable and 'It Should Have Been You', containing what would become a typical Mike Scott rage against unrealised potential with its ambiguous subject most likely being Scott himself.

But the masterpieces of the record are left until the end of side two. The studied piano-led fantasy of 'The Girl in the Swing' with its title borrowed from the book by Richard Adams, and its allusion to the controversial apocalyptic SF novella of Harlan Ellison, 'A Boy and his Dog'[12], and Scott's most notable foray into Native American mythology 'Savage Earth Heart'. "It was written in a spirit of revelation!" he told Richard Cook. "I was sitting in my flat on a Sunday, thinking about all these things, the nature of inspiration, the muse... and I pinned it down to three words. It summed up the nature of... of me. It came out without thought." Later he would see this song as succeeding in a live environment, telling Valerie Rosner and John Wilde that, "'Savage Earth Heart' has about four climaxes at the end—just rising and rising in these peaks where we throw everything to the song. It's more extreme than the album version even!" But for the moment the release of the LP and its singles ('December' followed, appropriately enough, in December 1983 as the band's second 45rpm release[13]) would be the public representation of The Waterboys, TV appearances aside.

Colin Irwin, later to become quite a champion of the band and one of their regular interviewers and correspondents, thought that through the development of Scott's skills, the first LP would be taken, in hindsight, as being "an interesting, occasionally inspired but ultimately disjointed document."

---

12 Originally published in the April 1969 issue of the British SF magazine *New Worlds*. 'It took a long time before I stopped hearing her calling my head. Asking me, *do you know what love is?* Sure I know. A boy loves his dog.' Often labelled as misogynistic (Ellison prefers to describe it as misanthrope ... 'I treat male and female with equal monstrousness in this work') it is both a cautionary tale for the Cold War nuclear age in which it was written and something of a study of middle-class, middle-America mores.

13 The B-side of 'December' was a curious, plaintive, track called 'Where Are You Now When I Need You?' which appears to encompass some dialogue to his mother that suggests a need to impress upon her the importance of their relationship and bond. The song seemed to take on the air of something of an embarrassment to Scott, who later told Richard Cook it was "a sad song and it's my business. I put it out, but I wouldn't broadcast it."

"Like a young racehorse, he probably needed the outing," Irwin considered. Identifying the need for a producer to cut back on some of Scott's excesses and 'hyperactive studio sense' he at least heard "Scott's own character [managing] to seep unerringly through even this motley collection." Released in the USA as a five-track mini-album in the summer of 1984 (eschewing 'The Girl in the Swing', 'The Three Day Man' and 'Gala') it attracted the attention of Parke Puterbaugh in *Rolling Stone*. Drawing a comparison with U2 ('voice and guitar sound eerily like Bono and the Edge') 'I Will Not Follow', was described as having an "anti-war, anti-draft diatribe." This was, at least in part, a misinterpretation as enforced National Service had long since disappeared from the British military, although the US Draft system continued. "Scott's wandering pitch, feverish poesy and bracing, minor-key music make his a vision worth sharing," Puterbaugh concluded.

3

GOODBYE, SHADOWLANDS

With the first album released but only lightly promoted, The Waterboys reconvened to complete work on their second album. This time, instead of the urban environment of Redshop, they were in the quite different atmosphere of Kingsley Ward's residential Rockfield Studios in the Wye Valley, near the town of Monmouth in Wales. What was emerging was the definitive line-up and sound that would come to be characterised as the 'Big Music' era of the band.

During September 1983, Scott, Thistlethwaite, Wallinger and Wilkinson cut at least another five tracks, three of which ('A Pagan Place', 'The Big Music' and 'Rags') were destined for the new album. Another two songs recorded at this session, 'The Madness is Here Again' and 'Love That Kills', later appeared on the remastered and extended reissue of the album and *The Secret Life Of The Waterboys* respectively. The following month, at Farmyard, Roddy Lorimer, making his first of many appearances for the band, joined them when they completed overdubs for 'Love That Kills'. In fact, this presaged another round of recordings, overdubbings and mixings that stretched on through most of the first half of the following year. "I wasn't aware of who was playing what, apart from Mike obviously," comments Lorimer. "It's not like being in a live situation; you're working in isolation in a recording situation. You're turning up and there's a lot there already down so you're just adding your bit without being aware of who's playing what. Mike would say what he wanted and I'd try and make that work by thinking about who should be playing what and in what way—and what Mike wanted sometimes was literally impossible. He'd want the horns to play and then suspend a chord for thirty-six bars [laughs] but, y'know, human beings can't exhale for that long! So we had to close-fade, record the note for as long as we could, then in unison back off the mike slightly and stop playing. Then we'd record the same part and just as it was backing-off we'd come in off-microphone and start playing again and try and match the two things up."

"In any musical situation, it's always going to be the case that the guy who writes the songs is going to have a preconceived idea of how it's going to go," Thistlethwaite adds. "The drummer might say, 'Well, we could have this rhythm', but the guy who's written the song, he might say 'Oh, that's better than I imagined' or 'Oh, don't like that, it's spoiling the picture for me.' So there's always give and take, you have to be generous to make it work. Sometimes you have to be really generous with Mike… when we recorded 'The Big Music', we'd done the backing track in Wales, then we were at Farmyard Studios outside London and it was time for me and Roddy to do the horn lines for the song. We went off with the cassette of the backing track and made up three or four different lines that could have gone with the song. We decided which was the best, the one we'd like to use, but if we play it to Mike first, he's going to say, 'Oh, I don't want that' because he wants the power of making the decision. So we'd play a couple of the ones we didn't like first, not our favourites, so he could say, 'What else have you got?' and that would give him the delight of thinking he'd decided what it was, but we got the one we wanted. Sometimes you had to throw something away to bolster his ego."

'The Big Music' was the defining track. In the NME Andrew Collins exclaimed, 'What a concept and what an albatross. A lilting anthem with grand cymbal splashes, soulful backing… a lazy, meandering essay.' Recorded at Rockfield and at Farmyard between September and October 1983 it is a bold, brassy mission statement, a marker of intent dominated by Wallinger's up-front piano with Scott's passionate, almost sermon-like delivery of the vocals underpinned by the backing-vocals of future Fairground Attraction lead-singer Eddi Reader. "I played bass and did the horns with Roddy, and the sax solo, so there's a lot of me in that record," recalls Thistlethwaite. "Eddi Reader was a friend of mine and I got her in to do the backing vocals—kind of my band if you like!"

The multi-layered wall-of-sound of 'The Big Music' demonstrated just how far Scott had come in such a short space of time from the demo-like, under-produced first album. He was looking for new techniques and ways of building from the basic blocks of a demo track with just Wilkinson or Thistlethwaite, into a song with resonance and depth. "On *The Roots* bootleg of John Lennon there was a version of 'Be My Baby', where he's using the Phil Spector wall of sound. The instruments come in one by one. It starts off with the wall of acoustic guitars and the bass comes… piano comes in, then the reverb electric guitar and the drums and horns… so you hear the construction of the wall of sound. On 'A Pagan Place' I did my own version of it."

For the song's coda, a triumphant and purposeful counterpoint to some of his more smoky, mournful, horn playing, Roddy Lorimer came up with "really, a combination of rock and classical—actually very much a classical thing but with rock folds coming off of it, baroque trumpet." Once again it showed the confident sophistication that was now distinguishing the sound of the band from the days of APF or Funhouse.

Taken as a whole *A Pagan Place* is very far removed from the syndrome of 'difficult second album' (perhaps partly by having been worked on concurrently with *The Waterboys*). If it wasn't for the strength and passion of the song writing on the first LP, it would be tempting to see the band as really beginning with this record. Partly this is because the themes that Scott was starting to explore in his writings were becoming more rounded and delivered with increasing confidence and eloquence. And partly it was due to having finally established around him a pool of musicians of the standard that Thistlethwaite saw that Scott needed at their very first meeting. In Thistlethwaite he had found someone very hard-working, talented but willing to bend those talents in his service, someone who saw that he had something with which to embellish Scott's obvious genius. Lorimer, who was never formally a member of the band, brought with him "the classical background and my influences from black music where the horn players were the rhythm section." This offered the possibility of "not so much rhythm guitar, but you got the backing riffs from horns. Related to The Waterboys this gave me a rather odd take on things, because I actually ended up using a lot of my classical training. A lot of things, like 'The Whole of the Moon', 'World Party'... had strictly classical trumpet playing."

With Wallinger, Scott had the opportunity to work with someone of no mean song-writing ability of his own—and a person who would perhaps be a foil to Scott's more introspective nature. "Karl's a clever, creative bloke full of ideas and jokes and stuff—a really entertaining guy and it's kind of a relief to have someone else... it meant I could relax a bit more," suggests Thistlethwaite, a contrast to Lorimer's commentary on Scott. "Mike's a lovely person, but very much a deep thinker, you didn't laugh and joke as much with Mike, he was really quite serious. But writing the most beautiful things, very few people are greater lyricists than Mike, I really think that highly of him, and an incredible performer."

Combined with what Scott once described as Wilkinson's "killer drumming" the first 'classic' Waterboys line-up was essentially complete. Though the occupancy of the drummer's stool was always an ad-hoc affair, Thistlethwaite notes how, "Mike had to get Kevin back—for the first record, the second, the third and the fourth, which just shows how good he was." Their perfection of Scott's vision was embodied in *A Pagan Place*. Released in June 1984, the same month that the band made their first appearance at the Glastonbury Festival[14], it's a collage

---

14   Interviewed for the *Independent*, Scott recalled his first experience of playing at the Glastonbury Festival as being "thrilling ... we were the first band to play the Pyramid stage on the opening day." Afterwards, along with Kevin Wilkinson, he wandered the festival's intimate highways and byways, drinking in its atmosphere ("a transient town") and finally seeing the sunrise over Glastonbury Tor. "Everyone who goes there gets touched by its sense of inclusiveness ... Glastonbury unifies us all."

of rock, jazz and classical tones, epic in its soundscapes and at the same time introspective in its moods.

A Pagan Place opens with 'Church Not Made With Hands', Scott's racing acoustic guitars melding with Lorimer's clean and regal trumpets and a paraphrase of C. S. Lewis from *The Last Battle*. Scott used a highly controversial quote—in the context of the book it seems to enjoy a sentimentalised delight in death and resurrection to Heaven— the song is a mystical celebration of paganism. It's extolling the basic and primitive divinity that exists in everything ('the oceans and the sand'), religious and spiritual and all encompassing. Here is something that can't be owned or built upon, something that has its existence in the concept of Mother Earth and has an ancestral approach to religion. And it takes in and embraces the feminine side of divinity, pluralistic in its acceptance of the wider pantheon of paganism.

For the title track, always claimed to only coincidentally echo the name of a novel by Edna O'Brien, Scott noted that it has "lodged in my brain as some sort of essence. The adventures that I had in the time between Another Pretty Face and The Waterboys, and the thoughts about life, me, all that stuff, brought me to a fresh place. I had come to a pagan place—I don't mean Godless, or heathen. Further than that."[15]

In a retrospective article in *Uncut*, Jon Wilde noted that following the release of the first Waterboys' album, Scott could be found 'holed up in his London flat [he was living in Notting Hill, on Aldridge Road Villas at that time] immersed in books about meditation, paganism and Buddhism.' Always the most literary-minded of songwriters, he was absorbing the work of Dion Fortune[16], a leading occultist whose writings blended hermetic lore with Freudian and Jungian psychology. "I was reading lots of far-out books all through the early 80s. Loads of occult stuff. *The Cosmic Eye* by Peter Lemesurier, and Aleister Crowley—though I was never big for him. Dion Fortune, she was a great writer." One account of Fortune's life describes her as having 'studied with, taught or bumped horns with the most well-known

15 Interviewed by Richard Cook circa *A Pagan Place*.
16 Pen name of Violet Mary Firth (1891-1946). Derived from the expression 'Deo Non Fortuna' ('by God, not by chance' or 'God, not fate').

occultists of our century: MacGregor Mathers, Robert King, W.B. Yeats, Aleister Crowley, W.E. Butler, Gareth Knight and Christine Hartley.' The commentator goes on to note that 'Crowley, widely acknowledged to be highly egotistical and downright abusive, was known to admire her and sought unsuccessfully on several occasions to draw her into his work.' Fortune lived for a time in Glastonbury, drawing on its traditional place in Arthurian legend when writing *Avalon of the Heart*. In her fictional works, often cited by occultists and witches as being of greater importance than her non-fiction dissertations, she drew heavily on the imagery of paganism, the use of the Horned God Pan in *The Goat-Foot God* would be highly influential on Scott's own writing. As another critic, Mike Hammer, put it: 'especially prevalent [in Fortune's fiction] is the notion that perhaps Nature has it right—a freed person is a happier, more fulfilled, more productive person in the long run than one repressed and squeezed into a socially acceptable mold.'

"It was the beginning of a period of deepened learning," Scott explained. "Suddenly a door had opened and I saw the world in a different light. When I sing about hearing 'The Big Music' I'm singing about having a complete spiritual awakening, something so pure having called my name." Earlier, he'd talked about this concept as being concerned with "seeing the divine in nature or art, or otherwise abroad in the world." Others, however, saw 'The Big Music' as having been rooted in the musical language that the band was adopting. "The Big Music—I can see what it was," Anto claims. "Think back to *Dark Side of the Moon*, a record with a great expanse of sound to it and big ambitions in the lyrics—and also almost a kind of spiritual aspect to it, implied but not defined."

In addition, Lorimer also considers the broader pictures that were being painted and the lineage that was underlying what became effectively became a Celtic rock (or, at times, folk-rock) movement. While anchored with a broad-church spirituality, it was also informed by the wild, harsh granite beauty that the Celtic nations stand-upon across the British Isles from Scotland to Cornwall. Lorimer, though, traces the wide-vistas of U2 and Simple Minds and Big Country (all of whom were also linked to this sound) to more Anglo-Saxon beginnings. "The thing that the Big Music bands had in common was that they were anthemic. But I think it was a genre that The Who had started. I've worked with The Who, and I've played in Pete Townshend's band as well, and Pete talked about actually changing the way he wrote music when he started playing in stadiums. He said that you couldn't play intimate music in stadiums; you have to go for this big anthemic thing. And that's where the Big Music probably started. But of course it didn't start with him, it started with Wagner! Music for huge production values—that's part of the wider picture of music. But The Waterboys weren't just about Big Music, if you look at Mike's songs about Native Americans and their tribes, though that was concurrent with "Big Music", it was very intimate—'Custer's Blues', 'Bury My Heart', songs that you'd ideally want to play to three hundred people..."

"It's really difficult to describe something there are no words for," Scott told Paul Du Noyer. "It's not about music; more like religious thing. And it's a very serious song. You see I guess if I could explain what the song was about just like that, then I wouldn't need to write the song. So I write the song instead." At other times he would try and dismiss the term as simply labelling "because they are full of wide-screen songs with a prominent brass section and multiple, layered guitars and pianos."[17] Often he would draw a parallel with C. S. Lewis and use Lewis' words as a way of explaining the themes on which he would draw upon and write about. "I write the books I want to read, because no one else does."

The intimate moments of *A Pagan Place* have Mike Scott very focused on personal events. Though he'd enthused about the opportunities the breakdown in his relationship with Mairi and with former musical colleagues had offered, within the LP there are moments of introspection and flashes of impatience, frustration and anger. All of these emotions had already appeared as touchstones for his writings over the years but they are really brought out for deliberation and inspection in this record. Like 'Father' during the APF days they

17 *Musician* magazine, 1990.

show Scott always prepared to wear his heart on his sleeve. In 'All the Things she Gave Me' and again on 'The Thrill is Gone' he's burning his bridges and walking away, making things final and starting over again. Perhaps that's why he follows these songs up with the far more upbeat and optimistic 'Somebody Might Wave Back', inspired by a line from the Elvis Presley film G. I. Blues and seemingly signalling fresh starts and a sense of openness.

The Waterboys finally trod the boards for the first time on 19th February, 1984, when they played at the Batschkapp Club in Frankfurt and followed it up the next night with another German show, this time in Munich. As a temporary measure the band included Eddi Reader and, making a final return to Scott's fold, John Caldwell. On bass, Scott had recruited Martyn Swain[18], whilst the rest of the band was drawn from the contributors to A Pagan Place: Thistlethwaite, Wallinger, Wilkinson and Lorimer.

Though it was, to say the least, unusual that a band could be afforded as long a development period before venturing out into the live circuit, Thistlethwaite notes the advantages this had. "Nigel and Chris deserve a lot of credit for giving Mike those two years to germinate in London, smoke his dope and write those songs. So by the time we went out on tour we'd been friends for two years instead of meeting one week and touring the next." They made up for lost time though right throughout 1984. 'The Big Music' was issued as the band's third single in March and the following month The Waterboys took to the road for their first UK tour, kicking-off at The Heathery in Wishaw where the support act, Woza, featured future Deacon Blue leader Ricky Ross. Ross, who like Scott was an admirer of Springsteen and Dylan, recalled the impact The Waterboys had on him to Q's Mat Snow. "Here was someone who's playing with the same energy, the same passion as Bob Dylan; it was like, punk's over after people had been trying to live in that image for years."

18 Swain, who later played with World Party, Julian Lennon and David Bowie, was a regular fixture in the early Waterboys' line-up. He later went on to a highly successful career as a composer of scores for film and television, earning two Emmy Awards for his work on the BBC Timewatch documentary series ('Allied to the Mafia' and 'The True Story of the Roman Empire'). He also scored the classic children's serials The Moon Dial and Century Falls, the BBC's revival of Auf Wiedersehen Pet and the Corporation's adaptation of Jonathan Coe's novel The Rotters' Club.

A slot opening for Simple Minds at Poole Arts Centre on 10th May was followed by a European tour supporting the Pretenders. This ran from 22nd May until 19th June and was followed by the band's first appearance at Glastonbury Festival, on the Pyramid Stage on 23rd June. Scott saw the live environment as an opportunity to grow and expand songs, to treat them continually as never-finished work-in-progress and, remembering his dissatisfaction at discovering the regimented routines of the set-list and banter of Stiff Little Fingers, began to let his own set-lists change on a nightly basis. "I don't ever want to be in the sort of band that comes along and does the same show every night, saying the same things between the songs," he told *The Beat* magazine. "Shows should grow and change."

This approach to his work, evolving and expanding the constituent parts of his music canon, came of out a need to explore the work in much the same way as an actor on a stage might refine or flesh-out a character during a play's run. "Improvising in rehearsals or on stage, that's pretty good," he told Marc Issue. "Things happen that you never foresaw. That happens when the music is working." In the studio though, he was hearing the work in a very different way. "When I hear final mixes I'm always freaking out, wondering why the music doesn't sound like how I wanted it to. I'm never satisfied with my own recordings."

"Every gig was a unique event," Lorimer confirms. "None of this going on stage and doing the same number again. You might do the same number but it would *never* sound the same." Because of his other commitments, notably the Kick Horns, Lorimer would not always be available for specific gigs, could not guarantee to be on call for every show on a tour itinerary. "Mike once said, 'It's great when you're there because it's different. And it's great when you're not there because we have to fill the gaps—and that's different too.' Don't confuse that lack of attendance with lack of wonder at The Waterboys phenomenon. Sometimes I'd fly to America, do a couple of gigs and fly home again. It was extraordinary, none of us had much money but I'd get a flight to Cincinnati, or wherever, do a couple of shows and fly home again to do some session work."

These tours were often chaotic, shoestring affairs, Lorimer describing how he found himself on one occasion "turning up somewhere in North America and getting to the hotel" to be told, 'No, The Waterboys aren't here and you're not booked in.' Eventually a tour manager turned up and got me, but it was quite naive stuff." Or another time, "being skint and saying, 'Well, what do you want to do,' and somebody said, 'Well, we'll get a beer somewhere,' so we went to some grotty little café, absolutely horrible, and had a couple of beers. We thought, no, this is just too awful so we went back to the hotel and found out that Bob Dylan was having a party and had sent a limo for us—but there you go!"[19]

The opportunity to play in the USA came out of a fortuitous slot on U2's British tour in November 1984, which also saw The Waterboys enjoying some high-profile gigs in the UK—Brixton Academy on 2nd and 3rd November, Birmingham's N.E.C on 12th November and two nights at Wembley Arena. "Originally we supported them around the UK," recalls Lorimer. "At the end of that tour we ended-up in Glasgow, at the Holiday Inn or somewhere—and of course they were big stars and we weren't. But Bono asked us down to the bar for a drink, and said, 'This has just been fantastic, such a great tour and I've loved you guys playing. We're going to be doing a US tour next and I don't want our manager speaking to your manager because we're all musicians here. Let's stick together, I'd love you guys to do it—would *you* love to do it?' Of course, we all looked at Mike and Mike said, 'Yeah!' but it was so nice that Bono wanted to do it personally, he is such a nice guy."

Following a short trip to Germany to record an appearance on the television show *Rock Pop* on 21st November, The Waterboys joined U2's North American tour from 1st to 16th December. This was only interrupted by a solo show at the El Mocambo Club in Toronto on 6th December, a show at Irving Plaza, New York on the 12th and one more the following night at the Hollywood Palace, Los Angeles.

19 Scott had some opportunities to play with Bob Dylan, a performer who he greatly admired. "I played with him in a studio in London in 1985," he told Martin Aston in *Q*. "I had this old, beat-up out-of-tune guitar. I'm playing with Bob Dylan and my guitar won't go in tune, which was like a funny dream." To Colin Irwin in *Melody Maker* he added that "He was doing some stuff with Dave Stewart and we were in for a few hours ... they played us some backing tapes and we jammed along. I've no idea what it was for."

Lorimer recalls that, "U2 were such big fans of The Waterboys, you'd often find them sitting at the side of the stage watching our set." Bono listed 'December' as one of his Top 10 Favourites of 1983 in a survey for *Rolling Stone*, along with 'Summit'; by Irish band In Tua Nua who would have a major significance in The Waterboys' story just a couple of years later. Geoff Parkyn of the U2 Info Service network commented in the summer 1984 issue of *U2 Magazine* that, 'As for The Waterboys, if you haven't caught up with them yet, then I suggest you investigate further. They are firm favourites of all of U2 and if you listen to Mike Scott's songs it's not hard to see why'. And U2's The Edge confirmed to Mark Ellen, writing for *Word* magazine (in 2005) that he considered Mike Scott to be "a great talent," adding that "It's not about internal performance, not about trying to maintain your cool. All that left me with an instinct about what's required to put on a great concert[20], where there's never a dull moment."

"U2 are a positive group, they're a positive force," Scott told Mat Smith in *Melody Maker*. "The ideas that they're giving out have a lot to do with hope and faith and goodness and pride in good things. That's something I learned from watching them when we toured with them, how important it is to send out positive ideas."

Though Scott had some insight into the demands that success placed upon a musician from the modest success of Another Pretty Face, the trappings that came with this were not particularly appealing or desired. Just as he had been dismissive of the recognition that appearing with APF on the front cover of *Sounds*, the increased profile and promotional requirements that were manifesting themselves throughout 1984 were difficult to reconcile with Scott's artistic view of what he was trying to achieve. Interviewed by Valerie Rosner and John Wilde the following year he was at pains to describe the angst that was created in his attempt to remain a private figure despite the significant boost to his profile. "I don't get a thrill from seeing my picture in the paper [though] I used to when I was nineteen. I want to make records and I want a lot of people to hear them, but I don't really want to be famous." He seemed almost to believe that he could

20   The Edge was specifically recalling a Waterboys show at the Top Hat, Dublin a few years later.

separate himself from the rigours and demands of selling records, as though he thought he could remain aloof from the machinations of the music business. "I've never done it for any ambitions. I've always loved guitars and making a noise. Hearing two sounds and putting them together to make something new."

Partly this was born out of the frustration of being constantly on the road, regurgitating songs from *The Waterboys* and *A Pagan Place* rather than immersing himself in new writings. It's quite telling that 1985 was almost a mirror image of the previous year, being much more dedicated to creating new songs. And then again it was in part the effect of being thrust into the limelight; the U2 support-tour, coming back to Britain and finding his press coverage expanded, his picture in the music papers and having to absorb what was being written about him. "It's difficult not to think about all that when I'm writing," he confessed in his open and frank discussion with Rosner and Wilde. "1984 was a work year, not an inspirational year. 1982 and 1983 were the inspirational ones for me. But last year was a workhorse year."

At the same time, he was in the position of having to start to think about what the Big Music meant to him and where it should be taking him. U2, arguably the most comparable band of the moment to The Waterboys, were already well on their way to the very heights of rock stardom and Scott had to define within himself whether this was a route that he wanted to take. "That was never my intention, to be a stadium rock band," he told BBC Radio 2's Marc Radcliffe many years later. "I just wanted to be great, to give people shivers up the spine like I got when I listened to records. For me, the music was first. And I got to a stage in my life where to get success I had to make compromises and I wasn't prepared to do that. I needed to go where the music was sending me and it sent me some queer twists and turns but it was just where I had to go." And at the time he was rejecting comparisons with the likes of Big Country or The Alarm. "We're definitely not another Big-guitar band," he claimed.

Whilst on tour with U2 he'd taken a withering look at the contemporary music scene and dismissed it. "It seems very much like music is going through that mid-70s kind of thing, when it was very boring. I think that good things are happening, the way that African music has come to the West recently—like reggae came in the '70s. We're seeing sort of a melting pot; all the cultures are coming together. We're going through a dull period just now, but there's going to be a definite explosion within a year's time."

4

THIS IS THE SEA

Though the genesis of the third Waterboys' album would be found in all night sessions between Scott and Wallinger at Wallinger's Seaview Studios in North London, work on what would become *This is the Sea*, really began in earnest at Park Gates Studios in Hastings during February and March 1985. Scott would be joined there as producer by John Brand and also Mick Glossop, who Scott admired for his work with Van Morrison. Though the association with Glossop actually proved frustrating for Scott, he noted to Mat Smith that, "Working with Glossop I knew the sound would never fall below a certain high standard. He was like a safety net on which I could bounce around and try out new ideas." The working method was at times comparable to the sessions that produced *The Waterboys*; Scott entering the studio with material that he had worked on at home in Ladbroke Grove and building up a collection of demo tracks with Thistlethwaite, Wallinger and Lorimer arriving later to glue on their contributions. Drums were provided by incumbent live drummer Chris Whitten and by Kevin Wilkinson, brought back for specific tracks, whilst bass lines were generally provided by Wallinger's keyboards. At other times the approach would be more in keeping with the later work on

A Pagan Place with the entire "band" in the studio cutting tracks 'as live' and with a number of musicians filling in on an ad-hoc basis. "The band was Mike, Karl and Anto at that time, everybody else was hired in for a tour, an album, a track on an album," notes Lorimer. "They were the ones who were signed to the record company, I don't think anyone else was."

During the initial work at Park Gates, a substantial number of basic tracks were laid down, most receiving overdubs when the recordings relocated to Livingstone and Townhouse studios during the summer. From the original sessions came 'Spirit', 'The Pan Within', 'Medicine Bow' and 'Be My Enemy'[21], all of which would make the final selection for the album. At the same time, a large amount of material landed on the cutting room floor, only to be finally resurrected for a double-CD reissue of the album in 2004. 'Beverly Penn', which will be discussed later in this chapter, 'Sleek White Schooner' (a heavy rocking number with a prominent lead saxophone), the strident 'Medicine Jack' and the band's first take on Van Morrison's 'Sweet Thing' had their origins in the formative *This is the Sea* sessions. Asked by *Rolling Stone* as to whether Scott saw himself as a poet, he referenced 'Spirit': "I have done—but never very good poetry, I don't think; otherwise I'd have been a poet. One song on the record, 'Spirit', was a poem, and I set it to music in the studio, just by chance." In the same conversation he noted that, "Words aren't the salad dressing on top of the meal of music. Words are the first thing for me. I like having a finished lyric that I'm pleased with and letting the music flow from there."

'Medicine Bow', one of the songs to have been initially worked-up by Scott at his flat at 91E St. Mark's Road featured a co-credit for Thistlethwaite. "I went round to Mike's place and he was strumming away. He had two acoustic guitars and he was playing 'Medicine Bow'. He had the lyrics and the tune but he was playing it at half-speed, like a slow song. I started playing with him and it turned into a different rhythm, twice the beats per minute that he was playing in. And I put the ascending line in to the chorus when I heard what he was playing.

---

21 'Be My Enemy' had started out life during the *Pagan Place* recordings as 'The Madness Is Here Again'. This exists in at least two forms, a raw demo track with vocals on the 2002 CD reissue of *A Pagan Place* and as an even rawer instrumental version that circulates on a bootleg from the sessions. A cut of 'Trumpets', presumably the original take at Good Earth Studios can also be located on this bootleg.

When Mike's put in a co-credit, it means an acknowledgement of a contribution to the music. In publishing there's the lyrics and then there is the music—so it might be credited to two names but three-quarters of it belongs to Mike, he would have written all the words. In fact it was very generous of him to credit me on any of the co-writes."

On 'Medicine Bow', and an appearance on *Whistle Test*, The Waterboys were joined on bass by Lu Edmonds who had previously been a member of the Damned, playing as second guitarist on their *Music For Pleasure* album. Edmonds recalls his contribution to 'Medicine Bow' as being "Recorded with Mick Glossop in a studio in Vauxhall [the bass part was overdubbed at Townhouse 3 in April]. It was my first attempt on the bass. I forget how it went but there were very large monitor speakers that made low bass emit and then in fact when I played it on my own little system it was inaudible! I thought they had deliberately mixed it out! Great song anyway and it was made in three weeks when I was in the band to do an *OGWT* and other stuff. Looking back it was a very good band—Karl, Chris and Anto—and many others!"

In an interview with Ian Anderson he recalled his connection to the band as having been made by then Waterboys' manager Jim Chapman: "Mike Scott—what a singer! He actually met me when I was in the Damned and he came and interviewed the band in Edinburgh. I vaguely remembered him as being this very intense young chap." For the *Whistle Test* performance, disingenuously introduced by presenter Ro Newton as 'The band of 1983, The band of 1984 and The band of 1985. But they're not sunk yet', The Waterboys performed an extended version of the album's title track. Nikki Sudden recalled the performance to Dimitri Monroe. "I think Mike is good at using people—using their ideas—trying to empty them and then discarding them. But so are many artists. I was watching the *Old Grey Whistle Test*. The Waterboys came on and watching Mike was like watching myself. The velvet jacket, the scarves, the hair, the lot."

Also initially recorded at Park Gates was a song called 'That Was the River', featuring Tom Verlaine of Television on lead guitar. This was either planned to be the opening track for the album (according to the sleeve-notes accompanying its appearance on the *Secret Life Of The Waterboys* CD) or, as Scott suggested to Liam Mackey, the alternative single version of 'This is the Sea'. Its doppelganger was cut the following month at Townhouse. That both of these possible outlets for 'That Was the River' failed to come to fruition was, Scott considered, because "at the time I had some complaint about the recording—some stupid thing." A faster, heavier counterpoint to 'This is the Sea' it uses the same lyrics but has a very different, more exuberant tone and has since turned up occasionally in the live set.

Taking the place of 'That Was the River' was a song cut at Livingstone Studios, 'Don't Bang the Drum' itself a ferocious rock-out with a dramatic, haunting and atmospheric piano and trumpet intro which U2 adopted for a time as their play-on music for their own live shows. "I'd do a very wide vibrato flourish on the trumpet, on things like 'Don't Bang the Drum' which has the big trumpet intro that's almost two minutes long," notes Lorimer. "I was never a fan of that sort of Spanish trumpet thing at all, it wasn't planned it just came out that way. But I never questioned improvised session work too much anyway. I ended up getting so many jobs after that, being asked to do Spanish solos. Phil Manzanera, the guitarist from Roxy Music, who's of Portuguese/South American origin, used to produce a lot of music for South American bands. He would ask me to do the Spanish trumpet—very successful albums that sold well to Latino people in the USA, but being played by this Jock!"

"Really love that one," noted Scott of 'Don't Bang the Drum'. "I love the trumpet intro. I wrote the lyrics and gave it to Karl Wallinger to put it to music. He did a version that I still have on tape, which is slightly different, some different chords. And I rewrote it myself—sculpted it and changed around."

At Livingstone in May the band also recorded 'The Whole of the Moon' and completed work on 'Trumpets', a song that had been started a whole year previously at Good Earth. The previous month at Townhouse they'd already recorded 'This is the Sea', which had already joined the live set, having been first performed at California's Long Beach Arena (16th December, 1984) and 'Old England', a rare political diatribe from the most romanticised of songwriters. And, at the last moment, there was a chance to revise 'The Pan Within' to include the fiddle playing of Dublin-based musician Steve Wickham. Wickham was at the time blending traditional Celtic music with rock in the Irish band In Tua Nua and, in 1982, had played on U2's *War* album. In a moment of pure serendipity, Scott had heard Wickham at work on a demo for Sinèad O'Connor that Wallinger had been preparing at Seaview. "Sinèad was in my first band, In Tua Nua," recalled Wickham. "Sinèad had written a song, 'Take My Hand', which we'd recorded for Island Records, but she'd come over to do her own thing, Karl was doing the demo, and she asked me to play some fiddle. Mike heard the demo and called me."

Ensign had been interested in O'Connor and as Wallinger recalled, "I had some gear at home—so they said, "Why don't you demo her songs? We want to hear what she's like." For Mike Scott, though, the discovery of the playing of Steve Wickham was almost a 'road to Damascus' revelation. One that, admittedly, arrived too late to influence much of the new album, but which would open up new possibilities and very soon send him and The Waterboys on a totally new route.

With the majority of tracks laid down, Scott was in a position to assess how the tone and feel of the band was evolving, noting to *Jamming* that, "There's much less lead guitar, much less triumphant brass section. There were no premeditated reasons for the change, they just happened." The previous year Springsteen had culled *Born in the USA* from a mammoth collection of recordings and had left what would have been a quite different album on the cutting-room floor. Likewise, Scott's prolific creativity had afforded him the opportunity to condense down from some forty songs a distillation of metaphysical and ethereal tracks. Unlike some of Springsteen's choices, Scott's selections would be thoughtful and considered and gathered up for him a commercial, mainstream album that was accessible without pandering to its audience and which would reward its listeners with its depths and mysteries. All it needed to lift The Waterboys out of the fringes and into the higher echelons of public recognition would be a radio-friendly single.

The sleeve notes for the 2004 reissue of *This is the Sea* reveal that by the time the sessions for the album commenced, Scott had an almost complete songbook prepared. The exception was a work-in-progress that he had begun making notes for in New York but which would be not be fully realised until the band reached Livingstone Studios in May 1985—'The Whole of the Moon'. Interviewed by Stuart Davis in 2005, Scott looked back on this pivotal song and considered that at the time he was "a young man floundering around trying to find reason and direction in life."

This song was worked-out in a three day session with only the sound engineer and Roddy Lorimer as accomplices. "I think it was a Celtic thing," Roddy. "Mike wanted a friend with him while musing about the lyrics. He talked about the lyrics, and there's a specific line—'I saw the rain dirty valley, you saw Brigadoon' or should it be 'I saw the mist in the valley', and I said, 'Oh definitely 'the mist in the valley'. But that says everything about Mike, it wasn't going to be 'the mist in the valley' after that! We'd talk about stuff like that, or he'd say that he wanted trumpets in the middle part. Normally in The Waterboys, I'd play something and Mike would say "like it" or "didn't like it," but in this instance I said, "Get me a tape and I'll take it home and get a look at it". And I actually worked it out on piano instead of trumpet, perhaps to try and harmonise the thing. When you compose or write on an instrument other than what your second nature is, you tend to do different things. Which is why it came out slightly differently—and I had a piccolo trumpet as well as my b-flat trumpet. The idea came out of a piccolo trumpet on one side of the stereo and a piccolo answering it with an ordinary trumpet under it and it just worked. Then I put some classical trumpets on at the end answering each other and to this day so many people know me as that guy who did that. But I also did the backing vocals—though I didn't realise it! I thought it was just me and Mike coming up with ideas. Six months after it came out, I went, 'Wait a minute!'—and of course I was a session musician, not signed to the record company [laughs] and I didn't charge for it!"

'The Whole of the Moon' would become The Waterboys' most recognisable recording, making two chart appearances and essentially being their crossover single—on the one hand radio-friendly and highly commercial, on the other a summation of Mike's cabalistic literary influences. With its wide vista of myth and mystic (unicorns, comets, and of course the enchanted Brigadoon[22]) it has a resonance and depth that belies its catchy, easy listening overtones. Scott later attributed the feel of his lyrics for the song to his reading the works of Mark Helprin, an American writer, born in 1947, who, following spells in the British Merchant Navy and both the Israeli airforce and army, became a writer on politics and aesthetics and a novelist. Although Scott has noted that 'The Whole of the Moon' was not written about Helprin, the author did have a profound impact on him and there is some imagery from his opus work *Winter's Tale* clearly influencing the flow of the song. In particular, a sequence in the novel where the terminally-ill central female character, Beverly Penn, gazes from her rooftop apartment at the night-time sky, though not explicitly referenced in the song, resonates in some of the lyrical imagery.

Winter's Tale had, in fact, already provided both the characters and narrative for the song 'Beverly Penn', cut during the early *This is the Sea* sessions at Park Gates Studio. This track actually opens with the sequence involving Beverly, laid-out on the roof of her father's mansion in furs and covers watching the stars before encountering Peter Lake ('a thief on a horse') who falls in love with her and in whose arms she dies. Like the Shakespearean work from which the book takes its title, it is a novel of redemption and transformation through a long and solitary journey. The book's opening line 'I have been to another world, and come back' would later be paraphrased for the song 'Crown' on The Waterboys 2001 album *A Rock in the Weary Land*.

'The Whole of the Moon' is influenced by, rather than a reference to, Helprin's work. Many listeners have sought in vain for the identities of the people to whom it relates, with Mike Scott merely acknowledging that it has something of C.S. Lewis it in. Indeed, the dream-like quality of the narrative, wherein the dull and the mundane are

22   A Scottish village that legend says is hidden by magical mists and becomes visible only once every hundred years
     to shield its inhabitants from the outside world

contrasted and juxtaposed with something altogether more brilliant and alive, has something of the tone that permeates through the closing sequences of *The Last Battle*. There is also a story that circulates regularly amongst Waterboys' followers that claims how, in a drunken moment, Mike claimed that the song was written about Nikki Sudden. The source of this notion was the song's backing vocalist Max Edie, also known as 'Lizard' but originally born Elizabeth Mary Fairborn Wilcocks, who had previously contributed backing vocals on Nikki's first three solo LPs. Many years after, Sudden asked Mike about this but he had no recollection of ever telling Max this tale. "It's written about various people—C.S. Lewis and others—but definitely not you." Mike had also once, apparently, described 'It Should Have Been You' as partly about Sudden as well as Johnny Thunders, though he also later recanted this, advising Nikki that his place in Waterboys' folklore was actually as the inspiration of the second verse of 'The Late Train To Heaven'.[23]

"I remember sitting in the studio listening to 'The Whole of the Moon' and thinking that the whole world was gonna love this," said Scott. "The comet explosion—KABOOM—that's my favourite bit. And when the sax files out of the comet. The comet goes screeching by the earth and this comes out. A parachuting saxophone!"[24]

With 'The Whole of the Moon' being a standout it was a potential single, but there was some serious consideration of how it should be translated into a promotional video. Although The Waterboys had previously made promo films, Scott was not an enthusiast, claiming to prefer the pictures that the music inspired in the listener's mind to any visual presentation that could be made to accompany his work. He felt that to put his songs as a soundtrack to a video actually devalued them, that they became something secondary and subservient to the visuals.

---

23 ' The Late Train To Heaven', written while Scott was still resident in Aldridge Road Villas, Notting Hill Gate, was originally released as the b-side to 'A Girl Called Johnny'. It is clearly written about Mike's pre-Waterboys associations, with John Caldwell making an appearance in the first verse and Sudden ('dressed in velvet and scarf') clearly delineated in the second. A version of the song, described in the sleeve notes as recorded at Redshop Studios in 1982 and completed at Rockfield the following year, appears as a bonus track on the 2002 reissue of *A Pagan Place*.

24 Quote of unknown origin.

Roddy Lorimer had, with The Kick Horns, been working on Pete Townshend's album *White City.* "With the album, Pete did a film, and we were involved in that as well. Two of the songs we did in the film were shot at Poplar Swimming Baths, because they'd boarded over the pool so you had a stage with the band at the deep end! A few months later, I was up in the West End and bumped into Richard Lowenstein, the director of the film. He said, "Wow, I saw you guys the other night at the Town & Country Club with The Waterboys—fantastic, what a band, I'd love to do a video with them sometime." So I locked that away. When Mike was talking about the video for 'The Whole of the Moon', he wanted it to be *different.* I said, "I've just bumped into the producer for Pete Townshend's film, and Pete actually played guitar and sang live to a backing track." Mike said, "That'd be brilliant," so I gave him the phone number—and that's how that great video for 'The Whole of the Moon' came about."

"But, it was almost a disaster. Mike said, 'I want to re-record the backing track for the film.' Fair enough, we'd do it at Highbury Studios in Islington. I got there mid-afternoon and Mike said, 'Ah, Roddy, come in, we're working on the backing track and I've come up with this whole new concept… I'm not doing it with the rhythm section, I'm doing it with accordion and tambourine!' I said, 'Mike, I've never done this before but I'm telling you I disagree with this completely—you can't do this, you'll kill it.' He obviously realised I was sincere because he went back to the original twenty-four track recording." Visually there couldn't be a shot of one person appearing to play the layered, four-trumpet section. "For the video I did a solo version of that with a slightly Latin trumpet, so that when you see one player—it *is* just one player. The great thing about that video, why it's still so popular today, is that Mike is singing and playing live which makes it very special."

As part of their manifesto, the Clash famously refused to appear on the BBC's flagship music show, *Top of the Pops.* Marcus Gray notes in his biography of the band, "The Clash had thrown in their lot with the music press" as an alternative because the programme "required bands to mime along to a pre-recorded backing track and was therefore deemed inauthentic." Interviewed for Gray's book, *The Last Gang in Town*, NME journalist Tony Parsons considered the stance had "masses of contradictions. We were all part of the music business." *Top of the Pops* didn't have the power to make or break an act *entirely*, The Clash managed fourteen top forty singles between April 1977 and October 1985. However the restriction to just one, hilarious, representation of a Clash single by dance-troupe Legs & Co ('Bank Robber' on the 21st August 1980 edition) must have contributed to their highest chart-position, during the band's lifetime, being an underwhelming eleven for 'London Calling'.

None of the other notable Punk bands followed this particular line. The Stranglers had no qualms about miming along to 'Go Buddy Go' in May 1977, being beaten to the dubious accolade of first Punk/New Wave act on the show by the Jam's 'In the City' the previous week. The Buzzcocks didn't mind doing 'I Don't Mind' in 1978 and the Damned happily performed 'Just can't be Happy Today' in 1979. The Sex Pistols were never going to have the opportunity during their original run, though they did perform a double-header of 'New York' and 'Pretty Vacant' on the 28th June 1996 edition during one of their erratic reunions. Nevertheless, the stance taken by the Clash formed an important impression on Mike Scott and he seemed determined to follow their example when the opportunity arose, despite having already mimed on other television shows.

Once 'The Whole of the Moon' headed for the higher steps of the charts, Scott's refusal to appear on *Top of the Pops* had potentially far-reaching consequences for their record label Ensign and onwards to their distributor, Island Records. Dave Robinson had originally made his mark alongside business partner Jake Riviera signing Elvis Costello and the Damned to their fledgling Stiff Records label in 1976. By the time *This is the Sea* was released he was employed by Island and enduring Scott's lack of adaptability in the promotional stakes.

"Ensign did a licence deal with Island," Robinson recalls. "I arrived at Island at the end of 1983 and Ensign were there. In those days, if you had a small label you would licence them to a bigger label and they would pay your costs and your royalty. You were the A&R source

and the basic shape of the label but they would have the rights internationally to your output. So a small label would sell to a bigger label
in a hopefully agreeable sort of partnership to make something work."
This 'agreeable partnership' would, of course, need to extend to the
acts signed to the source label but Scott was already uncomfortable
with the direction that Ensign were going in and had a clear personality clash in his dealings with Robinson at Island. "Mike and I did
not hit it off—he irritated me to a degree because I thought it was
such a waste of what he had. He wanted fame but pretended he was
above it all, though quite honestly he was very ambitious. It was difficult to get him to talk sense because he was a bit spoilt and thought
that the artist should control everything, which is a good attitude if
the artist is bright about business and marketing matters and he just
wasn't." Robinson saw the root cause of Mike's awkwardness when
it came to promotional activity deriving from the way his talent had
been indulged by Nigel Grainge at Ensign. However, Mike's disdain
of record industry control ("He resented authority of any kind," comments Robinson) almost certainly travelled back much further, to the
rejection of the APF album by Virgin. "Nigel was very good at bringing along talent, but they always seemed to be problematical at the
end of the day. I think part of the problem was that he was excited
by their talent—he's a very good picker—but at the end of the day
he may have spoilt them a little and that was a drawback both for his
record label and the artists themselves. You've got to teach them what
it's about—it's a learning process, people don't just get discovered with
gold ingots in their teeth. People call it paying your dues, but that's
not the essence of it, you learn a certain stage-craft or professionalism
and it never hurts to be nice to people, it doesn't cost anything at all."

The issue came to a head by April 1984 when it was clear that, in
'The Whole of the Moon', The Waterboys had produced something
special. It was a single that could stand as both a commercially attrac-
tive, radio-friendly work and as a metaphor for the wider strand of
Celtic rock that was being categorised under the 'Big Music' banner.

"This is the Sea was the most commercial Waterboys album—but
there wasn't any sell-out in that, it just had so many great songs on

it that nobody could ignore it," considers Roddy. "But you did have a situation where Mike was not self-destructive, but as near as damn it. He refused to toe the company line and do what the record company wanted. When 'The Whole of the Moon' was released he said we'll do it [*Top of the Pops*] if we can do it live, but at that time there was no live performances on it, it was all mimed. So he said, 'Well, we're not doing it.' So they did relent and said, 'You can do it live,' and I think Mike said, 'We want to do it live from a barn in Gloucestershire.' Fuck Off.' So, no *Top of the Pops*, no hit—though it did eventually become a hit because [DJs] just didn't stop playing it for the next ten years."

Thistlethwaite recalls the events and the decision, which, as he notes, would have been a decision for Scott alone. "I think they said we could play live. But then Mike said, 'but I don't want any effects in the background or dancing people in our way.'"

"There was a famous *Top of the Pops* situation where he got an offer to do it, and didn't want to do it, but eventually agreed he would," adds Robinson, "But, obviously he *didn't* want to do it and was prepared to mess it about. If he just didn't do it, that's one thing! *Top of the Pops* in those days was a very powerful show, with a very powerful producer in Michael Hurll. He had the biggest show on TV for music, and so had a certain attitude of his own. At the end of it he called me to say he wouldn't have any Island or Ensign, or Stiff, acts ever again on his show—which is the sort of thing you don't want to hear![25] So that was a bit of a blow, and the first of many. Mike didn't really want to promote—he wanted the success and the fame and complained when it seemed like the record company wasn't doing enough—but he didn't understand that the record company had to go out on a limb, had to spend money, had to have an attitude. I always tell artists that they motivate the record company—but that's a double-edged sword,

25 To be fair, Hurll had been something of a two-headed dragon in his stewardship of *Top of the Pops*. He'd brought John Peel back into the presenter's fold—Peel's previous attempt at presenting it in 1968 was a disaster—and would (ironically) reintroduce live performances during his tenure. On the other hand, Hurll came to the show from a strictly light-entertainment background (his previous producership was for the Friday teatime slapstick kid's show *Crackerjack*) and was responsible for taking *Top of the Pops* downmarket with a flashy and trashy overtone. In an article for the website *Off The Telly*, Steve Williams sums up his tenure as having "wit and charm to tone down the more vulgar aspects, and it could be argued that the early 1980s were the programme's finest hour. Certainly, the viewing figures seemed to bear this out."

you could motivate the record company to not want to do things and that's pretty much the situation we ended-up which was a shame when you consider how good he was."

'The Whole of the Moon' failed to appear on *Top of the Pops* during its first run in the UK charts. It reached number twenty-six during November 1985, the best showing a Waterboys single would make during the Big Music era. At the same time, other bands associated with the genre were starting to make their own commercial mark: U2 reached number six a few months earlier with 'The Unforgettable Fire', Simple Minds achieved two top seven records during the year in 'Don't You (Forget About Me)' and 'Alive and Kicking'. Even the Alarm, whose singles chart success was as modest as The Waterboys, made twenty-two early the following year with 'Spirit of 76'.

"He's inclined to entice you in, he likes the romance of it, then he turns you down when you set-up something," says Dave Robinson. "That's difficult for anyone to go along with but it's a kind of technique that he has had—if he just said no, you'd know where you stood. He wants to get somewhere, so he wants to appease to a degree but when it comes down to factual details he wants to oppose what your ideas are. It's a shame, there have been a few of them like that but not quite as talented as him. He had the potential to become a huge international act, and that kind of music would have been great, a big music that would have been marvellous to have had on the international record market because it would have opened the door to a lot of other people. Big Country had a little bit of it, but not to the talent extent that he had."

A lot has been made of Mike's failure to embrace *Top of the Pops*. Twenty years on from the decision, it is still a favourite story for journalists and has received an enormous amount of coverage. This is for good reason. Today *Top of the Pops* is a spent force. At the time of writing it had finally been cancelled, having previously been reallocated a Sunday evening BBC2 slot, displacing it from its traditional BBC1 prime-time dominance that it had enjoyed since New Year's Day 1964. But in the 1980s it was still at its height, pre-MTV, pre-CD: UK, the most visible showcase for music in the UK. In rejecting the programme Mike Scott was making a conscious decision to eschew fame and fortune. Unlike the Clash, he didn't have a substantial music press crusade in his favour and neither was he being swept along in a radical revision of the UK music scene.

"Eventually Ensign left Island and signed to Chrysalis," notes Robinson. "But he never really got where he wanted to get, he never really got to the place where, probably, with his talent he should have got." He attributes this as being "down to the anchors he threw out constantly along the way in terms of opposing any kind of record company involvement or marketing. He was an anti-guy rather than a positive guy."

'The Whole of the Moon' did achieve a second lease of life in 1991, when it reached the top three, with the promotional film finally receiving an airing on *Top of the Pops*. It appeared on the 4th April programme and again on the prestigious Christmas Day review of the year edition. The *NME* summed up the song's revival as: "One of these happy coincidences in late '88 when club DJs like Andy Weatherall and Terry Farley began playing 'The Whole of the Moon' at clubs like Phuture and Chaos. Mike's blissful outpourings fitting in with the sunny Balearic ideal."

Extracted from its mammoth collection of demo recordings, *This is the Sea* demonstrates both continuity with and closure from *The Waterboys* and *A Pagan Place*. Throughout the album there is a feeling of shifting sands, of frustration, of dissatisfaction and a sense of an end being sought after and reached. The tone is angry, accusatory and the range of targets for Scott's bile and vitriol wide-ranging, even though he would claim to *Melody Maker*'s Mat Smith that "I don't think there is anything particularly unhappy about [*This is the Sea*]. Except of course 'Old England' but that's not to do with personal unhappiness as many of the older songs were."

On 'Don't Bang the Drum' Scott is both challenging his subject and dejected about the protagonist's ability to deliver—calling upon that person to live up to their surroundings and possibilities. There is a stark sense of underachievement. Not only is Scott demanding that somebody rise to the moment, bare their soul, but, Hamlet-like, there is a father's ghost also trying to guide the right path, though never is there a feeling that inner-ambition will lead to anything more than a primitive response to (perhaps) divine surroundings.

The atmosphere is transposed and reversed on Scott's first mainstream classic, 'The Whole of the Moon', with its spirit of admiration and awe of someone taking every chance and opportunity, daring to follow their dreams and absolutely prepared to reach high and far in pursuit of them. The lyrics might seem a direct counterpoint to 'Don't Bang the Drum' but in fact they resonate in time with the following tracks, 'Spirit' and, most particularly, 'The Pan Within'. Both of these feel as though the tables have been turned, that the observer who is so impressed with the personality described in 'The Whole of the Moon' is now himself being fêted and urged onwards—'put your face to my window / breathe a night full of treasure'. Come on, take a deep breath, surrender yourself and follow a new path, I can show you the way. Scott pondered the significance of 'Spirit' to Merle Ginsberg. "The song is looking up. I'm not saying you *could* be much better. I'm saying you *will* be. There are various methods of achieving that that have been known since the dawn of civilisation."

Though by mid-album Scott is painting a mystical, spiritual route that can be attained simply through letting-go of the mundane and trusting to the sanctity of the inner-self, much of the second-half revisits the angst and anger of the opening song. In 'Medicine Bow', Scott is once again dissatisfied and restless, any colours that he has previously nailed to his mast have to be changed and everything he has created before has to be consigned to the fire. Yet again, as previously with 'All the Things She Gave Me' and 'Rags' Scott was seeing something redemptive and cleansing in the flames. He has to go back to year-one, put himself to extreme test, break free of his chains, prove and renew his character and creative abilities. Standing to one side, Scott then, in a rare and awkward political moment, surveys the state of 'Old England' at the height of Margaret Thatcher's administration. The track nearly ended-up on the cutting-room floor because, as Scott explained to Marc Issue in a 1985 copy of *Beat*, "it was a bit negative, and what the world needs right now is a lot of positive feelings."

However, it was probably retained because, he said, "I still sort of... believe in it." In *Vox* magazine he recalled that, "It was really about Thatcher's Britain, 1984. She'd just won that second election. I didn't like what the Tories were doing. I felt they were dismantling a lot of the structure of the society of the country. I also thought there was a lot of jingoism after the Falklands War."

In itself, 'Old England' is an adaptable and pliable "State of the Nation" summing up. The version committed to vinyl rounds up and pokes at the usual suspects—the dirty blue of "Old England's" clothes must represent the Conservative Government, the alluded to Empire song and England's naval strength a metaphor for the Falklands War. But elsewhere in the official version, Scott's targets are clumsy, obvious and generic: criminals, politicians, and journalists. Outside of the LP's cut of the song, the coda set its sights wider. A session for the radio show *Saturday Live* in February 1985 produced a stunning and in hindsight precognitive blast at former Labour MP and then recently installed owner of the *Daily Mirror*, Robert Maxwell[26], claiming that 'many things are right / but you're all wrong'. At Glastonbury in 1986, though the coda followed more closely the version from *This is the Sea*, Scott additionally demanded 'tear it down—throw up the new one'—and in another rare political gesture dedicated 'Be My Enemy' to "Mr. President Ronnie Reagan". On *This is the Sea*, the target of 'Be My Enemy' is less clear, possibly a vitriolic stab at a disaffected lover, perhaps an attack on someone that Scott saw as holding him back, maybe a sweeping statement about the destructive power of negativity. It's strong, black and gut-wrenching, the narrator seemingly lost in a downward spiral of hate and antipathy and prepared to do anything to his declared enemy, including injury or murder—though it's this referencing of physical violence that most leads the listener to accept the sentiment as metaphorical. Certainly the mood abruptly changes, 'Trumpets' and the LP's title (and final) track having an altogether different ambience, one a celebration of consuming joy and love, the other really an optimistic summing up of the album's disparate, almost schizophrenic moods. There are, of course, no actual trumpets

---

26 Maxwell of course achieved enduring notoriety after his death in 1991, attributed to accidental drowning but almost certainly suicide in anticipation of the discovery of his impending bankruptcy.

on 'Trumpets'. "That would be too obvious, and Mike would never go for the obvious," notes Lorimer. "My impressions are that Mike found them noble, bright, pure, these sort of words. So, 'My love feels like trumpets'... I understood it at that level. It's such an ancient instrument, a marshal instrument. Amongst swords and spears and shields being clattered about, someone sounds the trumpet and everyone hears it. It's the clarion call, the clarity of it finds its way through."

"I can be very self-critical," Scott told Martin Aston in Q magazine years later. "I can cut myself off before I get started, telling myself that what I've done isn't good enough." From the viewpoint of 'This is the Sea', there is an instruction to throw away the old and embrace the new, catch that train, see the previous existence as something old and gone. It's as though there is a split personality, the war raging inside the head, the mental anguish and internal argument. This song gets right back into the thrust of 'Don't Bang the Drum' and comes full circle, rejecting the soulless existence painted in the LP's opening moments and treating it as a journey, comparable with the travelling of the river into the sea. It's really the sentiment of somebody making a huge adjustment in their life and that really elucidates the themes of the album and points to a crossroads in Mike Scott's creative thinking. "There's a romanticism in these songs that's seldom found elsewhere in popular music," wrote George Byrne in a contemporary review of the LP. "Scott seems to be striving for something that will always be just out of reach... God? Love? I really don't know, and I'm not sure if I want to find out."

This is the Sea hasn't necessarily stood the test of time better than its predecessors, its big production values ("Diamond-hard yet crystal clear, full but not slick," wrote one music critic) rooting some of the material squarely into the mid-80s. It was, in any case, Scott's last application of that 'wall-of-sound' technique for another fifteen years. "I finished with that kind of music to achieve whatever it was I was trying to achieve with that album," he told Alain Gales. "That overdubbed big sounding music, I didn't need to do it anymore." But because of its intimate complexities and its rewarding study of an artist in turmoil, seeking out new horizons and destinations it is a cornerstone in understanding Mike Scott's emotional and creative journey. On release it merited some unfavourable comparisons with *A Pagan Place*, Andy Strickland (who saw it veering "dangerously towards just another Waterboys' album rather than a step forward") noting, for example, that it lacked "the triumphant feel and classic consistency of its elder brother." But Scott was starting to come to terms with his position in the world and recognising both his strength and fallibility. "In the days of Another Pretty Face I never had any self-doubt," he mused to Dave Sprague. "The music I made was too self-assured, too breast-beating. As I get older, I find out I know less and less."

What was fascinating about Andy Strickland's critique of the album was his on-the-nail identification that "it may be time for Mike Scott to allow a little more outside influence on his work." By the time the next Waterboys' album appeared, Scott would have embraced a whole new range of collaborators and influences that retrospectively allows the first three albums to be placed in a collective context that Scott had exploited in full and moved on from.

Lorimer saw some of this in the background of differing ambitions within the band itself. "Anto just loved Mike as a person and as a musician and he was happy to just be part of it, I was more on the outside and as a session player not intimately involved in it. But for Karl, it must have been grating because as you can hear from his band, World Party, he is a great individual writer/singer/performer. And so for *This is the Sea* his playing was so much a big part of it and he influenced the album greatly."

The Waterboys had been entirely focused on the sessions for *This is the Sea* throughout 1985, with only one live appearance during the first eight months of the year, at a benefit concert for the Miners at South London Polytechnic on 15th February. October saw the band gearing up to promote the new album with a run of dates in the UK leading to their first headlining North American tour the following month. By this time Martyn Swain had departed from the line-up, with bass duties taken-up by Marco Sin, originally from Queens, New York). Sin had previously been a member of CBGB's regulars Dirty Looks, who had relocated to England to record their eponymous first album for Stiff Records in 1979. He stayed with The Waterboys through to a tour of Europe in December, leaving the band after a show in France due to a cocaine overdose. He later spent time being active in support of Alcoholics Anonymous and Narcotics Anonymous and working in support of victims of sexual abuse, though his recurring problems with drugs eventually led to his untimely death from heart failure in October 1995.

Steve Wickham joined the promotional tour on sabbatical from In Tua Nua, though as events would turn out he wasn't to return to their ranks. For the band's gig at London's Town & Country Club, backing-vocals on 'The Big Music' were provided by Sinéad O'Connor, making her first UK live appearance. Lorimer recalls this particular show with much affection. "Tim Sanders from the Kick Horns came to see The Waterboys play at the Town & Country Club up in Kentish Town, and afterwards he said a great thing to me: 'That was so brilliant, it reminded me of why I want to play music.' What the band gave off not just in a musical sense but an emotional sense was completely captivating. The Waterboys never played a number in the same way twice, so each performance was completely unique. That could be a nightmare because you never knew what was going to happen. I remember one night going onto stage and Mike took me aside as we went on and said, 'Roddy, in the second song, when I nod at you I want you to answer back musically, and we'll keep answering each other.' And I spent the whole of the number waiting for him to nod—and he's out there bobbing around everywhere—and it's that seat-of-the-pants feel, you never thought it was going to be comfortable *ever*, and it shouldn't be." Scott commented to *Rock On* that, "Some songs always stay the same but others lend themselves to change. I always liked to hear Bruce Springsteen do totally different versions of his songs. With 'Thunder Road' he could do it like on the album with the band, and then he could do it just on the piano."

"For a few months at least we had Roddy and I on horns, Karl on keyboards and Steve doing fiddle—and I thought it was fantastic, like we were Gods!" enthuses Thistlethwaite. "And they were all people I respected as well."

"We'd done a show in Canada; Toronto I think, and it was just sublime—we all knew it was great and afterwards we were hugging each other, it was such a feeling," Lorimer adds. "The next day on the tour bus somebody said, 'Oh, put the desk tape on and we'll listen to it', but by this time we'd done another show and the ashen-faced sound engineer said, 'Actually, I recorded over it.' But someone, Mike or Anto, said, 'It doesn't matter—that show will always be that great—if we listened to the desk tape it might not have been that great, but it'll never change now.' I think it was the night that some of the Native Americans came backstage afterwards with harmonicas, blues harps and guitars and we had a jam backstage with them, an amazing feeling. This was the sort of thing that would happen with Waterboys' shows—like you could find yourself out on San Francisco bay with the Greenpeace protestors!"

As late as October 1985 Mike Scott was openly claiming that The Waterboys' line-up, though always in a state of flux and change, would continue to be centralised around the 'Big Music' nucleus that had polished *A Pagan Place* and created *This is the Sea*. "Some of the guys, like Karl Wallinger and Anthony Thistlethwaite seem like they're here to stay. And if others come along that were right then obviously I'd like them to stay, but I do like switching about in the studio, and having people from different towns joining in when we're touring. I like the idea of having a big pool of musicians I can rely on." Under this assurance of continuity there was Scott, within himself getting ready for the next twist in his journey of discovery and Wallinger becoming increasingly disillusioned with the opportunities The Waterboys afforded him. As Scott had previously noted to Harold DeMuir, "It's my songs and my group, basically. It's my vision of things that gets followed and I've got control over everything."

Karl Wallinger left The Waterboys after the final date of the American tour, at Irving Plaza, New York, on 16th November 1985, frustrated with the lack of input he was able to bring to the direction of the band. Perhaps, also, he had foreseen that the additional of Steve Wickham, and Scott's obvious affinity with him, would further marginalise his own contribution to the band. Brimming with his own ideas and songs, The Waterboys, so clearly focused around the sublime talents of Mike Scott to the virtual exclusion of all others, was never going to be enough to satisfy Wallinger's immense ambitions and abilities. And, of course, Scott had seen himself as very firmly the captain of the ship ever since Another Pretty Face. "It was precisely because I didn't really like the fact that it was his football and he was choosing the teams that I left," Wallinger later commented.

"The only person it ever created problems with was Karl Wallinger who would've liked more authority than I was prepared to give," Scott considered. "The Waterboys was never his band, we'd made two albums before he came along [sic]. He was the keyboard player but he had bandleader quality in him. So he went off and did his own thing, forming World Party." Guy Chambers replaced Wallinger for their final commitments of 1985, fourteen dates opening for fellow Big Music exponents Simple Minds on a European tour that took in Holland, France and Belgium. Interestingly he also went on to play in Wallinger's World Party before becoming, most notably, Robbie Williams' co-songwriter. "Karl was a mentor for me," he told Spencer Leigh in Record Collector. "He is an extraordinary talent. He has an incredible memory for songs and would memorise hundreds of lyrics. He made me realise how important words were, that they are just as important as music."

"Karl was a huge part of what the band was then, and I think the frustration of not being able to make all the final decisions was one of the things that lead to him leaving the band and going out on his own," claims Roddy Lorimer. "Karl had decided to leave the band. Perhaps it was a bit lacking in feeling but during the tour, Karl had decided that and Mike started to audition piano players in New York. Now, I'm not signed to the band so I'm not involved in auditioning piano players, so I said to Karl, 'Let's go for a walk'. So we went to Strawberry Fields in Central Park, the garden dedicated to John Lennon, and as you can hear from Karl's music he's a big Lennon fan. We just walked about, talked about Lennon and what had happened and it's just across from the Dakota Buildings where it happened, so we walked across there. Just at the spot where Lennon was killed there were a lot of pigeons, then a dog barked or a car backfired—a noise of some sort—and the pigeons all flew away except there was one that flew right at us and it was a white dove. It flew right up and over the buildings and we just looked at each other and thought *Jesus*. Just one of those magical moments that happen in your life and it doesn't matter why, coincidence or whatever; it's just the effect it has on you, this mystical thing."

"Karl was a joker who used to wind me up at times," adds Lorimer. "Once he locked me outside on a balcony in Toronto in the middle of winter, and I'd just washed my hair. There was a strange looking sign outside and I went out, but saying, "Look, I've got a cold, I don't want it all tour so don't shut the door. Of course, Karl being Karl shut the door and locked it. He's rolling about in laughter and I'm 'Open the fucking door!' and lost my temper and kicked in a plate glass window—and I've never been prone to violence in life! I got a dressing down from the record company, but I think they quite liked it as well"!

Wallinger and Scott have been cool in tone towards each other ever since their split. A few years after he'd left the band, Wallinger made the suggestion that he should produce some of Scott's studio work, but, according to Mat Snow, "Mike didn't even bother to return the call." Wallinger thought, "He's in his own world, doing his own thing, and good luck to him." Many have seen Scott's response to Wallinger in a song recorded in 1985 and partly credited to Wallinger himself, 'World Party' though Scott denied that he had been the subject of the song despite the many clues within the song pointing in that direction. "My song 'World Party' is about Live Aid, it's not written about Karl at all," Scott claimed. "We both wrote songs called 'World Party' around about the same time. It's not meant to be a "how do you sleep" attack on Karl, I wouldn't waste my time doing something like that." Lorimer recalls this song and agrees with Scott's assessment. "'World Party' was about Live Aid, Mike would really have loved to have been involved in it. We were touring with U2 and Bono had to fly back quickly to London to do 'Feed the World'. It was new, this idea of music as a force for good in a global sense and I think Mike was hurt to have missed out in being asked to do Live Aid. But it's tough, it's your profile and I suppose The Waterboys' profile was deliberately low and thus he didn't get it. But that's why he wrote 'get yourself along to the world party.'"

Wallinger himself posted to an Internet discussion in 2000 on the subject, explaining that he'd come across the phrase written on a piece of graphic by his brother, Tim, which inspired him to write a song using 'World Party' as the title. "I don't know when exactly I played it to [Mike Scott]," he wrote, "but Mike and I had both been to Live Aid and that kind of world vibe was kind of happening or rather we thought it was anyway." But there certainly appeared to be some rancour on the matter, as he went on to comment that "Unfortunately he just thought I was a kind of extra brain for him to have access to in a way."

Wallinger and Scott seem to be more alike underneath than they ever would appear to be on the surface, despite Wallinger being consistently characterised as the ebullient joker and Scott the dour and introverted artist. Both have established bands that are very much expressions of where they are, emotionally or inspirationally, rather than collective ensembles in the traditional sense. Karl's principal post-Waterboys project, World Party[27], though he has relied on friends from past endeavours as guest musicians (Steve Wickham, Anthony Thistlethwaite and Chris Whitten have all been called upon to serve) is essentially a one-man-band, appropriately enough. And, indeed, during their Waterboys association Wallinger certainly seems to have become wrapped-up in some of the same underlying mystical back-story that fascinated Mike Scott. "When I was with The Waterboys, and when I came out of that and did my first album I was very much in the esoteric mist, Glastonbury Tor, the red rose, the esoteric philosophies of life that are very popular amongst fey gothic types. But it is a real thing and it can be very inspiring if you can locate the essence of it, it really is an angle to life. William Blake's outpourings are inspirational, people do have a thrill sometimes when they sing 'Jerusalem',

27 Still seemingly raw about the use of the phrase 'World Party', Wallinger noted that "I thought it was a bit rich to nick a title and do his own song ... or I *think* I thought that then, you see! Suffice it to say that I think his version came out first so people kind of thought that I'd named my band after a Waterboys' song."

you can get carried away by it all, 'Bring me my sword', the symbolism of it stirs something within the subconscious."[28]

Despite the all-night creative sessions at Seaview Studios with Wallinger, and the apparent camaraderie with Thistlethwaite, Scott still cut a lonely and solitary figure throughout the Big Music era. Though he had a relationship with photographer Lynn Goldsmith[29] during 1985, sending her a name-check from the stage at Irving Plaza, he was still fundamentally obsessed with his song-writing career over-and-above any associations outside of the music business as he acknowledged to John Milward in *USA Today*. "I realised that my work had taken over my life to the exclusion of everything else. I can't honestly say I've resolved what to do about it." Whilst that awareness of his position had been declared in 1985, it reflected the way Scott had been totally focused on maintaining his creative energies right through the first half of the decade.

In the way that Scott described his way of life, little had changed since the earliest days of The Waterboys when Anthony Thistlethwaite was observing Scott holed-up in his flat making probably more phone calls than was strictly necessary and having little other contact with the world at large. "When I go home after a hard day's work I go home to an empty place," he told Chris Heath of *Jamming* magazine, exuding a forlorn and distant tone. "There aren't many mates there playing a new record they just bought, or telling me about what they just read, so I don't have any normal communications like that." He claimed to actually prefer this lifestyle. "I live on my own and I do most of my thinking on my own. And my best friends are the musicians that I play with." Nevertheless, it appears that the undercurrent was of somebody only really able to connect with a satisfying lyric, a well-honed stanza or a musical progression that elucidated or expanded on his word-craft. "I don't enjoy life when my world is unsuccessful, but then I've been in the studio, in the darkened room with pen and paper. My experience is blinkered; I haven't been out in the world doing things

28 Radio interview.
29 Goldsmith, who photographed Scott for the cover of *This is the Sea*, also enjoyed her own musical career in the early 1980s under the nom-de-plume Will Powers. She achieved a high of number seventeen in October 1983 with the single 'Kissing With Confidence' before going on to a career as a major rock photographer.

and seeing how people live." Heath observed this in Scott's output, delineating the unifying idea or message in his music as being 'one of searching, glimpsing possibilities, waving in the hope that someone will wave back. The roar with a vision of something better. Or, to put it another way, the reek of disappointment, of unfulfilment.'

This self-imposed isolation from the world was surely compounding his discomfort with both the trappings of popular success and its demands. "I just haven't got enough time to go to the places I want to go to or read the books I want to read," he complained to *Melody Maker's* Mat Smith. "I've been chasing the tail of this record ever since the end of last year and it feels like I'm living in a vacuum. Every waking moment I have seems to be dedicated to work, there just isn't enough time for other things and that bothers me a lot 'cos outside influences are where inspiration comes from." But the addition of Steve Wickham to the band made a huge difference to how Scott wanted the band to progress and opened up a whole new index of possibilities to consider. Interviewed by Dave Sprague late into 1985 he realised that, "I've achieved everything I set out to do with the type of music I've been making—I'm hearing different sounds in my head now. Really different. I've been working with rolling piano, violin, sax, trumpet all playing lead at once. A synth playing a constant 'whaaaa' behind. And bells. But I don't have any metaphors for it."

And so this was Mike Scott at the mid-point of the 1980s having reached a milestone in his personal odyssey. After 1984's year of consolidation, of working the touring circuit and developing a reputation for The Waterboys as an exciting, epic live sound and the intensive writing and recording of '85, Scott's music was firmly established as a leading part of a Celtic rock movement. Loosely defined, certainly, convenient labelling, no doubt. But the fact was that The Waterboys as an idea, as a unit and as a force had found a place that was far more than the niche that they'd occupied previously. They were now a recognisable and marketable rock act that could build on their achievements during the remainder of the eighties. Not surprising then, based on Scott's character and internal motivations, that at the very cusp of substantial mainstream success, he would look for the interesting or unexplored tributary and steer his boat in quite the opposite direction to the flow of the tide.

5

FISHERMAN'S BLUES

"I would love to be successful in America!" Given the unwelcome pressures that the accomplishment of 'The Whole of the Moon' and *This is
the Sea* had placed on Mike Scott it was somewhat surprising to read
in *Beat* magazine that his next target could be an assault on the home
of rock'n'roll. "I'm fascinated by the place," he explained. "I just can't
get enough of the place. Everything is happening, all the time! As a
musician you only see [these places] in the context of tours. Your time
isn't as open for adventure as you'd like it to be."

At the end of 1985, Scott was clearly harbouring a desire to find
the next stage of his journey in the epic landscapes that had fired his
imagination from the music of Dylan and Springsteen to the spiritual
ethos of the Native American culture. He'd declared to Mat Smith,
in his typically dreamy and idealised way that he'd, "like to change
my circumstances, maybe move to New York, It's time for a change
of scenery. I think it will be an inspiring move. I just figure there are
people there I want to work with and be with."

His change of circumstances actually developed in a much more
organic way and not in the intended direction. It would lead Scott
far away from the introverted city life that he'd lived through the first

years of The Waterboys. For the rest of the eighties he could almost be characterised as having absconded to Ireland, certainly in the way that he effectively tore-up his route-map and relocated to the Emerald Isle. And he immersed himself in a musical scene that was as much about finding comradeship and community as it was about understanding tradition and the influence of geography. He continued to be plagued by self-doubt and the difficulties of balancing the feeding of his ever-demanding muse with a real ache for fulfilment in his relationships. But, on the other side of the scales, he would find both satisfaction and personal development in seeing out his inner-demons through a difficult year and then consolidating his, quite unexpected, position in a burgeoning Irish music scene.

He was painfully honest about the reasons for needing to find a new start in life, telling long-time observer of Irish music, Colin Irwin, how he was "in bits at the end of our last tour and Steve said, 'come over and stay, man.' So I went over and stayed and that was it. I'd moved to Ireland." To Jon Wilde, in *Uncut* many years later, he recalled that "before I went off to Ireland, it was like being caught in a cross-fire. There was pressure from all sides. Everyone around me seemed to know what I should and shouldn't be doing next. I felt like so many people wanted to own me and live my life for me." But there were other influences coming to bear. He'd become totally captivated with the possibilities that Steve Wickham's presence in the band offered, identifying with a kindred spirit much more than he ever had with Wallinger's joker-in-the-pack mentality. "I had this big relationship with Steve, a musical love story," Scott commented. "I followed the fellow who fiddles. But I was also pretty unhappy in London. I wasn't enjoying myself at all." That said, a certain amount of expediency was also at work. "I went to stay with Steve because I was homeless at the time. The landlord was selling the flat I was staying at in London, so I had to get out and that was in the middle of a tour. So when the tour finished it was Christmas and I went home to my mum. And then after the New Year I had to go somewhere so the Wick asked me over to Dublin."[30]

30 *NME*, September 1990.

Steve Wickham was born in 1960 in Rotunda, Dublin and was always going to be a professional musician, having learned the violin at the age of four and attending the College of Music in Chatham Row from seven until he was fifteen. But that creative path wasn't clear to him when embarked on a three-year career with the Bank of Ireland at their Dublin head office on Baggot Street which, according to an interview with Jim Carroll in the *Dublin City Review*, was "pretty good fun." Despite the incongruity of such a job, Wickham explained that "I was a musician even then. I knew I wouldn't be in that job for the rest of my life." He was playing in a few bands but when those didn't work out the wanderlust struck him, sending him off with his cousin to busk the streets of Europe, taking in Italy, Greece and France with stopovers in London and Copenhagen.

'All we did was play music, no other work to get money,' he told Carroll. 'Irish tunes, Bob Dylan tunes, everything. You just open your case and play where you can. That's the kind of busking we would do—play all day and people would give us money and we would survive on that.' Encountering the Edge at a bus stop, he had the opportunity to play on U2's *War* album and joined them on tour in support of that LP. 'I used to come on and play 'Sunday Bloody Sunday', and on the odd night or two, one or two others.'

Wickham really came to prominence with his membership of In Tua Nua, following a meeting with the band's guitarist Ivan O'Shea. Playing a mixture of traditional and rock flavoured music, Wickham's association lasted no more than a couple of years. Jim Carroll noted in a *Hot Press* interview after the departure of Wickham and the band's tin whistle player Vinnie Kilduff "an amount of bitterness existed." But Wickham saw it as a crossroads in his musical development, "between going out having adventures, which is what The Waterboys thing is, and staying home."[31]

Scott's arrival in Dublin, though the intention was that it would be simply a break, a New Year stopover, in hindsight ushered in the next incarnation of The Waterboys. But it also once again affirmed a practically universal truth. However any one person might believe them-

31 Interviewed by Paddy Kehoe.

selves to be the captain of the ship or the guiding light of a creative enterprise, there is a reality inherent in collaboration. It means that for even a band with such a firm hand as Scott's holding the tiller, being in a group entails a partnership where inspiration and technique would be drawn from one another in a sort of symbiotic alliance. In the case of The Waterboys, it effectively drills down into each phase of the group being Scott's guiding vision supported by another member's own intuition and imagination binding together to create the concept of the band at that moment in time. Anto saw this right at the start and acknowledges how this evolved. "Mike needed a foil and for a while I was probably that man, then we met Karl and I was kind of happy to pass on the job. In a way it suited me, because it's rather tiring. Mike is very single-minded and he wants a lot from you, it's a demanding position to be in."

"The next era was very much Mike and Steve," adds Roddy Lorimer, though he emphasises, "Mike was looking to move on anyway. It wasn't all down to Steve, although Steve is such a magical performer and he added so much. I have great admiration for him as an extraordinary musician. He's not a laugher and a joker, he's a very serious person—he thinks about what he is doing and it's deep and meaningful to him. Mike saw that and loved that. And also, it was different from what Mike did—that folk violin—and so Mike could just give Steve his head and didn't really need to instruct him what to do, Steve could just go off and do his magical thing." And that was really the rub of what was going to drive the new Waterboys' sound, replacing the lead guitars and heavy keyboard sound of the Big Music with acoustic instruments. This allowed the band to take on a very different challenge. It could now incorporate a wider vista of styles and tones. It could head off into a whole new way of making music and a completely different approach to creating it, being liberated by the idea of making The Waterboys an acoustic band that could play anywhere and with anyone. It would start them on what Anto describes as, "a thing between Mike, Steve and myself—a three-way band of gypsies or something, a funny little adventure."

Right at that moment, then, it wasn't just Scott who was relishing a chance to take on a new direction, as Anto describes. "At the beginning of January [1986] we went over and stayed with Steve, who had a flat in Central Dublin, Mike and I—we slept on the floor in the front room. I had already been playing mandolin, I'd played it on 'Red Army Blues', so I had that and the saxophone, Mike had his acoustic guitar. The mandolin, the fiddle and the guitar made a good three-piece! We'd sit in pubs and play songs and the country-folky sort of aspect suddenly came out, and this suited me fine because in fact it's less physical to play the mandolin rather than pumping into a great big saxophone, kind of relaxing, so that was nice." The three of them may have found a different pace of life in Dublin (though unlike Scott, Thistlethwaite never fully relocated to Ireland preferring to retain his London home and use a flat in Dublin rented by the band), but there were commercial pressures again lurking in the background. "There was a time there [in Dublin] where things were not difficult and all three of us were having a ball, free of all chains; a moment that was fantastic. I don't know how long it lasted because there was this cloud of having to make another record."

The recordings for the next Waterboys' album, *Fisherman's Blues*, got off to a flying and deceptively straightforward start, with a day's rehearsal in England where bass player Trevor Hutchinson and drummer Peter McKinney, who had played together in the band Kathmandu, joined the core trio. This quintet then reassembled on 23rd January 1986 at Dublin's Windmill Lane Studios.

"This was a really good thing that Mike did," Anto recalls. "We'd been sleeping at Steve's, playing a few old songs, very relaxed. One day Mike said, 'I'm going down to Windmill Lane Studios tomorrow lunchtime to have a look at it, why don't you meet me there because perhaps we could do some recording there one day.' So Steve and me arrived at lunchtime and walked into the main recording studio and our amps and our instruments were all there. We'd been playing with Trevor and Peter and had spent a day rehearsing with them, really just jamming at this really cheap studio in London. Mike had booked the studio at Windmill for a day and got someone to take all our gear

Above: Mike Scott, perennial Waterboy in New York. *Photo: © Ebet Roberts/Redferns*

Opposite top: Another Pretty Face.

Opposite left: 'You be Mick Jones, I'll be Joe Strummer'. John Caldwell & Mike Scott.

Above: Mike Scott: Portrait of the singer as an Angry Young Man.

Right: Another Pretty Face in the studio.
All photos © Mick Mercer

Above: The Red & The Black. Big Music. Big Hair. Anto Thistlethwaite & Mike Scott, Ad-Lib Club, London, May 1982. *Photographer unknown.*
Below: Mike, Steve & Anto, Tel Aviv May 1986. © *Gil Steiner*

Above: Playing anywhere at the drop of a hat. Anto, Mike & Steve in Jerusalem, May 1986. *Collection of Gil Steiner, photographer unknown.*
Below left: 'As soon as we'd finished we'd go back to the dressing room and the instruments would come back out'. *Colin Blakey Collection*
Below right: Colin Blakey with recorder. *Colin Blakey Collection*

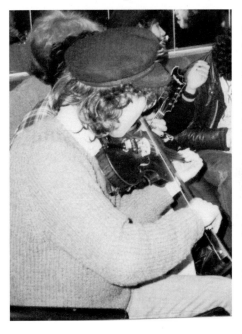

Above: The Kick Horns see the whole of the moon (Roddy Lorimer, centre),
Autumn 1990. *Collection of Roddy Lorimer*
Below left: Colin Blakey with bagpipes! *Colin Blakey Collection*
Below right: Roddy Lorimer: Trumpet for hire. *Roddy Lorimer Collection*

Above: 'They played on the island, doing a benefit for the Hall which I thought was very good of them'. Mike, Colin and Steve. Easdale, Scotland, July 2003. *Colin Blakey collection.*
Below: The Waterboys Trio with electric add-ons: Carlos Hercules (drums) and Steve Walters (bass) join Mike, Steve and Richard. © *Alwies Meuleman*

Above: Findhorn's own Contemporary Bard. © *Alwies Meuleman*

down without telling us. He'd told Trevor and Peter to get there earlier so that when we arrived, the drums and bass had been sound checked and all our gear set up. All we had to do was sit down and play—and in that day we recorded maybe ten songs. One was 'Fisherman's Blues', which we recorded in ten minutes; and we did 'Sweet Thing', and some country songs, some of Mike's gentle ballads. It was a great thing to do, like a present for Steve and me, and we had such a great day doing something together. However complicated it was with Mike, if you have one day like that every now and then, you always hope there'll be another one because they are fantastic times."

'Fisherman's Blues' was Scott's most sweeping, epic song since 'The Whole of the Moon'. Harking from his period of introspection and re-evaluation prior to arriving in Dublin, he described it as having been written, "at a time when I would have given anything to have had a simple, normal, down-to-earth lifestyle—which I assumed fishermen lived." It received its public premiere a couple of nights later when the new Waterboys made a low key start to their live career by open-ing for Light A Big Fire at one of U2's earliest haunts, The Baggot Inn. Bill Graham, reviewing for *Hot Press* noted that the support slot contained "all the performance power required to capture stadia audi-ences compressed into a fiercely burning set that almost over-loaded the Baggot's intimate surroundings." It certainly demonstrated that the band was shaking off much of its previously acquired baggage and looking to country and folk as the new road to follow. Aside from the Gogi Grant classic 'The Wayward Wind'[32] there were covers of songs by Hank Williams ('I'm so Lonesome I Could Cry') and Dylan ('I'll Be Your Baby Tonight' and 'Girl From the North Country').

When they revealed themselves to the wider audience on Channel 4's *The Tube* and BBC Belfast's *Video Gossip* during April 1986 the regeneration of the band to raggle-taggle, anarchic mayhem was complete. A fast and furious cacophony of mandolins and acoustic guitars, and at the very heart of the sound, Steve Wickham's fiddle and presence dancing figuratively and literally across the songs and the stage. Energising the band, giving it new meaning and definition

32 Written in 1956 by Stan Lebowsky and Herb Newman and covered by, amongst, others, Rex Ritter, Patsy Cline, Neil Young and legendary DJ Jimmy Young.

and becoming the central point from which all the new strands of Scott's vision would burst through. 'Fisherman's Blues'—honest and straightforward —and 'Meet You at the Station' its traditional spiritual words rewritten and expanded by Scott whilst retaining a gospel aura of integrity and fellowship. "It was always a splintered group," he told Colin Irwin. "A car with four wheels not pointing the same way so it just goes round and round. But now... we're facing the same way." With Dave Ruffy behind the drums and Hutchinson brought in full-time on bass, Scott, Thistlethwaite and Wickham played their new repertoire and their freshly discovered sense of traditional-infused rock across Ireland and the UK during April. And then on to shows in Israel in May with crowded houses at Tel Aviv's Liquid Club, Scott appealing to the audience to "be mellow". An impromptu acoustic set comprised of mainly folk-rock covers outside of Jerusalem's National Hall emphasising that this incarnation of the band was ready and able to play anywhere, anytime, at the drop of a hat—as Scott famously put it, "usually Steve's."

From there, festivals across Europe—and the definitive Waterboys' performance on the Pyramid Stage at Glastonbury on a warm and sunny afternoon, a thing of joy and beauty that would be remembered and talked about, then released as a bootleg appropriately called *A Golden Day*. Mike and Anto cherished their previous visit to the festival, and for Mike it was partly the music and partly the whole mystical backdrop. "It's a power area, thick in legend," he told Hayley Bartlett. "They say King Arthur's buried there, that Jesus went there and that the first Christian church in Britain was built there. For us, it was the gig of the year. It's always been one of my favourite tapes of any gig. I have the bootleg on CD—it's great." One reviewer, describing the band as "one of the best received Main Stage acts of the whole weekend," delineated Scott's music as being "about honour, and magic, and emotions... strength... love".

That love at times didn't always extend to the paying audience. Scott, a most demanding performer, appeared from reviews and events to be somewhat on edge and taking negatives as well as positives from the crowds he was pulling in. In *Melody Maker* Colin Irwin noted an outburst at a show at the Sardine Club in Oslo (a three-night residency from 2nd to 4th June 1986) during a blisteringly heavy rendition of 'This is the Sea'. It ended with Scott grabbing the microphone, glaring into the audience and yelling "Fucking Asshole!" at a particular member of the crowd who, it transpired, had wound him up with constant shouts for 'Red Army Blues'. Exit Scott in silence, only to later return with an apology and a "Now we'll forget that and roll up the fucking joint, right?" Tom Morton, reviewing the band at a Scottish AIDS benefit show in Edinburgh (2nd April 1987) related how "the crowd eventually [caused] Scott to lose his temper, throwing down his guitar during 'Has Anybody Here Seen Hank' and lashing the piano in a frenzy of rage." A show at The Studio, Bristol was cancelled on the night of the show, in the words of their record label, Chrysalis, because "there was a *Saturday Night Fever* type rig at the venue with flashing neon lights which they [the band] were told they couldn't turn off. They found the lights were putting them off and also because they play on an extended stage the rig would have blocked the fan's view. So they cancelled the gig." The perfectionist in action.

The same perfectionist was in evidence at Windmill Lane as the sessions for the next Waterboys' album developed, grew, multiplied and eventually became lost to all perspective and cohesion. A morass of styles and musicians with numerous friends and new associates passing through, adding their own influences and magic moments and moving out of the recordings again.

Colin Blakey hailed originally from Central Scotland, but like many that gravitated towards The Waterboys had become well-travelled in pursuit of his musical interests. "I learned music originally from my parents; classical flute when I was in my early teens, then piano at school but also I was interested in electronica. I was building my own little circuits and treating the sound of the piano and stuff like that, primitive multi-track recording, which was when I was fifteen or sixteen—probably like a lot of other people—a lot of other anoraks sitting in their bedrooms making strange noises! I really liked the sound of the Moog synthesiser—I think the first time I ever heard it was Roxy Music, Eno doing that funny thing in 'Virginia Plain'. I

just loved it—'What *is* that noise!' I built an electric guitar with my
Granddad, he delighted in woodwork so I found the design and he
did the wood and it worked well enough to learn to play it. Then a
friend of my Dad came back from Ireland with a couple of tin whis-
tles. I got one and my sister did as well and we figured out how to play
them, which opened up the whole thing of traditional music—you
could play it on a wee instrument which you could carry around with
you, which was great."

Blakey's life started to follow a fairly mundane path. "I did the traditional thing of going off to college and played in a few bands. I played
in Edinburgh with a guy called Lenny Helsing who is still doing a lot
of stuff in and around Scotland in a band called the Green Telescope,
which later became the Thanes. Following this he moved to Spain going
to live "up in the mountains, in Galicia," a Celtic area in the Northwest
corner of the country where he became fascinated with the traditional
music of the area. "I just wanted a change from Edinburgh and I didn't
know what I wanted to do. But it was that time where everybody was
saying, 'I'm going off travelling' or 'I'm just back from travelling', so I
did that thing of setting off with my rucksack, with my tin whistle
and my flute and did a lot of busking. I got to Madrid and met these
young fellows in the park where I was busking and they told me about
Galicia, gave me a tape of Galician music and I just had to go there.
It was amazing, the northwest corner of the Iberian Peninsula, above
Portugal, and there I discovered this wonderful music. For me, it was
this completely undiscovered part of Europe, nobody I knew, knew
anything about it. Now of course it's much more open and all these
characters are coming out of there. This would have been 1983. I'd
have been twenty-three. I spent a whole year there."

Though he'd always enjoyed a catholic taste in music, everything
from blues through rock'n'roll and on to more experimental sounds,
his experiences in Spain led him to want to discover more about
the musical heritage of his homeland. When he returned home to
Scotland he travelled out to Shetland with this in mind, though he
did also keep his eclecticism at work as well. "I went to Shetland and
got into the traditional music there, but also I played keyboards in a

reggae band called John Bibby's Dog. Then went to Manchester and lived there for a bit, where I got into playing improvised music with a very talented guy called Andi Chappell, who I'm still in touch with. We tried to avoid the existing structures of music, playing outside of chord structure. What you'd normally think of doing with music, we tried not to do! For example we'd try not to repeat anything, the drummer would keep going but he wouldn't repeat any rhythms or patterns and we would try and play outside melody, or harmony… it was bedlam really, what a noise, but really liberating to play. I was working on an archaeological dig, digging up Romans, and met a lot of interesting people. But it was a melting pot at that time of strange and wonderful people involved with music. With Manchester being a centre of Irish traditional music I came across that a fair bit, and as a home of reggae and Jamaican music, which to this day I have a great love it. Then I went back to Edinburgh and it was there that I met We Free Kings."

"At the time, We Free Kings—everybody said, "Oh, you sound like the Pogues," which was very unfortunate because I thought we sounded completely different! The Pogues were doing noisy, mental versions of Irish traditional songs, whereas we were making up our own songs which were Punk Rock played on acoustic instruments—mandolin, cello, acoustic guitars and a drum-set. Nice and loud, fast and furious, everybody playing at the same time, it was wild! Sometimes it ended-up in a similar place [to the Pogues] but it came from a completely different direction. We were writing songs from a very different angle. Maybe I was responsible for making it sound a bit Pogue-ish because I brought the tin whistle in and there is only certain kinds of lines you can play on a whistle. I'd have probably preferred to play the saxophone or something! I was always jealous of Anto because he played sax!"

We Free Kings found themselves an enthusiastic audience of their particular blend of Celtic Punk Rock in Ireland. "We did four [Irish] tours, and each one seemed to be longer than the one before it. We ended-up spending a two-month period there in a thatched cottage by the beach in Laytown, County Meath which had barely room for all seven of us and yet we had a continual stream of people coming to stay and it became a hub of some sort."

Joe Kingman, the band's singer and lyricist, had at one time shared a flat with Mike Scott in London so that when We Free Kings arrived to play in Dublin it was quite natural that they would find accommodation with him. Having been out of the UK music scene for sometime because of his travels around Spain, Blakey arrived quite unaware of who Scott was—"I just thought Mike was a mate of Joe's. I was in relative isolation, being in far-flung corners and not really listening to mainstream music other than that which I came across through the people I met. I would just make sessions or recordings and learn to play tunes and ask people for transcriptions, so I was unaware of eighties' popular culture in its many manifestations. I hadn't heard of The Waterboys or had any awareness of their stature or standing."

Scott though took a very keen interest in We Free Kings and became a good friend and supporter of the band. "His influence was behind making the tour happen for us, helping open up a few venues to our onslaught. And, indeed, Mike and Steve came around with us and played at a few venues with us, doing a few numbers—which was hilarious! They were tremendously supportive. They'd been stuck in the studio for months and months, and it wasn't just them that came out, John [Dunford] and Jimmy [Hickey] from the crew came out as well. So we had a really strong team helping us and looking after us, and teaching us—particularly Jimmy Hickey, showing us the ropes really. Mike seemed to be interested in the energy of what we were doing, I think he found it inspiring—and it was a two-way thing."

Scott, with his by now substantial experience of the music business, was increasingly happy to act as a mentor to musicians and bands that he found interesting. At a 'Lark in the Park' show in Galway he befriended a young guitarist, Leo Moran, who appeared on stage with Scott that day and who would go on to be a significant player in the Irish music scene as a founder member of Tuam band the Saw Doctors. When Scott gravitated to Ireland's West Coast he took great pleasure in catching Moran's band. "I used to go watch them play in The Quays and down in The Claddagh Hall," he told Kevin McGuire of the *Galway Advertiser*. "I was utterly charmed by them. They had wonderful songs like 'N17', 'The Streets of Galway' and others." This growing friendship led to Scott inviting the Saw Doctors to tour as support to The Waterboys and Scott producing their first single, 'N17'.

"If we hadn't been seen by Mike Scott we might never have got out of Galway," claimed Saw Doctors' lead singer Davy Carton, whilst Moran recalled the impact that touring with The Waterboys had on the ambitions of the band. "The Waterboys put us moving when Mike came to see us," he explained to Kevin McGuire. "Mike asked us to do a six week tour of Britain… this was a dream come true, doing dates in venues that you only ever read about in the music press."

The impression that Colin Blakey had at Windmill Lane studios, when he was invited in to play on a couple of tracks with The Waterboys, was of "a lot of people moving through and Mike trying out different tactics and strategies for writing songs and getting music to happen. I think he was very resourceful, very clever, the way he used the studio. People say it was very expensive but I don't think really… he certainly didn't waste any time. He was always very focused—he worked the studio and he worked the people in it. Whether he got the results he wanted I don't know, but he'd ask the right questions musically, and impose the right conditions for things to happen. He'd have a song written and say, "What can we do with this?" but he wouldn't give you crap parts, he'd say, "What can you add to this?" and you'd suggest something and he'd look at it. It was as though we were putting the flesh on the bones of his song-writing."

Blakey had been called in to play on the Salvation Army meets New Orleans jazz rabble-rouser 'On my Way to Heaven' and the wide-eyed and gently whimsical 'Strange Boat'. The later is a Scott/Thistlethwaite attributed song, though again Anto is at pains to impress the generosity of this co-credit. "On 'Strange Boat', Mike had written the song and got to the bridge and had the first chord but not the second. So he said to me, 'Anto, where shall I go now?' I said, 'Oh, F-Sharp-Minor, or something.' He tried it and said, 'Oh, that's good', so again the contribution was actually very minimal but he was generous with the acknowledgement."

"That was lovely to play," recalls Blakey. "I played piano, and came up with a gentle line, a kind of response to the melody. He sings a line and I go 'plink, plink', sort of a question and answer thing, though it's very far back in the mix on the album of course. Mike tends to mix in a very dynamic way. What I mean by that, some of his mixes only really make sense if you turn the music up loud so that the music becomes more three-dimensional as you turn it up. You have the groove, and I love the way he has the vocals right at the front so that you get every single word, that's very important and a lot of singers at that time weren't doing that. But all the other layers… like the way Eno talks about music as a landscape painting where you have these different kinds of horizons going back into the distance. The distance is where you put things in the mix, the level at which you have things to create three-dimensionality to the music. Especially with the multi-lyric music like The Waterboys, sometimes there was quite a lot of layers and it was almost like a symphonic structure, like 'The Stolen Child' which had a lot of different things running through it."

Also brought-in to play on 'Strange Boat' was the former Fleadh Cowboys' drummer Fran Breen. He'd first played with Mike Scott at the same Galway 'Lark in the Park' festival which had seen the young Leo Moran guest with the band. Breen was already a highly experienced player, having started his career "playing around show bands and stuff" which led to him "working with a guy called Rob Strong. From there I went to a band called Stagger Lee and then to another good singer-songwriter called Earl Lee, who was the singer in a band called Lapland. Then I went to work with Paul Brady, did his first rock work, *Hard Station*, and from there just bits and pieces until I ended up with the Fleadh Cowboys run by Pete Cummins and Frank Lane. If my memory serves me right, we started off doing a late-night gig in the Olympia Theatre in Dublin—the first rock night in Dublin actually. We'd do late night Friday or Saturday night. We did a 'Lark in the Park', the Fleadh Cowboys, and Mike might have got up and done a couple of songs. Then I got a phone call. Mike was using different people in the studio for different songs, seeing what would work and what wouldn't work. I played on 'Strange Boat' at Windmill Lane, ran it a couple of times and we had a take."

Roddy Lorimer, who would come-in to record on various bits and pieces during the Dublin sessions recalls some "wonderful nights arriving in Dublin, in the studio, and it was like 'where is everybody?' and they'd be in the pub. I'd be sitting there for five hours waiting to do my session and the doors open and everybody would be coming in with crates of Guinness. 'Right, Ok, put the horns section in the toilet and we'll take leads through and put microphones in,' and we'd have great jam sessions all night long and it would be *mad*."

"We would get a call to be in a certain rehearsal studio, in Dublin, and we'd be there at 11 o'clock," Breen adds. "No sign of Mike, so we'd do a bit of playing and hang around and Mike would come and sit at the piano. And I don't know but it seemed like there was a sort of triangle there with Mike, Steve and Anto. So there was always this kind of... well, I didn't know what was because I was just asked to come and rehearse but I couldn't see what was beyond this thing between these three guys[33]. So, Mike would come in and... well, I put it down to him being up all night writing [laughs] but he'd come in, look around, play about three notes and go home! And, at the end of the day, you're thinking—what's this all about? The singer-songwriters are a very odd breed of people, y'know? I worked with Lucinda Williams and it was kind of the same deal, you never really knew what person would be coming at you. She'd get up in the morning; 'Why do I have to do this?' We'd go: 'You've just got a Grammy, you're in the charts, and your record is *selling*. You've got sell-out shows. You're on the crest of a wave!' Now, I know it goes beyond all that but at the same time these are part of your reward, the money gives you a bit of surety."

The surety that Mike Scott could surround himself with at this point was the confidence that Chrysalis Records, who had by now acquired the contract for Ensign, had in him. No greater demonstra-

---

33 Writing for *Melody Maker*, Colin Irwin observed how "the three of them will tell you at great length that there is an empathy, an *instinct* between them that goes far beyond the simple practicality of three guys in a band making music."

tion of this was in the way that they were prepared to let the Dublin sessions for the new album run and run. As Breen notes, "There was no end to that fishing line was there? It was like, "let it go, let it go, let it go…" Would you get that anymore from any record company?" Scott himself commented to Liam Mackey, "There was nobody telling us to hurry up; putting a deadline on us. I wasn't on great terms with the guys who ran Ensign and so I decided to deal directly with Chrysalis." The end result was that "Chrysalis gave us a free hand." Reflecting on the situation many years removed he recalled, "I was in a position of great power. Doug D'Arcy [Managing Director of Chrysalis] said, 'You can have whatever you want and however long you want.'"[34] That wasn't necessarily such a good thing as by the time 1986 stretched into 1987 Scott was piled high with songs and recordings and had reached a point where he was entirely unable to see the wood for the trees. "We were recording everything live—there were hardly any overdubs," he explained in the NME in 1990. "We'd go in there with whoever was our latest drummer, and we might play ten songs in a day or work on one seriously. It was wild and woolly. Nobody was saying 'look, take a break and think about what you are doing.' It was just getting wilder and wilder." And to Alain Gale in Melody Maker he confessed how he'd "lost my point completely on that album. It was too long, too many songs and too many different kinds of music. We had folky traditional music; we had rock'n'roll, bluesy music and lots of country & western stuff that never came out. We could have done anything and I didn't know what to choose." Though he was playing in and out, and around, a varied cross-section of genres, there was something within these sessions that anchored the band back to the tradition of The Waterboys that wouldn't be so apparent in later recordings.

"There were bits of everything," notes Roddy Lorimer. "You've got to remember that Mike taped everything, just recorded things to keep. The drunken sessions are still there, Mike's got everything, which is lovely." Fran Breen recalls how, "We'd do a show in Dublin and the next morning he'd go off and pick up a bootleg! I don't know how they

34 Interviewed by Alan Pattullo, Scotland on Sunday.

got away with selling them, forget about the music—some of them sounded like shit—recorded at the back of the hall."

This archivist mentality in Scott also extended to the live shows, providing Lorimer with one particularly happy and cherished memory of his association with the band. "There was an Irish tour and we were going to be there between Christmas and New Year. It was my son's first birthday on 30th December so I said, 'No Mike, sorry mate, I'm not going to be away for his birthday.' So Mike said, 'Well, what if we get them across for the tour', to which I replied, 'that's not very fair on my wife is it... come on tour and every night go back to your hotel and look after your kid!' Mike said, 'Well, get a nanny.' So, we ended up getting a nanny and Kate, my wife, and Alex came across to Ireland. Now, there are no wives or girlfriends on the tour bus so Kate and Alex are being driven around Ireland in a chauffeur-driven limo and I'm on a rickety old bus! We played Cork on Alex's birthday, three thousand people. Mike came out on stage to start the show with an old recording Walkman and put it on the front of the stage. He stood up with his guitar and said, 'We've got a very special guest tonight, who can't be here—he's in the hotel along the road and it's his first birthday. So I want you all to sing 'Happy Birthday to Alex'.' He sent me a copy of it about three years ago, he still had it on the desk tape, and I can now give it to my son. It's like, Alex can play saxophone and soprano-sax, piano and guitar and things like that, but he's also got this 'born in a suitcase' vibe!"

In between the sessions at Windmill, the band continued to develop their sound and new sense of identity both on tour and at ad-hoc shows. Peter McKinney sat behind the drum kit during April 1987 when Scott brought The Waterboys back to Scotland with two shows in Edinburgh (one of which was a opening set for We Free Kings) and the next month made way for Fran Breen to become the latest Waterboys drummer.

Breen: "I was glad to be there for all of them [the live shows] though I didn't think I particularly suited what he was doing, [ponders this] or maybe it wasn't what I was supposed to be doing, though every one was something special." That month the band played a benefit for

Greenpeace on board the *Sirius*, harboured at the docks in Dublin
and then were joined by Roddy Lorimer at the Pictish Festival back in
Scotland. "Greenpeace? We played on this boat in the harbour, and it
was obviously a rally for Greenpeace," recalls Breen. "Mike was really
into all that stuff so he just kind of lent his talent to that. We just
set-up on this ship and played to the people on the quayside. Then
we went off and did this gig at the Pictish Festival, in Scotland, and I
didn't even know what the Picts were!"

There were more and varied shows, line-ups coming and going like
summer breezes—really developing that sense of whoever showed
up could bring their own magic moments into play. Gigs in Galway
for the North Atlantic Network and at Dublin's Olympic Ballroom
for the Irish Green Alliance. Mike going down to Clifden, County
Galway with Wickham's In Tua Nua colleague Vinnie Kilduff and
performing at a school there. And fabulous shows throughout Ireland
in December 1987 culminating with New Year's Eve at the Top Hat
in Dublin—the last night of a three-night residency. Breen again:
"There was a real, special, vibe there then. Such a great vibe."

But what had seemed so simple and easy going when the band first
set-up at Windmill and came away from a day's work there with three
fully-formed and usable songs had become ever more complicated and
unwieldy. Legion were the number of musicians who came and went,
numerous were the styles and tones that the band played in. Early on
in the sessions, producer Bob Johnston[35] had been drafted in, overseeing one song that would make the final selection for *Fisherman's Blues*,
the furiously feisty 'We will not be Lovers'. In this instance, Scott had
entered the studio with the basic structure of the song worked out
and the words having been written. "It was a very chaotic day," he
recalled. "There was a very frantic, awkward atmosphere in the studio... I plugged into that atmosphere." Believing that the tone that
had beset the sessions at that time would be perfect for this particular

---

35 Bob Johnston, whose Grandmother had, curiously, once co-written songs with the author of 'When Irish Eyes Are
    Smiling', was a music industry legend having produced Dylan's *Highway 61* when Dylan had a falling-out with his
    previous producer Tom Wilson. He worked again with Dylan down in Nashville for *Blonde on Blonde* and was
    also behind the desk for Simon & Garfunkel's *Sounds of Silence* and *Parsley, Sage, Rosemary & Thyme* and Leonard
    Cohen's *Songs From A Room*. In his highly distinguished career, he also played a significant part in the rehabilita-
    tion of Johnny Cash with live albums recorded at Folsom Prison and San Quentin.

song, Scott kicked-off and "the band just came in, and that's the way we hear it on the record."

Johnston's overseeing of the recordings lasted only one week, in March 1986, though Scott, Thistlethwaite and Wickham would have the opportunity for a further collaboration with him when they travelled to San Francisco for some additional recordings at Fantasy Studios in December. But as 1986 moved into 1987 it was clear there was no end in sight and not a hope of a cohesive follow-up to *This is the Sea* being released anytime soon. Stories began to circulate of massive studio bills and awards being issued by tape manufacturers for the sheer volume of recording media being consumed. At the same time, the arrival of The Waterboys in Ireland created a sense of competition—particularly with U2 who Scott in hindsight saw as moving to occupy some of his own ground. "U2 clocked what we did, just as they later clocked the Stone Roses… Oasis… Beck," he recalled to Alan Patullo. "We were one of the cherries off the tree that they picked." Despite the continued camaraderie between the two bands (Scott recalls visiting Bono in Dublin and playing him cuts of 'Strange Boat' and hearing an early take of 'Where the Streets Have No Name' in return) there was that competitive edge to their relationship. "A jostling one [though] friendly and quite loving," as Scott described it, but this aside, the relocation of The Waterboys to Ireland and the developing expectation for their new album naturally created a situation in which some rivalry had to be perceived. "I was very aware we were the only band [in Ireland] that could take U2 on," Scott told Pattullo. "I know they recognised this too."

And, on top of this, Scott was again suffering from a generally unsettled and unhappy period in his life. He'd started a relationship with Irene Keogh, who worked as a studio manager at Windmill Studios, and this would lead to his first marriage in June 1990. But in 1987 he'd not reached the place he wanted to be and the combination of personal and creative pressures were driving him to a fairly low-point. "My life was in chaos," he explained. "I was fighting with my girlfriend all the time and I didn't know what to do, and there were vibes going down with the band and with the crew. And I just went west where it's all quiet and pastoral and I just sorted myself out for four months." To Liam Mackey he noted further that, "I did have my difficult year, 1987. I went through a lot of demons and things—personal things— but I came out the other side with a much greater sense of content- ment." He saw it as partly reluctance, almost a fear of settling down and making commitments. "I was terrified of tying my life down in the sense I might live permanently anywhere or be permanently with anyone—be that my girlfriend or other musicians."

Scott had already visited Ireland's West Coast. But his love affair with the area and its music really began to take hold of him and, working its magic, he shook-off some of the demons that he shoul- dered when he and Irene took in Galway, Dingle and Clifden whilst on holiday in 1987. In particular, Mackey notes, "His immersion in the Clifden Fleadh was a turning-point."

This was indeed a cornerstone of Scott's Irish adventure as he delved further and deeper into the traditional music of Ireland, open- ing up a whole new range of possibilities much broader than he could have anticipated when he embarked on this phase of his journey two years earlier. "It's just music that comes out of the land, pure music," he claimed, "not done for commercial reasons." In fact he found himself immersed in something that resonated with his anti-establishment, anti-music-business ethos to the extent that it effectively closed-off the recording of *Fisherman's Blues* at Windmill, a line drawn at the end of side-one, and blossomed into the more folky contentment of the LP's second-side.

6

A CELTIC SUMMER

"In Ireland, there were a lot of things that I learnt that were completely new to me like traditional Irish music, all the tunes, I never knew or understood that," Scott told Alain Gales. The particular way of play-ing in acoustic mode wasn't virgin territory—it had been a part of The Waterboys right back to their early days with Anto's mandolin play-ing—'Red Army Blues', 'The Thrill is Gone'. It was a key part of their early experiments with folk rock sounds on 'Billy Sparks' at Redshop in 1982. So he could reasonably claim of his immersion in traditional Irish music that, "All of this was new, but also very natural."

Partly, of course, the responsibility for this new and passionate enthusiasm could be laid squarely at Steve Wickham's door. Scott talked about some of his own musical education being solely to enable him to play alongside this man whose talent had captivated him in a unique and special way that no other collaborator had quite reached in him. "When [Steve] introduced me to Irish traditional music and got out his fiddle... we could just make music in room, the two of us," he told Matthew Magee. "Country music was open to me, blues was there, gospel." But there were other people leading Scott down this particular pathway, and there was nothing like being in the living heart of the reels and jigs out on the West Coast.

"I think right from the outset Mike found himself in the lap of the best traditional music there," Colin Blakey considers. "His landlord when he first moved there was Charlie Lennon who is one of Ireland's top traditional musicians and tune writers and he would drag Mike down to sessions—in at the deep-end, no excuse, you're a musician grab your guitar, come on. And that was the way it went, and for all of us meeting people there in our own ways." He also became a close friend of Vinnie Kilduff, often claimed to be Ireland's greatest tin-whistle player and a former band-mate of Wickham's from In Tua Nua, another person who could ease Mike's way into the sessions and pubs of Ireland. And in The Waterboys' sound engineer John Dunford he found someone stepped in the musical heritage of Ireland, who'd worked with the perennially changing West Coast folksters De Dannan. In De Dannan, Scott could hear the entire gamut of tradi-tional influences and ways of playing that would heavily influence the writing and recording of both the second side of *Fisherman's Blues* and its folk-lite successor *Room to Roam*.

Earle Hitchner, writer for the *Irish Echo*, claimed that, "Any serious discussion of the evolution of Irish traditional music… must include the enormous contribution of De Dannan." They came out of exactly the atmosphere and the informal way of making music that Mike Scott had found down in Galway. Playing at sessions in Hughes Pub, Spiddal in County Galway and the Cellar Bar in Galway, Frankie Gavin's fiddle and Yorkshireman Alec Finn's bouzouki came together to create a band that would eventually epitomise the session made large and brought out to the masses.[36] But they also, like Scott at Windmill, took from other traditions—Gavin having been described by Nuala O'Connor as having been "drawn at an early age towards the 78rpm recordings of Irish American musicians. The Flanagan broth-ers, John McKenna and Joe Derrane," which "had a liberating effect on his playing." This same liberating effect shone through in Mike Scott's

36 Mary Black, who at one time was a singer in De Dannan, described traditional music as having "its power in its passion. Traditional music has the ability to either get you up and dance or make you sit down and cry. They are the two emotions you want from music". [Interviewed by Brett Leigh Dicks and D. J. Palladino, *The Santa Barbara Independent*]

work once he'd thrown off the shackles and the bad vibes of 1987 and had taken himself off full-time to Spiddal in search of some order and meaning to the body of work that had been amassed in Dublin.

That came from the need to clear his head of all the work at Windmill and to try and get some perspective of exactly what he had and where he was on the new album. With John Dunford as his guide he went West to seek this calm, taking a holiday let from Charlie Lennon that looked way out over Galway Bay to the Aran Islands on the far horizon and where he discovered a sense of belonging that reached right down into his soul. From there, it was the most natural thing to build on his education, playing in the sessions, immersing himself in the music and the *history* of the music—making the connections between the Celtic traditions of home and the sounds and the feel of its Gaelic counterpart.

This led to the gradual westward drift of the rest of the core-members of the band. Anto travelled there, and onwards to the Aran Islands—the self-proclaimed 'Celtic Eden'—joining with Mike the sessions in The American Bar by Kilronan harbour. Steve Wickham was there, of course, and Trevor Hutchinson and sometimes band member Vinnie Kilduff. And so Scott was able to rediscover the passion to continue with *Fisherman's Blues* but in a different context—that index of possibilities opening up again—and so sought-out somewhere in Spiddal where the band could gather and work through what became the LP's second side. Most appropriately enough, the recommendation came from De Dannan's Alec Finn who knew of 'Spiddal House', a sizeable property set over Galway Bay which he believed would be available for renting from the then owner, Mrs. Buckley. Easter 1988 found The Waterboys assembled there and ready to record.

"There was a big house that we worked in, beautiful grounds with lots of space," recalls Colin Blakey, also called in for duty. "We all stayed in cottages nearby and we all had bicycles—hired at great expense by the record company I suspect [chuckles]. We'd all eat together, with caterers, in the big house." This idyllic-sounding arrangement lasted for two months whilst Scott continued the practice of bringing in musicians and trying out sounds. This time, though, it would be the players whose work he'd come to love and admire around Galway: Alec Finn, Frankie Gavin, his West Coast mentor and teacher Charlie Lennon and De Dannan accordionist Mairtin O'Connor.

At Spiddal the whole vibe of The Waterboys changed again, with Steve Wickham's fiddle and his fascination with the heritage of Irish music coming further to the front of the band's sound and identity. "Steve is an eclectic player," says Colin Blakey. "He has a lovely way of playing the traditional music but he's not just a traditional player, he's done quite a lot of jazz/swing stuff as well. He's so intuitive, when he's play-ing that fiddle it looks so much like its just become part of his body. He has such a relaxed way of playing. I was trying to learn the fiddle at that time. I was just so jealous, he could pick up my fiddle and play it and it would sound beautiful, then he'd give it back and it would sound like a screaming bag of cats!" He adds, "Having a fiddler in the band made the possibilities of the sessions all the stronger." Scott had explained to Colin Irwin in 1986 the route that The Waterboys were beginning to take, deliberating where the change had come from. "I don't know how much of it is to do with Ireland itself or just the opportunities Ireland has created with space and a normal lifestyle, but it has made things happen… fiddle and mandolin [have] taken over the sound and it's welcome."

Relocating the final *Fisherman's Blues* sessions from the more cos-mopolitan atmosphere of Dublin to the laid-back shores of Galway could only increase the effect that Ireland was having on the band. "It's a Gaeltacht area," explains Blakey. "You'd go down to the pub and they'd all be talking Gaelic—which makes you realise that you're in a different culture with a different way of thinking and that influences [the music]. There's a great openness and optimism with the people there, which may be something to do with the language. Perhaps if you speak in that language you have a slightly different take on the landscape and the weather, the light that's playing on the water and that can go into the music as well."

It's not hard to imagine Mike Scott, having identified the creative opportunities that this new environment offered him, becoming totally immersed and trying his utmost to become a part of the fabric of the scene. "Once I got ignored more for the way I made my entry than anything else," he recalled in the *NME* of one night's jam session in a public house. "I figured out what key they were playing in by peering through the window, and I walked in playing—a big vibe. That didn't go down too well." The music and songs that he wrote, and other's work that he chose to play reflected this. 'Jimmy Hickey's Waltz', named after a key member of the crew—a slow waltz that was assigned to Wickham, Thistlethwaite and Scott, with Scott taking only third on the credits and seeing it as Wickham's instrumental, with Anto adding the middle-eight bridge. Wickham's 'Dunford Fancy', noted on the release as being simply Steve's fiddle with the bouzouki of Brendan O'Regan. Scott's litany of past lives and loves 'And a Bang on the Ear' with Mairtin O'Connor on accordion. His tribute to Hank Williams, 'Has Anybody Here Seen Hank' (again Anto receiving a co-write for the middle-eight). 'When will we be Married?', a traditional reel adapted and arranged by Scott and Wickham, and a ramshackle final track for the album (unlisted on the LP) covering Woody Guthrie's 'This Land is Your Land', tradition from another place and time but some how fitting and appropriate.

But the masterpiece of the original Spiddal sessions was the band's interpretation of the W. B. Yeats poem 'The Stolen Child'. Yeats had written the poem in 1886—a melancholic rumination on the death of his brother Robert (Bobbie) at the age of three, filled with Irish legend and Yeats' own interest in paganism and *faerie* mythology. For the vocals, the enunciation or recital of this work, Scott brought in 'Sean-nos' singer Tomas MacEoin who he'd discovered from a poetry tape that MacEoin had made and which was amongst a collection of Irish-based recordings that he'd been listening to at Spiddal[37].

MacEoin was about as far removed from the rock business as could possibly be imagined. Interviewed by Liam Fay about his work with The Waterboys he confessed that he had not previously been aware of the band and demonstrated just how sheltered he'd been from that

---

37 Lexicographer Seamus Mac Mathuna described 'Sean-nos' singing as being "the least often heard and the least understood part of Irish traditional music ... to some ears it sounds 'uncouth', 'untuneful' and 'unmusical." The term appears to have come into use at the start of the 20th Century and has wildly differing interpretations, though it developed into an accepted style of signing predominately in Connemara. It tends to represent an unaccompanied, stark, often devoid of rhythm, style of Gaeltacht singing that has almost a crossover into spoken word.

whole genre of music. "I'd heard of The Beatles and U2 and wasn't there The Rolling Stones?" When Anto and Steve Wickham sought him down at his small farm in Connemara, MacEoin was a man approaching his mid-fifties who was living by himself in what was once his family's cottage and enjoying a simple lifestyle from the modest income he could generate from the farm. He saw a resonance in the way he lived right back through the history of the Irish people. "Down the centuries people have put up with great hardship—still do—just to live in this paradise. That's God's truth."

On first visiting MacEoin, Wickham and Thistlethwaite found their timing somewhat off—MacEoin had just retired for the night and wasn't going to answer the door to anyone. But the band persevered; leaving messages and notes for him, until eventually he was persuaded to arrive at Spiddal House for the recital of the poem and to travel over to Wales for the mixing of the track at Rockfield. His deep, rich brogue can be heard breathing authenticity and honesty into Yeats' mystical evocation of the poem's County Sligo settings. The effect was such that even though the words were delivered in English, there was a Gaeltacht lilt and timbre to the recital that captured and described, beyond words, the atmosphere of the setting.

"There was quite a buzz recording it," recalls Blakey. "I suppose some people around the recording process, not the musicians but people looking on, had a few raised eyebrows because we were doing something that was so far away from rock'n'roll, something more like a tone poem. Mike had what he calls his doggy-paddle way of playing the piano where he plays one hand then the other really quickly with the sustain peddle down and you get this mad mix of harmonics when you do that. He was playing this thing and you could hear if you listened into the sound of the strings, it wasn't like a modern electric piano where you don't really get that effect so much, it was a properly strung piano and you could hear all these overtones interacting. It reminded me of a similar experience listening to some of Steve Reich's music, *Music for Six Pianos*, where if you hear it live you get this mesh of sound appearing that is almost visual, it comes from the overtones. So you could hear lines within it, Anto picked up a couple of riffs listening to it, sax parts that were there already in the chord progression Mike was playing. At the end Mike said to me, 'Would you go and do some flute' and I just went in and played and pretty much first take is what you hear, that very baroque line just came out, I don't know where from! And getting Tomas MacEoin, his presence was so beautiful. He was a real connection with the area, with the landscape, with the people and with the language. He would tell you about it, and you could sit for hours in the pub talking with him and asking questions."

The middle section of 'The Stolen Child' was created one evening by the self-styled 'Woodland Band', described here by Colin Blakey. "It's the bit in the 'The Stolen Child', where you hear a bouzouki and a bodhrán and I'm playing a funny little thing called the border horn, and I think there's a mandolin. It comes in from the distance and drifts through the music and then goes out again at one point, if you listen really closely you'll hear it. It was further forward in the mix that Mike used for a compilation that came out and had the Woodland Band a little more prominent. But it was recorded, at dusk, on the flat roof of one of the wings at Spiddal House. We built this turf fire on top of the roof—how it didn't melt the roof I'll never know. We used peat because that didn't crackle and it kept the midges off. John Dunford ran some microphones out with long leads and we sat around this thing playing with a couple of monitor speakers to hear what we were playing to for the overdub. And it was just so funny, sitting there at dusk on top of this roof with the peat smoke stinging our eyes, we were reeking by the time we were finished, but it was lovely though!"

Mixed at Rockfield Studios over the summer of 1988, *Fisherman's Blues* finally saw the light of day that October, its iconic and visually descriptive cover photography by Steve Meany proving that indeed a picture is worth a thousand words. Thistlethwaite, Scott and Wickham sit centre stage with their acoustic instruments, relaxed and raggle-taggle, surrounded by members of the road crew and production team (Jake Kennedy, Pat McCarthy, Jimmy Hickey and John Dunford) and by guest musicians (Blakey, Breen, Hutchinson). With the sheer volume of material recorded and the number of players who had contributed to the sessions both at Windmill Lane and in Spiddal, the appearance on the finished album was, for any of them, something of a pleasant surprise. "I was absolutely amazed I ended up on *Fisherman's Blues* at all" recalls Colin Blakey. "I didn't know until a friend phoned me up and said '*Fisherman's Blues* is out and you're on the cover'—'What? What?' I had no idea, and it was a lovely thing to happen." Fran Breen had a similar experience for the couple of songs that he'd contributed to. "The record came out and there were the two tracks on it and I was, 'Oh, Hey, that's nice', because Mike had recorded so many songs you just didn't know what was going to be on. I wasn't expecting any- thing… and there we all were on the cover of it!"

With so much material committed to tape and such a diversity of genres experimented with, the *Fisherman's Blues* sessions have proved to be a treasure-trove of recordings for record companies and bootleg- gers alike. "There was a room in Windmill Lane Studios, about the size of a moderate-sized bedroom. And it was wall-to-wall, ceiling-to- floor multi-track tapes," Scott told Stuart Baillie. Though an *NME* journalist once described seeing Mike Scott demolish a bootleg tape stall in London's Camden Market, Scott had actually been an avid collector of live and unreleased recordings of artists that interested him, and had been open and vocal about this over the years. In *The Beat* magazine he'd previously exclaimed, "I like the fact that there are a lot of bootlegs around, I think it's very healthy. I think it's bad that people can own songs. I have a publishing deal at the moment but I think it would be interesting when this deal ends not to sign a new one… just leave them in the public domain and see what happens."

There is a three-CD set, known simply and definitively as *The Complete Fisherman's Blues Sessions 86-88* that is by far the most com- prehensive bootleg collection of out-takes from the album's sessions. It doesn't contain much in the way of alternative takes of songs that made the final *Fisherman's Blues* selection. But it is an absolutely fas- cinating summation of a body of work that Scott described as being from a period when, "We would set up with a great sound in the stu- dio, turn the lights down low, and play for our pleasure and explora- tion." There are covers aplenty—particularly from Dylan's canon: 'Girl from the North Country' and 'I'll be your Baby Tonight', but also

'Lost Highway', made famous by Hank Williams, Williams' own 'I'm
So Lonesome I Could Cry' and the Western ballad 'Billy The Kid'.
There's also some of the quirky, personal observations that from Scott
can either be charmingly affectionate or bitingly sarcastic. There was
the honky-tonk style 'BP Villain', written about journalist and photographer B P Fallon, who'd been a major supporter of The Waterboys in
Ireland and with whom Scott, reportedly, had a public falling out with
at a gig at Dublin's Mountjoy Jail during the Jail's 'Art Week'. And, of
course, there are some of the great 'lost' Waterboys songs: 'Killing my
Heart', the reworking of 'On my Way to Heaven', 'Higher in Time' and
the fifteen-and-a-half minute 'Saints & Angels'.

For the less dedicated there circulate a couple of other valuable
compilations from this era of the band. The focus of *Fisherman's
Catch* is predominately on alternative versions of the selected tracks
from the official LP, though it also includes some of the more notable omitted songs, particularly 'Killing my Heart' and 'On my Way
to Heaven'. *The Windmill Lane Sessions*, on the other hand, is mainly
comprised of cover versions—partly redundant because so many are,
again, Dylan songs and a there also circulates a specific bootleg of
Dylan songs performed by The Waterboys. There has always been a
significant taping and trading culture around the band which, to his
credit, Scott has by and large indulged or turned a blind eye towards.
Like other bastions of audience taping, most famously the Grateful
Dead, there is that element of the band's live presentations that, due
to their varied and eclectic approach to redeveloping their material,
requires the dedicated fan to have multiple versions of songs to track
their evolution and development. And, because of Scott's prolific song
writing and covering, the only way to trawl through much of his output is to go to the live recordings to hear songs that have never made
it to official vinyl or CD.

Particular mystique has built up around the recording of *Fisherman's
Blues*, due in part to the apocryphal legend that so much tape was
consumed by the band at Windmill Lane that they received an award
from the manufacturer for being their best customer. In addition,
Scott had eschewed interviews for several years, giving the unheard

recordings an additional intriguing frisson. Not surprising, then, that a continual clamour for extended versions of the album or additional releases from the sessions continued unabated for many years. This wasn't a straightforward situation—the rights to release the work needed negotiating out of Chrysalis/EMI. But was partially sated by the release of *Too Close to Heaven* (RCA Records) in September 2001, which for the first time revealed to the wider audience just how far Scott had trawled his net during the initial work on *Fisherman's Blues*. In particular it demonstrated that in absorbing himself in the traditional music of Ireland, he'd also extended that influence much further, even though it hadn't necessarily worked its way through to the finished vinyl. Stuart Bailie, in *Mojo*, considered that it revealed "a band getting deliriously lost in the music" and appreciated "the verve of the original sessions."

Too Close to Heaven also serves to demonstrate how much different an album *Fisherman's Blues* could have been, with its collection of songs ranging from the upbeat hallelujah of 'On my Way to Heaven' through the defiant 'Higher in Time' and on to the introspection of 'Good Man Gone'. A number of the songs delineate the mood of depression that had hung over Scott during his early days in Ireland. Notably there was 'Good Man Gone'[38], which Sean Miller in his excellent appraisal of the album for his *Waterboysfans* website considered "distinctly personal, brutally honest," adding that "listening to the songs you start to feel the pain that Mike was clearly feeling at the time." Aside from the almost obligatory navel-gazing, it also demonstrated how the music of the band's Irish period still connected back through to some of the themes that had interested Scott in earlier days. There's the arrangement of 'A Home in the Meadow', which Scott had discovered from the classic Jimmy Stewart film *How the West was Won*, its frontier-stock lyrics made familiar by its use of the quintessentially English 'Greensleeves', and 'Custer's Blues' both driven from Scott's American West fascination. The later was actually written during the

38 The music for this song was recycled for 'Maggie, It's Time For You To Go' and played live by The Waterboys during 1989, another of Scott's rare and uncomfortable forays into politics. "I don't want to be involved in all of that, whether Maggie [Thatcher] goes or not. I don't want to make a statement and get called to account for it" he later commented. 'Good Man Gone' is very much a song of Scott's fractured sense of self during 1987, though it was never recorded for *Fisherman's Blues*; the version on *Too Close To Heaven* hails from demos recorded during February 1991 with overdubs recorded specifically for the compilation.

sessions for *This is the Sea*, as was 'The Ladder', noted by Bailie as, "a piece of sustained euphoria that reveals the Patti Smith fan in Scott," also included on the compilation. *Too Close to Heaven* is, taken as a whole though, an uneven record that reflects the way in which it was compiled at a distance of years rather than created contemporarily to flow as an album in its own right.

Scott later articulated the recording of *Fisherman's Blues* as "the powerful creative resonance of being connected to a battery of inspi-rational sources that went back beyond the birth of rock and roll." *Too Close to Heaven* went a long way to demonstrating that, but to put it into context required a further release, one that could chime the reso-nance between the faux-traditional Irish sound of the main album with the faux-Country of its out-takes sibling. "The earlier Waterboys was a great kind of rock/pop vehicle for his song-writing and there was a definite kind of magic there," comments Fran Breen. "I sup-pose when it disbanded, or whatever happened to it, he had to find another way of going. But then again, if he did a kind of country thing it wouldn't be *Country* country, he'd kind of rock it up. I think he's still kind of looking, though at the time I believe he wasn't happy with that either." The way, then, to hear this searching is to hear the story through the 2006 *Fisherman's Blues—Collector's Edition*, a remastered reissue of the original album with an accompanying second CD of material from the era. It was the result of Scott's painstaking trawl through the EMI archives supported by, according to Alan Pattullo in *Scotland on Sunday*, "a couple of overworked librarians in Abbey Road studios who documented each and every recording, with over 400 two-inch reels logged."

The result was a highly satisfying collection of the familiar and the unexpected. On hearing 'Carolan's Welcome', Waterboys' fan Jules Gray enthused to the band's Yahoo discussion group how he'd "loved it drenched in bootleg hiss" and then adored it "free from hiss on the remaster. It's stately, sweeping and epic. You can almost hear the sun shining through the windows of Spiddal House!" Shock and awe surrounded the inclusion of 'You In The Sky', an unheard song that had made none of the bootleg releases but which Gray considered "a bone-fide classic" and he also made special note of 'The Good Ship Sirius', a Wickham dominated reel. "Can you imagine how beautiful this would sound rising up at the end of 'Strange Boat'—its original home," he mused.

And yet, despite all of this, Scott is still keeping his eye firmly focused on getting the maximum amount of this material into the public arena. Comparing the work as being akin to his own personal version of Dylan's *The Basement Tapes* it seems something of a mission to him. "There's quite a lot more to come out," he told Alan Pattullo, "I'd be hard-pressed to condense it in a single CD."

The change in The Waterboys from the *Fisherman's Blues* record through to the second, and final, "Irish" album, *Room to Roam*, cannot be described better than by charting the changing live experience throughout 1989.

Fran Breen had amicably departed the line-up to follow his own dream of playing in America. "I've a lot of time for Mike and I think he's got a big heart. We had a meeting, at Mike's flat, and everybody in the band was there: "We're going to do a bunch of dates around Europe, then it looks like were going to do an American tour." It was gearing up so that basically we were going to be working for a year—which was the way he was kind of saying it. That was great, we all talked and off I went home. But then I got a phone call offering me the chance to go to America to record [with Nanci Griffiths, styled by *Rolling Stone* as 'The Queen of Folkabilly'], which I'd always wanted to do. So I talked to Trevor about it, 'I've got a real dilemma here, Trevor, I want to work with Mike, but I really want to do this.' But at the time it all worked out because something had happened with the tour—put off or something. So Mike said, 'No problem,' gave me a handshake and all the rest, a real gent."

Breen's intention was to remain resident in Ireland, making transatlantic crossings to work with Griffith and saw his life moving in that direction "for the next eight or nine years". But this changed dramatically because he actually, "spent eleven years in America living in Tennessee. The chance came to move to America, and that was what it was all about, I think it's a dream for all musicians. Records recorded in Ireland, or Britain, or America, they are all very different in technique, in feel and in approach. And I like the American approach; all that soul and blues music that came out of there has a real history to it that I wanted to explore." Breen's regard for Mike Scott remains undiminished through the years, though he has only played with him on one occasion since leaving The Waterboys. He admires Scott's ability to harness the creativity of the musicians he surrounds himself with ("Anyone who gives it 110% can't be far wrong. I must say, I was in awe of his ability to take everybody and move them in one direction."). And he looks back fondly on his association with the band. "I think when you're in that thing all the time, it's like being in a vortex or a tornado! Your hand comes out momentarily and then it's sucked back in [laughs]. It would be fantastic to have that in a cartoon of The Waterboys! The tornado with heads hanging out as it's going around!"

Since returning to Ireland in 2004, his American adventure at an end, Breen has drummed for the Saw Doctors—another little Waterboys connection. "The Saw Doctors are really good songwriters, never really got the kudos in Ireland that they deserved for their song-writing. I wish more people in Ireland, not the public but the journalists would *listen* to some of their songs." As to The Waterboys, he sums up his experience: "For my short period of being there, I have great respect for Mike. I think he's a great songwriter and I think he's a great performer. I suppose he's on that endless quest to find those ones he wants to stay on board his ship—you've got this guy who writes great songs and wants to try things out."

In place of Breen, Scott was fortunate in recruiting Patti Smith drummer Jay Dee Daugherty, who had already played on the sessions at Spiddal House, for a tour around the British Isles. The band also included occasional appearances by Vinnie Kilduff and Tomas MacEoin, and had Colin Blakey as a regular member of the line-up. "About a month after *Fisherman's Blues* came out, Mike gave me a call and said he was in Edinburgh. So I popped around to say 'hello', or met for a drink, and he said, 'We're going out on the road, would you like to come and play with the band?' I said, 'Yes' because things had pretty well lapsed with We Free Kings for me. So I went over for a week's rehearsal in Dublin and then we hit the road. It looked like a Chinese laundry between numbers, people scuttling around. Sometimes I'd play the Hammond organ, next number I'd be over on the piano, then I'd be on the flute—meanwhile Anto would be putting the saxophone down and sprinting over to the Hammond. It was just *ridiculous* but good fun, though you had to have a very clearly marked out set-list. But Mike would never do the same set two nights running. No 'put the set together and that's the way we'll do it until the end of the tour'. He'd the write the set before the gig in his hotel room and give it to you half an hour before you went on stage and you'd have to write your notes and make sure you could negotiate the stage—so never a dull moment!"

Although, as might be anticipated, the highlight of the shows featuring MacEoin was to be a live rendition of 'The Stolen Child' (it wouldn't be regularly featured in the set without his vocal contribution until 2006). But Scott once again also demonstrated his passionate support of musicians on the fringes by featuring MacEoin not as an opening act that could be ignored by the audience but taking the pace of the set down a level and having MacEoin as a feature of the main set. "When we brought Tomas MacEoin on, some people loved it but some thought we were mad," observes Blakey. "The bravest was Tomas for doing it, I don't know how he put up with it at all. I loved it, I thought it was a great thing to do. I suppose not everyone saw that, the people who liked their heads down, no nonsense, straight-ahead meat-and-potatoes rock'n'roll would be waiting for the time when Tomas went to the side of the stage again and we went back to playing 'Medicine Bow'. [Tomas] seemed to like it, he managed it fine and if he didn't drink too much… but that's the same for all of us, one hangover on a tour and you'll never catch your energy up. But he seemed pretty resilient!"

Interviewed by Jamie Davidson for the second issue of his Waterboys fanzine *Under the Skin*, MacEoin described the totally new experience of touring and performing before sizeable audiences. "The Waterboys have been so kind to me, I often wanted a few pints before

I did anything and they were really patient with me. Sometimes I may have had too many early on in the tour as I was so frightened." But he found the fans "really nice, lots of young people... I have even heard people calling to me in Irish." Steve Wickham summed him up to Liam Fay: "In the West of Ireland in the old days, 'Tall' was a word used to describe a handsome, strong and intelligent man. Tomas is very Irish, very gifted, very funny and very Tall. We're all very fond of him."

"When [the recording of 'The Stolen Child'] was over I thought it was the end of me and The Waterboys," MacEoin recalled. "Then came the letter saying they were going on tour. I got to see lots of places with them and they were very good to me." His appearances with the band were generally for two numbers played with a traditional Irish or Scottish arrangement. 'Down By the Sally Gardens' (a setting to music of another W. B. Yeats poem) and 'An Cailin Alainn' (noted on Scott's website as being played to the tune of 'The Mingulay Boat Song') or 'Bleann Na Bo', followed by the 'The Stolen Child'. MacEoin also performed 'Down By The Sally Gardens' and 'Bleann Na Bo' with The Waterboys as his support band, on Gay Byrne's *The Late Late Show* on Irish television station RTE in June 1989. It all served to demonstrate the direction in which the band was going. Although the set-list also included Thistlethwaite's 'Mr Customs Man', a far cry from raggle-taggle folk, and the drumming of Daugherty cracked the band along at a fair pace, the influences of Spiddal and the Irish West Coast were seeping in with ever-greater impact. By the time that the band were once again scuttling around Britain and Ireland over the summer of 1989, engaged in what became known as The Waterboys "Celtic Summer," they'd gained the services of accordionist Sharon Shannon and veteran Irish drummer Noel Bridgeman. And made the furthest step they would take away from the Big Music.

It was Steve Wickham who, perhaps unconsciously, set the band on the road to their most traditionally based folk period. In December 1987 he'd travelled out to the Northwest coast of Ireland, to Doolin, County Clare—a fishing village some forty-five miles from Galway that has enjoyed and relished its reputation as the music capital of

Ireland.[39] It's an area of a rich musical heritage, captured and recorded in the 1930s, akin to the work of Alan Lomax in America's Deep South, by Seamus O'Duillearga and maintained as an archive firstly by the Irish Folklore Commission and then by its successor, the Department of Irish Folklore UCD. But the area really came to prominence in the 1970s when the brothers Russell (Gussie and Pakie and, most famously, Micho) took its music to international prominence. Micho, a tin whistle player, toured in Europe and America, presenting a sound rich in what has been described as "an iconic Irish dimension… that had no precedent or equal on the concert stage." He and his brothers were captured live in Doolin at O'Connor's pub in January 1974 for a recording released by Topic Records the following year, whilst Micho also became a writer on the tunes, songs and folklore of County Clare. He died in a car accident in 1994. The village now commemorates him in the annual Micho Russell Festival Weekend.

It was at a session in one of Doolin's three pubs (aside from O'Connor's there is McGann's and McDermott's—they boast music all year round, nightly in the summer) that Wickham encountered a young accordionist, Sharon Shannon. She had grown up in Ruan, a small village in the predominately rural Corofin, born into a musical family. Her parents were dancers and, whilst she and her three siblings were versed in the tin whistle, Sharon, encouraged by her brother Gary, had taken-up the accordion by the time she was about eleven. "We were," she told Oliver Sweeny of *Hot Press*, "mad for music. My parents and all the neighbours were very encouraging. Then there was Frank Custy, who was a great music teacher. He used to run ceilidhs in Toonagh—near where my parents are from—every Friday night… 'twas the thing we looked forward to all week." She also became an accomplished fiddler under the tutelage of Custy, who recalled her as having, "a great natural talent, but she worked hard—very hard—at her playing. She had the golden touch." Moving to Doolin during her teenage years was a major factor in her musical education, as she explained to Tom Nelligan. "Musicians come there from all over the world. So I got to hear different traditional music, like Swedish,

39   And (the locals will insist) the inspiration for J.R.R. Tolkien's *The Lord of the Rings*.

American old-time music, and Cajun. I learned traditional music from all over the world."

She had opportunities outside of music; she was an enthusiastic show-jumper, brought-on by her father's love of horses, but she stopped competing when she was sixteen and, after a brief spell at Cork's University College, turned her focus on to her music. In her teenage years she had performed for producer Jim Sheridan in his staging of Brendan Behan's play *The Hostage* and been a member of former De Dannan bodhrán player Johnny McDonagh's traditional group Arcady. McDonagh explained to Lahri Bond[40] how previously he and Sharon, "used to play as a duo, while she was working with the Druid Theatre. I had not been playing with De Dannan for a while and I was looking to start a new band."

Arcady was quite an ensemble, "eight musicians and a manager and a sound guy". They played their first show together in the Point Depot, "the biggest place in Ireland—where U2 play" when they opened for Lyle Lovett at a show filmed for a TV series called *The Sessions*. The programme really set them on their way, though, as McDonagh noted, "it was too much really, because we were travelling to places like Iraq, Finland, Scotland and England. It was a big band and it wasn't really paying for itself. We recorded an album with that band that was never actually released." Though in his interview with Bond, McDonagh recalls Sharon has having left Arcady to join The Waterboys, she actually departed the band to start a solo career ("I wanted to do my thing"). She was twenty years old and more than ready and able to make her own mark on Irish culture. Supported by John Dunford, an album was planned, with a mobile unit sent down to the Kinvara's Winkles Hotel to record her live. With Scott and Wickham already on hand in nearby Spiddal it was only natural that they would come over for the session, which enjoyed further input and assistance from Adam Clayton, Sharon's sister Mary and Frank Custy's daughter, also Mary. Though the album, *Sharon Shannon* (Solid Records, 1991) was eventually completed at Windmill Lane, it was only a matter of time before the solo career, and the work on the album, was on hold and

40 *Dirty Linen # 59*, August/September 1995.

Sharon became the original 'Watergirl' in The Waterboys. "They came over for the fire crack. It ended up being a great three days music and two weeks later I was with The Waterboys."

"Sharon came in with fantastic technique, a beautiful smile, incredible youthful energy and a great curiosity about music," recalls Colin Blakey. "I don't think she liked my bagpipes very much, she used to wince a bit when I played them—but I probably wasn't very good with them then! It wasn't very Irish I guess."

There was some well-rounded serendipity in the timing of the precocious talent of the young Sharon Shannon's recruitment to the fold, coming as it did at when Scott also brought in someone who could well be described as the 'Grand Old Man' of Irish rock. Nollaug "Noel" Bridgeman, was a highly experienced and well-respected Irish drummer who'd played with just about *everybody* it seemed. Together with Gary Moore, Brendan Shiels and Bernhard Cheevers he'd formed Dublin-based progressive rock band Skid Row in 1967 (Phil Lynott had been their original singer) and played on the albums *Skid* and *34 Hours*. Their third album, recorded in 1972 but not released until 1990, saw Moore leave the band, though Bridgeman and Shiels struggled on with a succession of singers and guitarists. After Skid Row, Bridgeman established himself as a successful session player, appearing on recordings by Clannad and by Van Morrison.

"People would often ask me, 'What's it like backstage? What about the sex and the drugs and the rock'n'roll?' notes Blakey. "Really the thing that used to happen was that it was a session. Harry Isles, one of our tour managers, said that compared to any other band he'd worked with, we made them seem really uninterested in music! Because as soon as we'd finished we'd go back to the dressing room, a coffee or a beer, and the instruments would come back out—or they'd never have been put away in their cases in the first place—and the tunes would start. Often people had come backstage or had hung around afterwards who were fiddlers, banjo players, whatever, and so a tune would start, or Steve would say, 'I've just written a tune, what do you think of this?' Before long three or four hours would have gone by and you'd be staggering back to the hotel! Or, back at the hotel you'd here tunes coming out of hotel rooms—various members practising or working things out, or just having a tune. Noel Bridgeman introduced me to conga playing—I'd bought him a darabooka, a little African drum, in Oslo of all places, and bought myself one at the same time, and got him to show me a few conga grooves on it. Which didn't sound very good on the darabooka but when I got a set of congas I realised what a good teacher he'd been. I met up with him years and years later and got him to come and do some workshops at a samba school that I'd set up."

"It was quite delightful that it *was* a jumble, a collective," adds Thistlethwaite. "The thing was, we all had acoustic instruments so we could play in the dressing room and probably the music that went on in the dressing room, or on the bus on the way to the gig was just as important as what happened on stage. That was the differ-ence between the London 1985 band, because we weren't all jamming before we went on, so that was the beauty of what was going on. The Levellers came along afterwards and I thought, 'Oh, they're just us!'—they probably saw us at Glastonbury!"

Glastonbury, Cornwall[41], four sell-out nights at the Olympia Theatre in Dublin, a show for the benefit of the prisoners at Dublin's Mountjoy Prison, appearances at the French Inter-Celtique Festival, shows on the Aran Islands and in Galway, The Waterboys reeled and jigged across the Celtic heartlands. "You just play 'til the tunes stop chasing you," Sharon Shannon once said. Liam Mackie, reviewing one of the nights at the Olympia described the band as having struck a balance between "Bo Diddley and diddley-eye." After the show, he observed Sharon Shannon, Steve Wickham, Charlie Lennon and others striking up a session and it struck him. "It's loose and I'm being to see some light about where The Waterboys' world is heading," he wrote. He wasn't wrong.

---

41 An absolutely storming show on 15th June, watched, I'm pleased to say, by this author. Blakey: "We stayed in Fowey in this mad hotel on the cliff about two hundred yards above the sea, where we had a day-off. I loved it, went out and hired a boat and bought a hat! I knew which beach everyone was down on and went and picked them all up and went cruising around Fowey harbour and swimming off the back of the boat—it was great."

7

SPRING COMES TO SPIDDAL

The sessions for The Waterboys' second excursion into Irish traditional music were both more compressed in terms of the number of guest musicians contributing and, on first glance, with regard to the range of music being created. *Fisherman's Blues* had encompassed, with relish, a wide vista of rock, folk, traditional, gospel and jazz and painted, in its own way, a vivid picture of the influences and surroundings that had created it. In that sense it wasn't so far removed (certainly in respect of the songs that were laid down at Windmill Lane, whether selected for the album or ultimately discarded) from the roots of the band in the Big Music. It was neither afraid to go for the epic soundscapes or the drawn-out and studied mood pieces that characterised previous Waterboys records. The collection of seventeen short, sometimes almost abbreviated, tracks that comprised *Room to Roam* were, on the other hand, a thousand decibels and a million miles removed from the Big Music. "I'd been working on my song-writing, on getting songs more compact," Scott explained to Liam Mackey. "I was trying to say more with less words in less time and with more compact arrangements."

Reassembling at Spiddal House in February 1990 the 'Raggle Taggle' Waterboys were Scott, Thistlethwaite, Wickham, Hutchinson, Bridgeman, Blakey and Shannon. "We'd been touring the seven-piece band, with Colin and Sharon and Noel for about six months before we made the album and we'd worked on a lot of the songs so I think we all had a clear idea of what it was going to sound like," Scott recalled. Aside from the sessions at Windmill, and in San Francisco, with Bob Johnston, Scott had acted as the de-facto producer for *Fisherman's Blues*. The new album, though was to be overseen by Barry Beckett, an American producer born on 4th February 1943 in Birmingham, Alabama who had worked with Jerry Wexler on Dylan's *Slow Train Coming* and whose other production credits included recordings with Joan Baez, Dire Straits, Joe Cocker and Phish.

The recruitment of Beckett must surely have been on the strength of his association with Scott's hero Bob Dylan. The reason for doing so, rather than continuing the practice of Scott as producer as well as songwriter and arranger, lay in the dynamics of his association with the rest of the band during the recording of *Fisherman's Blues* and to his 'annus-horibilis' of 1987. He explained this in *Musician* magazine: "I felt my role as producer on *Fisherman's Blues* had strained my relationship with the others and I just wanted to be a member of the band for a while." The need to fit-in and be 'one of the boys' is noticeable, though what the reader would most understand from the quote is the qualification "for a while." There could be no mistaking that whilst Scott might want to liberate himself from the overseeing of the recordings the idea of taking a backseat could only ever be temporary.

"The room we were recording in, in Spiddal House, when we were doing four or five piece stuff for *Fisherman's Blues*, that room was big enough," Scott told Liam Mackey. "But when you put seven people in, it's a bit smaller and I think that was probably in Barry's mind when he split us up [for recording purposes]."

On the sleeve notes for the remastered CD release of *This is the Sea*, Scott notes, perhaps a little grandly, one of the components of his developing musical styles and techniques as being "my voice." That chimes with Barry Beckett's generalised comment, made in an interview with Robyn Taylor-Drake in 1999, describing the elements that made him want to work with any particular artist: "The sound of the voice, the timbre, whether the artist can be genuine in the interpretation, and overall taste and intelligence." In the same interview his declaration of approach appears akin to a perfectionist, something that Mike Scott must have had a significant affinity with. "You don't accept a vocal if you don't think it's right. You don't accept a guitar line if you don't think it's right." In Beckett's view, "If a song is not happening, you break it down, the most important element being the drums. The 'hi hat' is basically where you get your groove from. When you find a drummer that you love, and you find a great acoustic player that knows how to play with the hi hat, he's gonna play rhythmically."

"Barry Beckett? He'd try and get a consistency in terms of tempo," Blakey explains. "We'd find a tempo that was comfortable for us, then he'd come in with his metronome and we'd try and hold it at that speed, which generally we would because with Noel in charge of tempo—he's just so good." In fact, Colin credits Noel Bridgeman in generous terms for his presence and experience. "Noel was Groove Central. Not only did he play drums like an African man but also he had this ridiculous sense of groove, which I loved. He's quite a minimalist player; he could do it without overstating things. I was in awe of all of the drummers we played with. Jay Dee Dougherty, Fran Breen, I just loved them all, the differences in style. But I felt with Noel… he'd played on one or two of the Windmill session tracks that I did, I think he was on 'On My Way To Heaven' and one or two tracks that didn't see the light of day. The Grand Old Man of the Irish rock scene really, brilliant." Bridgeman's understated approach didn't suit every band member and the style in which the band had been playing through the second half of 1989 wasn't to the taste of some of Mike's longest associates.

Fran Breen, whilst having a great deal of respect for Noel Bridgeman, didn't necessarily consider him to be the appropriate driving force for the band. "I don't know how many drummers Mike has had play with him, but I honestly feel Dave Ruffy and Kevin Wilkinson, and also Peter McKinney, were the kind of players that really suited what he was doing." And Roddy Lorimer, although never an officially signed-up member of The Waterboys, was somebody who was as committed to the cause as anyone who'd played in the band and knew that the music the band produced in Ireland pushed his own contribution as a performer out to the margins. He notes simply that, "I had so little involvement in the Irish years because there was very little for me to do in the band. On *Room to Roam* I think I played on 'Spring Comes to Spiddal' and that was it, there was a trombone player and a clarinet player and we just did a little bit of trad-jazz behind it." He sums up the end results as being "unique, but it was unique with a genre where there were an awful lot of great performers playing Irish music, a lot of whom came and played with The Waterboys as well. But, it didn't give to music what the 'rock' Waterboys gave to music, there was so much originality—as much as there was a beauty in the folk thing that's not what I love. I love the excitement of rock music, and I missed that with The [Irish] Waterboys. When we were touring, with Martyn on bass, Chris Whitten on drums, Karl, Anto, Mike and I—that was the *greatest* Waterboys band. I remember coming back, doing *The Tube* at Christmas time when we'd just come off tour and I think that band was at the pinnacle and never reached these heights again. Mike obviously would have some very different opinions, because he thought it was at an end and had to move it on to something different. But it moved on to an area really that the trumpet didn't fit into, Irish folk music. It's not sour grapes, but a taste thing. There was nothing for me to contribute to it. So there's an obvious thing where I *wouldn't* find it… but I genuinely feel that what we had to offer the world as a rock band had a bigger appeal. A lot of people said we should have been bigger than U2, and I really believe it—had Mike decided to be."

"When we first went to Ireland it was great, but you see really my heart wasn't in playing all that stuff," notes Thistlethwaite. "I didn't join groups to play things like that [the raggle-taggle folk-music]. The blues or the Big Music I could go with one hundred percent, but… for Mike and Steve it was probably great, but it wasn't my cup of tea. I spent a lot of time after the initial excitement of recording *Fisherman's Blues* giving myself an apprenticeship in blues music. So we'd be on tour in America playing our folky stuff, but I'd be straight out after the gig playing blues music downtown, working away doing something else while all this was going on. Compared to what we'd done in the beginning, compared to *A Pagan Place* or *This is the Sea* it wasn't strong." This would eventually culminate in his first solo album, *Aesop Wrote a Fable*, which he describes as basically, a blues record. "I was seriously into that and working hard on it. It was a balance in my life, there was a lot of time where we weren't doing anything and I don't like to waste time." Recruiting guest session musicians for his solo projects led to a particular highlight in his work: "I was really rewarded on the albums that I made myself because Mick Taylor played guitar on all three—a dream come true."

On the other side of the coin, though, Scott had assembled a new set of musical allies for whom the whole essence of being in a place with the character and other-worldliness of Spiddal playing music with an immense history and tradition was everything. "There's 3,000 miles and then America," Scott enthused to the *NME* in September 1990, after his Irish adventure had essentially come to its conclusion. "It's the end of Europe, the end of Ireland... so it's the end of the world in that sense. I really love it. I feel at home there. It's such a free place, your imagination can really run riot." He reflected this breathless, mythological atmosphere in 'Song from the end of the World'. And in terms of what was being achieved at Spiddal, Colin Blakey, genuinely captivated by the surroundings and the way it was pushing the band ever further out from the sounds that it had made over the previous decade has much of the same sentiment. "It just sort of takes you over, you won't meet musicians like that anywhere else. The musicians in the west of Ireland are just second to none, and the tradition is so strong there. And that's me talking as a Scotsman and I love the Scottish traditional music as well. My heart was very much in the acoustic music by that stage, though I wasn't adverse to a bit of rock'n'roll either! So it really suited me, even though I didn't like the old sort of folk-rock that had been covered in the past, back in the seventies. This was a different approach, but an evolution also. Part of me knew that it wouldn't continue in that direction forever, because Mike just follows his own heart, that's the way it works."

Scott might have talked about *Room to Roam* as being a landmark recording in his development as a songwriter, but compared with every other album he has made it is a record that in essence feeds off and absorbs its surroundings, the culture and traditions of Irish folk music. That's not to suggest that there wasn't already an ingrained appreciation of what traditional Celtic (to spread the influence that little bit wider) could offer. Lorimer recalls how he saw this starting "a bit earlier [than The Waterboys Irish era]. I remember going down to Rockfield. I got a call late one night from Anto, could I be a Rockfield in the morning for a session for Mike. Train to Monmouth, car to the studio. Get there, nobody about. Sitting there, eventually an engineer arrives. I start setting up, figuring out where the good places and the bad places were, making sure I had the right sound in the right part of the studio. Got a bit of lunch and the band is all starting to wake up. Found Mike, big hugs, said, 'I've set up, checked out the sound, checked out the mikes, ready to go'. Mike said, 'Brilliant, Roddy. I want you to sing. I'm doing this old Scottish folk song called 'Twa Recruitin' Sergeants'[42] and I can't track myself, it'll sound too obvious, but I need somebody with a Scottish accent!' And it wasn't backing vocals. It was the two of us singing in Harmony. Mike said, 'I'm going to put that out one day.'"

Noting in this chapter that *Room to Roam* might appear 'on first glance' to be less wide-ranging in its construction than *Fisherman's Blues* is deliberate. In some ways, *Room to Roam* was one of Mike Scott's most experimental creations; however, the complexity of the record was not in his traditional literary allusions and spiritualist undertones but rather in the way that he would capitalise on his fascination with the Beatles during the recording sessions.

"It was partly my fault," Anto comments. "I'd bought Mike this terrific book about the early years of the Beatles by the guy who'd been their engineer in the studio, Mark Lewisohn, a *really* good book, tells

---

42' Twa Recruitin' Sergeants' is a traditional Scottish song pre-dating the Jacobite uprising of 1745 which describes how although the British Government were predisposed to using the fighting skills of the Highlanders in their regiments, they had a difficult task to persuade the Scots to take the King's shilling. The Waterboys included it in their touring set during 1989.

you all the edits and stuff. I gave it to Mike prior to making the *Room to Roam* record and he started doing loads of things that they'd done, it became his sort of inspiration. When we recorded 'How Long Will I Love You?' he wanted Paul McCartney to come and play bass on it!"

Lewisohn had written *The Beatles Live!* [1986], and then followed it up with *The Complete Beatles Recording Sessions* in 1988, the book that Scott had received in his Christmas stocking. They were later collected as, appropriately enough, *The Complete Beatles Chronicle*. In his own book on the Beatles (*Do You Want To Know A Secret?*), Newcastle journalist and broadcaster Keith Topping describes the Lewisohn volumes as "the standard reference works by which all other books on the Beatles will be judged."

Topping explains their relevance: "Mark Lewisohn was the first person outside of the immediate EMI staff to get complete access to their archives. He was the first guy to ever hear any of the unreleased stuff. He wrote a session-by-session breakdown of everything the Beatles recorded. Everything at EMI, and then he found the half a dozen sessions they recorded at other studios and managed to get access to them as well. It's *literally* 'on this day they recorded this song, and then they did this edit piece on this song.' He talks a lot to George Martin and Geoff Emerick, Phil Scott and Phil McDonald and various engineers who worked with them. McCartney does a big interview with him at the start of the book and goes into some of the song-writing. It's the trainspotter's guide to sessions if you like! If you're the slightest bit interested in how music is created in the studio, even if you're not particularly into the Beatles, you should have a copy of it—just to see how a band works in the studio, or did in the sixties. It doesn't tell you exactly how McCartney played the bass, but it would tell you what type he used on a particular song, different instrumentation that was used, stuff that had never been in the public domain before. Like, there'd been a harpsichord used on one song or a Hammond organ on another and you might have guessed that, but you never had confirmation. Remember that this is before Ian McDonald's *Revolution in the Head* and before nearly every band had a song-by-song analysis written—it's the forerunner of all of those. It's very well regarded in Beatles fandom."

As to what Mike Scott would have gained from the book, Topping considers that he would have had "an even greater understanding of how a record is put together. How edit pieces could be used. Normally when a band goes into the studio they'll do a basic foundation backing-track and then put vocals over the top of that. What *Sessions* describes is how, for example, when they were doing *Sgt. Peppers* there was thousands of little edit pieces, like a three-second guitar piece that they'd drop in. And of course, this was all pre-digital, done on tape as opposed to being played into a computer and then played back at a latter stage. So it's how to put a record together like a jigsaw puzzle, really."

"Mike was certainly exploring different treatments, and different styles of writing, different avenues," considers Colin Blakey. "I think there was more work afterwards on the tracks. Mike was reading a lot of stuff about the Beatles and George Martin, and was trying out a few of those ideas or finding different ways of using the studio. Running tapes backwards, odd effects. That sort of thing. The actual takes were done live, but there may have been some overdubs. For instance my flute solo in 'A Life of Sundays' I did by playing the flute through a massive distortion effect so it sounded like a crazy guitar solo and then Mike overdubbed some proper electric guitar over it, so it's a mish-mash of lead-lines."

In *Musician* magazine, Scott described the creation of what the interviewer called the "ethereal background sighs on the haunting 'Bigger Picture,'" as being "completely nicked from the techniques used on *Sgt. Pepper's*. You slow down the tape and sing along, then put it back up to normal speed and your voice comes out all echoey and breathy." Elsewhere he would try and paint *Room to Roam* as being his generation's *Sgt. Peppers*, or more specifically a *Celtic Sgt. Pepper's*.

Room to Roam drew strongly on the heritage of Celtic folk music, with Stuart Bailie of *Vox* describing it, appropriately enough, as "a magical mystery tour around the music of British Isles." Scott explained to Alain Gales in *Melody Maker* some of the cultural background that he was starting to plug into having not given much attention to whilst he was growing up. "I remember when I went back to Scotland for Christmas in 1987 I had a fantastic two weeks going around the shops, discovering the Scottish music. But it was the brother of Irish music. That was a great revelation [discovering] all this new culture I'd discovered in Ireland was actually my own culture, once removed."

So, and appropriately given the deep connection that Steve Wickham, his principal foil, also felt with traditional tunes, *Room to Roam* borrowed heavily. Most particularly, having played it live the previous year, The Waterboys committed to vinyl their cover of 'The Raggle Taggle Gypsy', a Scottish folk song but one also popular in Ireland. It tells a story, which is believed to have been based on a real event, of a lady who absconds from her affluent and comfortable life and her 'newly married lord', trading 'a goose-feather bed' to 'sleep in a cold open field'. In fact, Scott had become interested in the song after hearing a rendition by We Free Kings, "one of the traditional songs that they'd jazzed up. It turned out Steve Wickham knew the song very well and we decided to have a crack at it ourselves."

But *Room to Roam* wasn't dominated by Steve Wickham in the way that during *Fisherman's Blues* it could almost be thought that Scott's muse *was* the astonishing way that Wickham could weave his fiddle through the complexities of Scott's writing and arrangements. That emphasis on fiddle had left *Fisherman's Blues* with a dark winter tinge, but *Room to Roam* was a warm spring morning of a record and the newer element of Sharon Shannon's accordion and Colin Blakey's whistle and piano added that rather more easy going and sprightly step. "We had four or five musicians on *Fisherman's Blues* and on *Room to Roam* we had seven" Scott told *Musician*. "Steve tends to be a dark musician with his fiddle. The other musicians on this record tend to be light musicians… in the flavour of the sound they make. *Room to Roam* wound up having a certain lightness to it that didn't have as much to do with Steve's playing."

The lightness in the touch of *Room to Roam* reflected the origin of the phrase in the works of George MacDonald, who Scott cited alongside Lewis as an author influential in his own literary upbringing. Indeed, Lewis claimed that from MacDonald he had learned "the

beauty of goodness." One critic analysed MacDonald's adult fantasy
work, *Phantastes*, as having characters and places so interconnected
that "the two are often one and the same, or else they are so closely
linked that they cannot survive alone." As with the work of Lewis,
and of Mark Helprin, *Phantastes* has at its centre the idea of the
young man transported into another world and from it Scott rearranged MacDonald's wistful parting song:

Thou goest thine, and I go mine-
Many ways we wend;
Many days, and many ways,
Ending in one end.

Many a wrong, and its curing song;
Many a road, and many an inn;
Room to Roam, but only one home
For all the world to win.

From the idea of the interconnectivity between people and
places came a record that Scott described as being questing songs.
"Everybody's got to go on their own quest, their own adventure, and
those songs are mine."[43] The songs see the old Gods in the landscapes,
Scott's ever-present touchstone Pan appearing in 'Song from the End of
the World' and the Lewis-tinged 'Further Up, Further In'. They recon-
nect with traditional Scottish tunes in 'The Raggle Taggle Gypsy' and
'A Man is in Love' and with the heritage of his colleagues. 'The Trip to
Broadford' and 'Natural Bridge Blues' "are from the Sharon Shannon
repertoire," Scott noted to Stuart Bailie, adding that [Wickham's]
'Upon the Wind and Waves' was "a true song [about] real people that
we met." But Ian Gittins, writing in *Melody Maker* saw the songs in
a completely different light, calling them "disturbingly slack and trite"
and claiming the LP as a "trad stagger round a muddy meadow."
   "It's a picture we know by heart already," added Gittins. "It's an Irish
landscape… a sketch of his local area. A *good* sketch, admittedly, but
as such only of local interest. The Waterboys should be global."

43 ' Across the Tracks', *Vox* magazine November 1990, interviewed by Stuart Bailie.

The *Room to Roam* Waterboys made an appearance on the RTE/BBC co-produced television documentary series *Bring It All Back Home*, which traced the history of Irish music and its impact on the USA. The performance, recorded at Spiddal House, featured the band playing two tracks from the album, 'Song for the Life' and 'Spring Comes to Spiddal'; its importance though was that it marked the last time the raggle-taggle version of The Waterboys would appear together. It was an easy-going, comfortable, performance, particularly with 'Spring Comes To Spiddal' having been shot in the open-air, with Scott strumming in the summer sunshine, Blakey and Shannon in sandals relaxing on the doorstep of Spiddal House waiting for their cue. Such a presentation of the band, interspersed with long tracking shots of the countryside and water, posited something about The Waterboys that went beyond making music. It displayed a sort of charm and camaraderie—an atmosphere that was wrapped up in, or part of, the location and its ambience.

Though Mike Scott would continue to have a heartfelt passion for the people, music and geography of Ireland, the restless spirit had been reawakened. He married Irene Keogh in June 1990 and once again turned his attention stateside, planning another attempt at relocating to America. This, of course, was the very move that he had been on the brink of making those years back when, instead, he had chosen to "follow the fellow that fiddles" and in so doing embarked on his Irish adventure. Now it seemed that the original intention had been postponed the past six years rather than abandoned. And musically he was now looking to return to the days of lead guitar and away from the acoustic sound of the band's Celtic Summer. At the same time, both he and Thistlethwaite were unhappy with Bridgeman's drumming and had taken the decision to replace him—a decision that met with total opposition from Steve Wickham.

"I made a mistake you see," Wickham recalled sheepishly to Mark Radcliffe in 2005. "I went into the studio and things were shifting around and I got the feeling that Mike wanted to be in a rock'n'roll band." In the same interview, for Radio 2, Scott added, "Anthony and I were hankering for rock'n'roll again, I've got to tell the truth. And Steve has said to me that he just didn't want to go that way." But there were personal issues involved as well. Wickham was at a low point in his life, having divorced from his wife Barbara Lee and just embarked on his second marriage. And the hirings and firings that were part of The Waterboys' folklore had taken their toll on him and his enthusiasm for the band. He'd once described to Colin Irwin the need to "keep yourself emotionally well-fed in order to bring the songs to really good places every night." The situation with Bridgeman, for whom he had a particular affinity, was simply the last straw. "I just felt out of control of the situation," he told Peter Murphy of *Hot Press*. "One day my friend beside me, who's my best friend in the band, he's not there." He retreated to Ireland's West Coast, playing in local bands, still wanting the traditional music that he'd brought to The Waterboys, becoming a playwright and discovering the joys of fatherhood. Murphy considered the departure had been signposted: "On joining the band in 1985 he was a flamboyant whirling dervish of a performer, Scott's visual as well as musical foil. By 1989 he was rooted to the spot, an almost melancholic presence."

Soon after the split, and having broken his self-imposed moratorium on granting interviews, Scott noted to *Musician* magazine that his "reading of the situation is that Steve preferred to play traditional music." Once the band was moving back to their electric rock origins, Scott considered, Wickham would have felt, "that's not for him." But, with Wickham's departure, as far as Mike was concerned "the bottom completely fell out of the band and the game was up. I learned Irish music so that I could play with him. The man's a complete genius."

"Steve announced he was leaving," recalls Blakey. "He was the link between the rock'n'roll core and the kind of acoustic wing, which included Sharon and myself. With Steve gone a vital line of communication for Mike was lost, hence the dramatic decision on Mike's part to strip things down and move forward—that was his way of dealing with it." As Anto puts it, "It had gone as far as it could go. Steve said, 'If you're going to get rid of Noel then I'm going, I'm not going to put up with that.' So we found ourselves with tours booked for the *Room to Roam* record and basically there was Mike, Trevor and me. There was no point in having Sharon or Colin, you see, if Steve wasn't there.

And probably perversely as well, Mike could see the positive in the negative."

The biggest negative though was the critical response to *Room to Roam* once it was released, in September 1990. Though Katherine Dieckmann, writing for *Musician* magazine heard 'a collagistic assembly of ballads, rearranged traditional songs, carnivalistic bits and jazzy asides, with one college radio-ready rocker ('A Life of Sundays'), which nonetheless devolves into a wonderfully unwieldy guitar frenzy', others were not so enthusiastic. One reviewer wrote it off as an "exercise in cod-Irishness, with its lumbering odes to the simple life... the ultimate expression of Scott's love affair with the Emerald Isle." In the *NME*, Andrew Collins (retrospectively) dismissed it as highly irrelevant: "Despite folk music's significance in the history of the working classes, it cuts little mustard now that the Industrial Revolution's happened, and is largely the vanguard of civil servants." Scott, typically, was highly defensive of the album. "I love *Room to Roam*," he told David Cavanagh. "I get taken back immediately to the time and the atmosphere."

Another Waterboy disappointed with the response was Colin Blakey. "I'd hoped that *Room to Roam* would have been given a bit more of a thumbs-up because it was a really well-crafted album and had some amazing ideas on it. And it was challenging. But it was getting further and further away from the big sound of before. Maybe that album is the signal that Mike is never, ever, going to do what you'd predict and that he'll always change." But, again, the contrast is with Scott's longest serving band-mate, Thistlethwaite, who has no particular love for the album. "We'd started off well, but everything had started to go rather off-beam so I started doing stuff that would be on my first solo record [*Aesop Wrote A Fable*]. If you listen to the first track on that ['Muddy Waterboy'] you'll see where I was at, a hundred miles away!"

The tour that was, supposedly, in support of the *Room to Roam* album saw The Waterboys down to the core of Scott, Thistlethwaite and Hutchinson. They drafted in Kenneth Blevins, who'd drummed on John Hiatt's classic *Slow Turning* album with the intention of getting on the road with a revitalised, much heavier sound, turning away from reels and jigs and instead playing electric rock. "I really love playing rock'n'roll, electric guitar," Scott enthused to *Musician* magazine. "I was denying myself that pleasure for three or four years by only playing acoustic… relying on the musicians around me to take up all the solos and create textures in the sound."

"Then there were four of us and we had to go on tour," Anto observes. "So I had to play everything because we'd previously had a big band! We'd do 'All The Things She Gave Me' and I'd do electric mandolin and backing vocals, then pick up the sax for the sax-solo and then put it down and carry on with the mandolin—and I was playing Hammond organ as well. Running around just doing everything, because neither Trevor nor Kenny sang, or played anything else, so suddenly Mike and me are doing everything, but we somehow got away with it, though we could have done with one more person."

The newly slimmed-down and electrified Waterboys made their first appearance at the Hultsfred Festival in Sweden on 11th August 1990 before returning to Ireland for a trio of dates between 22nd and 24th of the month. They eschewed the traditional roots of the *Room to Roam* LP, with only 'A Life of Sundays', 'In Search of a Rose', 'Bigger Picture' and 'Room to Roam' initially making it from the vinyl to the live set. The Irish dates did, however, see the band joined for a guest appearance by Sharon Shannon. "There have been no rows at all in The Waterboys," Mike insisted. "Everybody's friends. Sharon has been playing the gigs with us. I've seen Steve loads of times since we split up and I'm still the best of friends with Noel and Colin."

The extensive *Room to Roam* world tour proper kicked off with a series of dates in Scotland, taking in the rest of the British Isles through September, a series of European shows during October and a substantial North American jaunt across November and December. The band finished with a return to Ireland for the by now traditional Christmas/New Year shows. By the time the tour reached Cardiff on 25th September the additional person that Thistlethwaite felt the band needed had been recruited, with long-time Waterboy Roddy Lorimer returning for one last tour. He'd never actually been an official member of the band—"I was never asked to join The Waterboys, but it was always clear I'd never leave the Kick Horns. That was my band as it were"—but in a lovely moment of serendipity he was able to combine his enthusiasm for the band with his Kick Horns duties.

"We were on tour with Deacon Blue in Scotland—and Mike was also there doing the Highlands and Islands tour and he phoned up and asked if I would do a European and US tour." This would have entailed a lot of time off from the Kick Horns as the tour was projected to run through to the end of the year. Though his fellow Kick Horns were understanding about this, it made Lorimer feel uncomfortable. "Twenty years the Kick Horns have been going, we've stuck to our guns and not taken the solo things, we've not compromised. We did an album for Jamiroquai—it was great, right up our street—then we got a call from Jamiroquai's management saying, 'You guys up for a world tour? But we only want two of you', well, no, we don't do that." But for this tour there would be a happy solution. "Mike said, 'how about asking them if they want to do it as well?' which would certainly solve the problem, they were big Waterboys' fans. So, we did it, and it was the last Waterboys tour of the old band as it were. Anto didn't play any sax, because we had a horn section. And we didn't do any folk songs at all—the heaviest set of The Waterboys you'd ever heard in your life—and all the audience turning up in Arran neck sweaters! For a Heavy Metal concert! But we had a ball, such a great time. If that was going to be the end of The Waterboys, at least I'd managed to marry it to the Kick Horns. I think Mike may have had that at the back of his mind as well, as a really deep thinker, so what I thought was a coincidental thing might have been Mike thinking it would be a nice thing to do. He would not use another trumpet player—I'd say, 'Get another player in when I'm not available', but Mike would say, 'No, it's you or nobody'. So it was a lovely honour that Mike did me by allowing my horn section to come and play with The Waterboys at the end.[44]"

44 Since his last appearances with The Waterboys Lorimer notes that he has "played with The Who, did three and a half months in America with them [on the Kick Horns website Lorimer notes that his career high point as "the first day rehearsing with The Who"]. I've done several US tours with Clapton, European tours, Worlds. There's a German artist who've I worked with, the last tour I did with him was twenty-odd dates of which the average audience was one hundred thousand a gig—a hundred and fifty thousand in Hamburg." At the time of interviewing (July 2005) he was gearing up for another world tour with Eric Clapton.

"The Kick Horns came on that tour, like the cavalry, but that wasn't quite right either, the whole thing wasn't really right." Thistlethwaite considers, giving the feeling that the 1990 tour had a whole 'end of an era' aura to it. However, before this era could close out, The Waterboys were present at the end of an infinitely more momentous piece of history, recalled here by Lorimer.

"We did a gig on Unification Day in Germany [October 3rd 1990], it was booked-in before it all happened—it all happened so quickly, a rush of blood, almost overnight. We decided to get a flight the day before so we could be there at the Reichstag for midnight, the party and all the fireworks. U2 were doing the *Achtung Baby* album, demoing it up in a house in Germany, in East Berlin. Coincidentally they were on the same flight as us, flying to Tegel airport. Of course, they were up in First Class and we were in cattle class but they rolled the champagne down the isles for us! We had nowhere to stay and they said, 'We've got this huge house, so come and stay with us.' In actual fact Berlin was at a standstill. You couldn't move anywhere and we actually ended up having to sleep on the bus, though apparently Bono and Adam Clayton were waiting up all night for us! The pilot of the plane came on when we landed and said, 'I've just heard from air traffic control, there are no more planes in the air. We are the last to touch down—and this is the last plane ever to fly over East Germany, in twenty-five minutes it ceases to exist.' In the rush to get to the Reichstag we all forgot to get our passports stamped, we just ran, got as close as we could, through the park and got there just in time—I've still got the photographs of that night."

The following night the band were recorded at Hamburg's 'Docks' venue, showing something of the style of the 1990 shows. A gentle and movingly thoughtful 'Something That Is Gone' with Lorimer blowing one of his most mournful and melancholy contributions over the parts where Wickham once held sway. Then Thistlethwaite's quirky bass lines counting in a blistering cover of Bob Dylan's 'Everything Is Broken'[45], one of the most memorable highlights from this incarnation of the band. It demonstrated not only Scott's rekindled passion

---

45   From *Oh Mercy*, released September 1989.

in wailing electric guitars but also the sharp drumming of Blevins driving the beat along at a pace rarely heard in The Waterboys before. Not broadcast, but played at Hamburg amongst other shows was 'Kiss The Wind' (a.k.a 'Once Upon A Time') which the *NME* described as, "A stuttering reprise on The Who's 'My Generation', stuffed with spiteful, kiss-off sentiments, aeons away from the winsome, raggle-taggle thing." Introduced into the set a few months earlier had been another curious insight into Scott's thinking, 'Karma'. The concept of Karma, essentially a Buddhist touchstone for the effect a person's actions have on their development and existence, had driven a lot of his writings over the years though never actually described as such. But in this song Scott spends a lot of time surveying his situation and it's a quite telling coda to his Irish years, metaphorically talking about paying back debts and, perhaps not so metaphorically, detoxing his system and his mind and becoming 'alive on the inside'. And he talks about the changing of his music, taking the traditional Waterboy allusion of the flowing river, a live affirming recognition of that constant renewal and regeneration that his followers had come to anticipate of him.

In this sense then, 'Karma' almost reflects the whole 'end of an era' feel of the 1990 Waterboys tour. Ramshackle at the outset, a somewhat enforced, but again in part orchestrated, U-turn that didn't exactly sign-off the original lineage of the band with anything like a flourish but still managed to encompass the group's comradeship with its sense of wanderlust and rootlessness. It wrapped up, appropriately enough, with a final end-of-year tour of Ireland, finishing at Galway's Leisureland on New Year's Eve with the band euphorically playing through the crash and swathe of 'Fisherman's Blues' on the chimes of midnight. But backstage afterwards, Scott and the band were identified as being downcast—as though they realised this was more than just the completion of a series of dates, but was actually a defining moment, a resolution. This time it was more than just the turning of a page—it brought a sense of finality and closure.

8

THE NEW LIFE

That final Waterboys show on New Year's Eve 1990 in Galway proved to be more than the wrapping up of an essentially chaotic and fraught touring schedule. Scott, through his desire to get back to playing electric guitar, might have thrown out many of the influences that had driven him through his Irish years but there was still a "rump-Waterboys" at least in name. It would take some time before he fully let go of the identity that had defined him in its different ways during the past decade.

Throughout 1991, though, that end of an era feeling remained hanging around, lingering but not receiving the final pay-off. Hutchinson departed in April, recruited to play on a permanent basis for Sharon Shannon's ensemble and left The Waterboys in the position of being effectively an on-hiatus duo.[46] The Waterboys' contract with Ensign Records expired and the label released a retrospective *Best of The Waterboys 1981—1990* and in so doing clearly drew a line under their relationship with Mike Scott.

"People at record companies perceive The Waterboys as this untouchable, unfriendly entity," Scott considered. He was reluctant

---

46   Trevor Hutchinson went on to become a founder member of Irish 'acoustic supergroup' Lunasa with whom he still performs a hectic touring and recording schedule.

to go along with a "Best of" record, seeing it as not particularly in the spirit of the band. However, he came to recognise that on reaching a turning point ("a new band is on the horizon—though I don't know what it is yet") perhaps a retrospective, a summing up of the journey so far wasn't such a bad thing. "After all our twists and turns people's idea of what The Waterboys is would actually be helped by a compilation album." So, contractually unable to prevent the release of the record he did the next best thing and took control himself, making the selections, regretting the songs he was unable to fit-in. "God only knows what it would have been like if [the record company] compiled it!" Perhaps also he saw it as part of the process of reconciliation within himself that he should take all these varying shades and textures and bring them all back into himself as a body of work. "Is it magic or clever sleight of hand, this obstinate Bohemian-in-a-basket sound of theirs?" asked Andrew Collins in his review of the album for *NME*, April 1991. "Mike Scott—muse or muso?"

Of course, Mike Scott just would not be Mike Scott unless he had the constantly shifting sands or an ebb and flow in fortunes and inspirations to define and spur him on. In the same month that both Hutchinson and Ensign Records departed from his story, Irene sent him off to the Caribbean where he started to kick his self-confessed heavy drinking habit. Drinking was something that he conceded to having "slid into" during his time in Ireland; regularly waking up with hangovers from Guinness-fuelled jamming sessions. And he was prepared to admit that he'd become focused on finding Dublin's best hostelries for the black nectar rather than on his creativity and work. It wasn't that his drinking made him "morose or depressed or violent" but that he considered himself "an amateur drinker," not a sound proposition in a culture of serious consumption. Removed from all of this, he told Allan Jones, he "got control of [his] own life" and from that feeling of empowerment and release came 'The New Life', a song he once claimed he'd like to have played at his own funeral as "It would be a good joke." But he saw the song as being "… about feeling. Have you ever had feeling of a whole new beginning? A new resolve? A closing of doors and an opening of new ones?" In it he wrote defiantly once again of burning his bridges and putting away all the things that held him back, of having a freshened clarity of purpose and being joyful in seeing his existence in a vibrant and emboldened way.

He was still talking about The Waterboys in the present tense. In his "come-back" interview with *Melody Maker*'s Alain Gale in May 1991 he talked about there still being a nucleus to the band of Thistlethwaite and "the American drummer who was on our last tour" and there were plans for further recordings and live dates as the year progressed. "I'll extend the line-up when we start recording," he claimed. "I don't know whether it will be guitars or Irish pipes, but it *will* extend and we'll go on tour… with maybe six people on stage."

"We've been undergoing a period of discovery and change and growth," he explained. It's good that we've been able to do that in our own time and our own way. I don't have any regrets." A clearer example of the 'Royal We' there is unlikely to be uttered. In fact by the standards of recording and touring achieved since his arrival in Ireland, 1991 was an unfocused and rather haphazard year despite the protestations of 'The New Life'. He'd worked with Anto, and others, during the early part of the year pulling together demos of previously unreleased tracks and had also cut demos of what would be his next studio album during the summer. His only formal live appearance was, though, under his own name at Dublin's Abbey Theatre performing musical interpretations of WB Yeats' poetry as part of the programme for The Yeats International Festival. "There's something about the rhythm of his lyrics that lends itself to music," Scott once told the BBC.

There were still the remnants of his Irish adventure and his personae of 'Scotland's greatest living Irishman.' Going down to Tuam, for example, and teaming-up with Saw Doctors' founder-member Padraig Stevens for a festival gig and then afterwards joining Anto and Leo Moran for a typically long and rambling set at a nearby hotel. But by the end of the year that was a part of his history and he was resident in New York's Greenwich Village and giving his first solo performance during a benefit show at the Beacon Theatre. "Recently I bought a book called *Pastures of Plenty*," he told his audience. "It's a collection of Woody Guthrie's [previously] unpublished writings…

and in amongst them is a poem called 'This Morning I Am Born Again'. When I read it, I fell in love with it and set it to music." With this thoughtful but low-key introduction on 12th October 1991 he celebrated his latest reinvention.

Allan Jones, writing for *Melody Maker* found Mike Scott firmly ensconced in the counterpoint to his Irish adventures, the hustle and bustle, and, yes, the sheer musical history of America[47]. Like Paddy McAloon in Prefab Sprout's 'The King of Rock'n'Roll' he was drinking in the atmosphere of his inspirations, wandering the same streets, dreaming the same dream. "Just walking around and thinking, 'God, Jimi Hendrix played here, Bob Dylan played here… it sharpens me. It sharpens all my edges." Or like Holly Golightly, Danish and coffee in hand, gazing in at the shining, shimmering jewellery at Tiffanys and daring to want to be something different, something *more*. "It's great to be completely unknown. I can be whoever I want to be."

Somewhere in the autumn of 1990 it had hit him. Ireland, Galway, had become cosy and comfortable. When that feeling had struck him, quite suddenly, he knew it was time to start over again. Time to follow his instincts and, just like arriving in Dublin for a short visit and staying six years, he had to be in a new place and have that new place drive his artistic vision. A short, tentative, visit to New York had convinced him that this was where the next phase should begin and that move, which he'd harboured dreams of many years previously became a reality.

Bohemian, he had relocated his new bride and himself to a first floor flat in the west of Greenwich Village where they lived "on a very loud street" and "there were huge garbage trucks going by at every hour of the day." David Cavanagh, tracking him down to the Café Fortuna (once a favoured spot for John Lennon), found him expressing a new focus and a clearly defined belief in God. And making changes: "I used to do things that I figured God wouldn't want me to do. Like drink all the time. I'm not meant to drink, I'm meant to be clear and to put music first in my life." He confessed that he found giving up the drink to be hard, but that he'd adopted meditation, "He's currently doing

47 *Melody Maker*, June 1993—'The New Life Starts Here'.

two twenty-minute sessions a day," noted Cavanagh and described it as contributing to Scott's "level of serenity and confidence."

Jones asked him exactly who he wanted to be. "Just the best Mike Scott I can be… That's what I'm working on right now." His new manifesto, his latest mission statement, that declaring of 'The New Life' would eventually rock-out on the opening of a new "Waterboys" album, a new chapter and a fresh start. There was a resonance with his countryman Roddy Lorimer so many years previously relocating from Scotland to London and leaving all behind him. Scott had, in his own words, burned his bridges.

Behind him were any and all of the musicians, compatriots and *friends* that had built on his artistic visions in the previous decade. Gone, of course, were all the Irish connections—it had come to the point where he could not walk the streets of Dublin without the increasingly weary comments and asides from passers-by. "Everybody knew me… 'Oh, there's yer man from The Waterboys.'" Gone too was the sound and the imagery, no longer away with the raggle-taggle gypsies, sometimes now cemented in noise, concrete and anonymity and at other times looking back wistfully to the essence of his home-land. Anything and anyone that rooted the concept of The Waterboys to those early recordings at The Farmyard and at Rockfield, the Big Music and *This is the Sea* had been expunged.

And gone was the man whom Scott would later describe as "My oldest musical friend." Scott's official website might now note simply "December 1991. Mike and Anthony split" but it was actually much more akin to Springsteen disbanding the E-Street Band and dispens-ing, coolly, calculatingly, with the services of his long-time saxophonist Clarence Clemons. "Mike just said, 'I don't want to work with you any-more,' and I don't know how that came about," recalls Thistlethwaite. All that time together focused on the musical journey, all that energy spent following Scott's creative twists and turns, all those moments of playing at the drop of a hat and in support of Scott's brilliant muse. "Anto and I had been together for about ten years," Scott explained to *Musician* magazine, recognising that both of them wanted to keep their association going. "We'd gone through a whole journey together and we were beginning to repeat ourselves. We were very much at ease with each other. But we'd have been keeping an old thing together for social reasons, not musical reasons and I don't think that would have been right." Thistlethwaite, phlegmatic and sincere, agrees with this assessment.

Like Clemons, the Big Man who knew he was becoming marginalised from Springsteen's ambitions and wasn't playing the sort of music he wanted to listen to, Anto's role in The Waterboys had diminished from creative foil to ever present workhorse. Sax, mandolin, keyboards, bass—Scott the Prime Minister reshuffling as required. But unlike Clemons, Thistlethwaite had no need to spend his time with his nose pressed up against the window of his past. He got on with things. "Six months later The Saw Doctors rang me, a founder member who'd played the mandolin in the band had left and soon after that I was on the road with them." With the passage of time it seems that Anto has accepted and written-off this severance of an alliance and the ten years of commitment behind it. He has released three solo albums and enjoyed two lengthy stints in the service of The Saw Doctors, a band that he still plays bass (and occasional sax) for today. He now lives in France with his wife, his two young children and two stepchildren and revels in the life of fatherhood.

Roddy Lorimer: "When Mike split The Waterboys up, my closest friend in the band was Anto and I could see it *was* a blow, because he'd invested everything of himself in the band and what the band stood for." It's because of this that Lorimer lists his career low point as being the disbanding of The Waterboys. "I grew to respect Anto so much as a man as well as a musician, he's a wonderful guy." Scott, however, saw his purpose to be seeking out and identifying new "Waterboys", seeing the concept of the band as his musical alter ego, this shifting and evolving creation, though, actually, perhaps not *evolving* because there was rarely evolution and always revolution.

"I was dissatisfied with the band," he commented to Allan Jones of the ramshackle 1990 line-up. "Not with any of the people in the band... I needed a new stimulus, new scenery. I needed to meet new musicians." Years later he would explain to Matthew Magee of the

Sunday Business Post his whole ethos on the perceived disposability of band-members generally. "Some people leave and some people I ask to leave," (Magee talks of him "picking his words slowly and carefully"). "If I ask them to leave generally it's because the music has changed, or because I want to play music that they don't play or because everything I could do with a musician we had done."

Meeting new musicians may have been his goal, forming a new incarnation of The Waterboys was, however, much more difficult than he had anticipated. He noted to *Musician* that, "I very much wanted to be in the middle of everything. I wanted to be where there were all these recording studios and lots of new musicians." But he'd also conceded just how daunting a task this was. "Starting a new life in a city as tough as New York is a very hard thing to do, and I resisted it for a while. I had a lot of fear. Would I be able to *make* it in New York?"

He'd commenced recordings for the next Waterboys record in New York during January 1992 and these sessions continued through to September. To co-produce with Scott, and engineer the work, Bill Price was recruited. Price had started his career in the 1960s working with Tom Jones and Englebert Humperdinck, though Scott would have known him chiefly for his engineering of Guy Stevens' work on The Clash's *London Calling*. In fact, Price had ended-up in an unaccredited co-production role on the album, along with Mick Jones, when Stevens alleged excesses became too much for the band to bear. He'd continued to work with The Clash, recording and mixing their triple-album indulgence *Sandinista!* and later overseeing the remastering of the band's complete back-catalogue for CD. Amongst his other notable work Price had engineered Chris Thomas's production of 'God Save The Queen' for the Sex Pistols and produced a number of the tracks for *Never Mind the Bollocks*. He had also been called upon for remixing and final production of the Sparks classic 'This Town Ain't Big Enough for Both of Us'.[48]

48   Price had actually started out in his working life working on guided missiles for the Plessey Company, before moving to Decca in the early 1960s as an engineer. "It was very handy to have some electronics background" he recalled in a rare interview in December 2000. "The ethos of Decco Studios was very much that engineers were expected to be just that—engineers." Later he moved to AIR Studios and worked on the sessions for Paul McCartney's theme for the James Bond film *Live & Let Die*.

Price was allocated the *Dream Harder* sessions through his relationship with Geffen Records, who had succeeded in the race to sign
the out-of-contract Scott. Geffen appealed to Scott *because* they were
prepared for a record that wasn't a return to The Waterboys of *A
Pagan Place* and *This is the Sea*, which others competing for the Scott
signature clearly wanted. "Just as I can't keep doing one kind of music
because of the audience, I can't keep doing one for the record company
either," he told Allan Jones. "Geffen were completely cool. They heard
the demos and liked them… there was no interference." There was,
though, a notion that Price had been assigned to the album to add a
commercial sheen to the record that was missing from *Room to Roam*
and to generally keep the sessions heading in the right direction for
Geffen. "I never got that feeling myself," insisted Scott. "Geffen knew
I wanted to do a gung-ho rock'n'roll album and suggested him. But it
was up to me… I was free to choose anyone. I was delighted to work
with him, pumping him for stories about Johnny Rotten."

What they came up with was a record so very clearly defined by
the opening balls-on-the-table mission statement, that declaration of
renewal and redefinition, 'The New Life'. It was punchy, it had attitude and it *rocked* like nothing since the Big Music days *rocked*. As an
album opener 'The New Life' must have woken-up the Arran-sweater
community looking for another *Room to Roam* in the way that *Room
to Roam* itself sent to sleep almost everybody else. It set the tone for
most of the first half of the album, being followed by the first perennial that Scott had committed to vinyl since 'Fisherman's Blues': 'The
Glastonbury Song'. This song had a eyes-wide-open sense of spiritual
fellowship and a warm, comfortable and almost schoolboy allusion
to Cecil F. Alexander's 'There Is A Green Hill Far Away' (which
Alexander had written after comparing a small grassy mound near
the old city walls of Derry in Ireland to Calvary). "I just found God
where he always was," Scott declared, taking the leap from writing
with a sense of spirituality to a time when the concept of God would
be an ever present force in his lyrics either as counsel, confidant or
inspiration. 'Preparing to Fly' thematically belonged with 'The New
Life' as it saw Scott ready to enter a relationship but not quite yet

'under my own steam'. He'd changed his address, he was head-over-heels and he'd found love—frankly he was exhilarated, but he was also confessing that he'd been wary of letting himself get back into an emotional connection and committing to someone.

And so these three opening tracks really sum-up autobiographically where Mike Scott was emotionally at the start of the 1990s. Looking to new surroundings and opportunities. Getting further in touch with his non-denominational religious beliefs (at one point in 'The Glastonbury Song' he appears to metaphorically glance over his shoulder at his fascination with the Native America spirit). Embarking on married life. These things are so deep, so intensely personal that from that point alone it is clear that this is a Mike Scott solo album in all but name. But Scott had not the courage at the time to present himself under his own name and needed The Waterboys as a smokescreen, as a crutch. "The record reflects what I was going through in 1991," he explained to Allan Jones. "My life was changing in a lot of ways and that's what I started writing about. I just write about… my own life. The only thing I can speak authoritatively about." He seemed to be finding a previously unheard of level of stability, talking about settling down, buying somewhere to live in a rural area. "I'd *love* to have a kid. Never really thought about it for an awful long time, but in the last few years I've thought about it a lot."

Getting further into *Dream Harder* is a hit-and-miss affair however. 'The Return of Pan' not only revisits Scott's fascination with the complexities of Pan as a character but also relates his and Irene's honeymoon in Arcadia, the heart of the Peloponnese, in some of the most beautiful landscapes anywhere in Greece—mountains, forests, flourishing vegetation. 'Love and Death' is Scott turning again to W.B. Yeats. This particular rendition was of a lesser-known poem from the Yeats canon, so that "when we sent a tape to the Yeats estate for approval they couldn't find it in their files." There is 'Spiritual City', an early Scott experiment with repetition and mantra[49] and 'Wonders

49 'Spiritual City', aside from its self-effacing outtro wherein a cockney-accented Scotsman is can be heard claiming, "I had that Dalai Lama in the back of me cab once", also includes some worldly wisdom from legendary Scottish comedian and actor Billy Connolly. Scot had encountered him when they both appeared on an edition of *The Late, Late Show* and had been struck by one particular comment from Connolly—"You're here to make babies and look after the place"—and subsequently obtained permission to use it in the song. "It was just when I was giving up drink," Scott recalled to Robert Sandall. "Billy had done the same thing … he just put it in such a way that I got a lot of strength from it."

of Lewis', recollections of a visit to the Scottish Isle of Lewis with his Grandmother. But there are some strange deviations as well, some of which work—the majestic 'Return of Jimi Hendrix'—and others which are out-and-out clunkers of which the cod-mysticism of 'Corn Circles' is by far the most inaccessible and unappealing. His breathless, whirling ode to Hendrix, though, was a minor triumph born out of a dream in which Hendrix came back down to Earth for just one night and played guitar with Scott. "I was at a friend's house recently," he explained on introducing the song to an audience for the first time, "and we were watching some videos of a half-black, half-Cherokee, left-handed guitar wizard, a fabulous character... that night I had a dream about him and wrote it down." To Dee Pilgrim, he expanded on this. "All the events that are in the song took place [in the dream]. Jimi was born out of an egg, came over to my house, checked out my guitar and we spent the afternoon together. Then he went wild rocking that night and that was my dream. When I woke up I wrote it down and took it in hand later by making a few bits rhyme and smoothed out a few lines and crafted it a bit."

Dream Harder was released in May 1993, having been preceded by the single release of 'The Return of Pan'; itself followed in July by 'The Glastonbury Song'. Earlier in the year Scott had begun working with Niko Bolas, a former motorcycle dealer and pit-crew manager who'd been involved with the establishment of California's Record One Studios and had been lead engineer there. He'd worked with Neil Young and would go on to record and produce, amongst others, Keith Richards (mixing his solo album *Main Offender*), Melissa Etheridge, Kiss and Herbie Hancock. But what probably appealed to Scott, and is evident throughout their association during the early to mid 1990s, was that Bolas particularly focuses on vocal production and in that respect may be responsible for the ever more exaggerated vocal performances of Mike Scott. It was certainly the start of a strong working relationship, Scott describing Bolas as "This great guy... a record producer from L.A. He was able to give me the feedback to tell me when I was playing great or when I sucked."

'The Glastonbury Song' saw Scott finally taking The Waterboys into the *Top of the Pops* studio. He appeared on the 22nd July 1993 edition of the show with *Dream Harder* session 'Waterboys'; Chris Bruce, Scott Thunes and Carla Azar. A video was also made to support the single, Scott's first since 'The Whole of the Moon'. This 'live' manifestation of the band was, though, something of a mirage—Scott had been auditioning for a new touring incarnation, advertising in the *Village Voice* as being a "band seeking bass and drums" and advising that the succesful applicants must be "into The Clash, Hendrix and The Waterboys." They didn't come and *Dream Harder* remained sidelined promotionally with no touring exposure. Between his brief 1991 solo show at the Beacon Theatre and what would prove to be his re-emergence into the live arena during the summer of 1994, Scott played only two live shows, both at New York's intimate Café Sin E on St. Mark's Street during November 1992. He also made one television appearance, on the Irish RTE channel's *Late, Late Show* which was broadcasting a tribute to Sharon Shannon and where, alongside the increasingly revered *Room to Roam* accordionist, he performed a version of Bob Dylan's 'Forever Young'.

With his marriage to Irene failing, *Dream Harder* having received only a lukewarm response from the critics and his career languishing in the doldrums, Scott's relocation to New York had begun to look like a dead-end. It clearly wasn't the first time that he'd found himself floundering and needing a new direction, in many ways the reason he was resident in America was just because of such a need. In the past this realignment had been found by surrounding himself with musicians who could take his work to the next level—Anto in 1982, Wickham in late 1985. This time, however, it was a place, a sense of community and a collection of ideas that sent him off on a completely unexpected track. His mother had undertaken what Scott later described as a "healing workshop" at a spiritual retreat perched way up on the Moray Firth and gazing out over the rugged beauty of Findhorn Bay.

The Findhorn Foundation has received an enormous amount of press scrutiny since Eileen and Peter Caddy and their friend Dorothy

MacLean established it in the 1950s. Some writers have thoughtfully considered its positive outlook, its focus on sustainable resources and its overarching sense of well being and mutual support. Others have been lured by the many ways in which the Foundation has been an easy target for sensationalist journalism. Partly that comes from the eccentricity of its beginnings and some of its more outlandish, even cranky, New Age philosophies. The story goes that the Caddys and MacLean were employed at the Cluny Hill Hotel in nearby Forres only to lose their positions when Peter Caddy cleared down a group of trees in preparation for the landing of Alien spacecraft. These unearthly visitors, it was claimed, would be coming to the rescue of mankind following nuclear meltdown. With their livelihood gone, Eileen Caddy heard the voice of God telling them to move to a caravan site on Findhorn Bay, and there in 1952 they established the Findhorn Community, growing their own vegetables and developing what has been described as a "pick and mix" approach to spiritualism. By the 1960s it had grown into an archetypal retreat, appearing to endorse, perhaps a little too enthusiastically considering Peter Caddy's alleged activities, the Summer of Love's approach to sex and so gaining a reputation as being just another 'Cult'.

There it might have stayed with its remoteness and its peculiarities combining to make it a curious but largely unnoticed haven for refugees from the trials and tribulations of modern life. Instead, it started to take itself seriously in a commercial sense and began to explain and educate, making valid associations to the growing concerns of the outside world. Writing for *Scotland on Sunday*, Dani Garavelli talked about how it had "connected with the zeitgeist" and gave as an example "its 'eco-village', a network of energy-efficient houses… farsighted rather than eccentric." As a development it burgeoned, its core values of mediation, peace, interpersonal dependency and ecological thinking, supported by a growing periphery of associated businesses, having something to offer a wide range of people and needs. It began to run 'Experience Week' programmes—seven-day residential introductions to its thinking and way of operating and then supplemented this with more focused courses on sustainable living or on community integration through sacred dances.

For Mike Scott, who had become increasingly interested in spiritual writings through the 1980s, the Foundation offered a gateway into a way of living that he'd seemed to be searching for. "I suppose spirituality has been a part of my life since 1992," he explained to Chris Short in *HM Magazine* (Jan/Feb 2002). "About 1983 I got turned on to spiritual literature and I found out about the whole world of spiritual wisdom and different spiritual systems from around the world... but it didn't become the central focus in my life until 1992." The enthusiasm communicated from his mother's experiences at Findhorn made him anxious to investigate what the community might have to offer him at that point in his life. "I checked out a video featuring Eileen Caddy," he told Steve Stockman. The message of gratitude and unconditional love resonated inside him and he "went there as quickly as I could and did an 'Experience Week' there during which God came down from my head into my heart." Visiting the Foundation for the first time, in October 1992 he found "a community of people living together, working with ecological principles but also a spiritual community, and a college too. People come in all the time to do courses on massage, meditation, healing or dance... a great learning place."[50]

Though he initially struggled to connect with the atmosphere and outlook of Findhorn, Scott found himself drawn to its meditative still-points, which he described to Dani Garavelli. "Wave upon wave of electrifying inspiration passed through me. I felt humbled... I'd been looking for this place all my life." Perhaps most poignantly, given the imminent breakdown of his marriage, he found that he realised "everyone really is the same deep underneath, with the same longing to love and be loved." In the grip of another of his emotional upheavals, he'd plugged into something that both shaped his view of the world and contributed to a new sense of inner-calm. "It's not mainly musicians or artists... It's all very dedicated people, dedicated to finding their path, and to working with spirituality in their lives" he told Chris Short.

50 Interviewed by KCRW radio, 1996.

He saw the road to Findhorn as a metaphorical journey, taking on board the message that Eileen Caddy was offering and seeing that as something that he needed to build upon. "Those were the hooks for me… things that I worked on a lot on my road to Findhorn because it took me about six months to get there," he explained to Maura MaCay in 1996. He eased himself gently into the place, visiting for just a couple of days at a time simply soaking up the atmosphere and getting to know how it worked and what it meant to its residents and visitors before taking the plunge and attending Experience Week. From then on, Findhorn became an ever more central part of his life, and in return he was able to offer his profile and endorsement in a positive way in promoting the Foundation. "During 1993 I went there three or four times for a week or two at a time. Then, I eventually went there and stayed." He left New York behind him during the August of 1993 and by January the following year was installed at Findhorn as a "long-term guest," finally making it a permanent arrangement in May that year.

Though he'd believed himself to be on a spiritual path for many years, the most striking effect that Findhorn induced was to accelerate this process. "I have had many lessons," he confessed to MacCay, "but they have been quite slow lessons. [At] Findhorn it was all speeded up for me. I lost some illusions and I got very grounded." And it *was* a great leveller, especially so for someone who'd come out of the often-indulgent trappings of success that the rock music business generates. At Findhorn, becoming part of the community meant immersing himself in the small details of day to day life—working in the organic gardens or preparing a meal in the kitchens. It was a long way, in more than just miles, of the world of different cities every night, eating different food everyday, having his bags carried and being indulged as only rock stars know how. "There was a lot in my life I was taking for granted," he recalled to Graeme Thomson. "When I approached it from a different perspective I realised that some great life truth was being presented to me."[51]

51 The Guide' *The Herald* 29th April 2006

Scott also saw that his time in Spiddal now came to represent, at least in some part, a component of the life education that had brought him out to Findhorn and drew some analogies between the two different environments. He described them as "similarly intense places" and talked about the "marvellous times [in Spiddal]" being "a bit of a training for Findhorn."[52] That part of the process was about living in small communities which he saw as needing "tricks of discretion and discernment and courtesy. I learned those in Spiddal."

Findhorn would come to inform his world-view probably more than any other influence on his life from the disappearance of his father to his own musical awakening in the Punk wars. It would provide both autobiographical material and much of the spirituality in his lyric writing. On spirituality, he commented to James Helfin of *The Advocate* that, "I am experiencing it and I always write about my own life, and [so] I actually can't *not* write about spirituality. It's too powerful a driving force for me. I've got to write about it." Considering the manner in which this would be received in the mainstream rock music world, he talked candidly about the ways in which it had already been a part of that scene. "I think in the 60s there was a lot of spirituality creeping into rock music, certainly idealism, and then I think it got hijacked by drugs and decadence and things I was probably doing myself at one time, and I don't think rock has quite come back from that yet."

---

52 Interviewed by Kevin McGuire, *The Galway Advertiser.*

9

FLYING SOLO

As the summer of 1994 eased into autumn, Scott reunited with Niko Bolas to record his first solo LP, reflecting the way he'd been working as a live performer during the year. Not seeking, as with *Dream Harder*, to create a full-blown rock sound but to turn things on their head again and record a pure, one-man, Mike Scott album; as different from his last work as that was, in turn, removed from *Room to Roam*. Though he came to see *Dream Harder* as a solo-album and at times seemed to regret having issued it under The Waterboys banner, he released *Bring 'Em All In* under his own name. He recalled to *Rolling Stone* that his decision was simply because, "It's not a Waterboys album if there's only one man on it." It was like embarking on a new adventure, this casting off of old preconceptions that came with the name. "That's the biggest thrill," he enthused to Brock Davis. "Being 'The Waterboys' was no longer an adventure, but being 'Mike Scott' most definitely is." He talked about there being "satisfaction from just standing under my own name and saying this is who I am and I believe in myself."

For the first time he set up in the sanctuary of Findhorn's Universal Hall and discovered the profound effect that it would have. "It gave me self-belief and helped me with my discipline," he claimed. "It effected the execution of the record, I was very focused and driven whilst making it." So, whilst the majority of the songs had been written during his time in New York the delivery and the tone was not of the cosmopolitan environment that he'd experienced in the previous few years but of intimacy and belonging. Looking back on his American stopover then, he could see what it had achieved for him and how it had refined and expanded him. "I had a few years in my life when I needed to get out of the music business and learn a few new tricks. I've always had these questions. Who am I? What am I doing in this world? What is the world for? So I decided to spend some quality time checking out those questions and trying to get the answers. I got some answers and some new and improved questions as well! Variations on the same theme but a little further along the road." In *Vox* magazine he enthused how "every time I get a new burst of information or a new discovery about life, it just opens up more doors, and there's more to find out."

Bring 'Em All In is as frank and confessional an album as Mike Scott has ever made, its bare, acoustic delivery in step with its raw and introspective mood. He explained how the title song represented him "singing back all the parts of myself; lost parts, happy parts, sad parts, nurtured parts, neglected parts, calling them all into my heart, effectively to touch them all with love—and the song can be taken in a universal way as well." During an interview with BBC Radio he expanded this further, describing a song that was in large part an attempt to come to terms with his personal relationship with himself. "It began when I was looking at some parts of myself that I don't normally like to look at, the sort of shadowy bits, the nasty bits or the jealous bits. And I thought, 'I'm going to stop trying to ignore those bits or sweep them under the carpet. I'm going to start bringing them in and accepting them and trying to love them regardless.' I spent a lot of time trying to love everyone else and accept everyone else and I came to a point where I was doing that fairly well but I wasn't doing the same thing to myself. I was criticising myself, putting myself down and I decided 'to Hell with that.' I'm going to starting loving myself and honouring myself in the way I believed I should do with everyone else. I decided to bring all the bits of myself into my heart."

There was an honest intensity to this. Another time he confessed that, "I've been manipulated myself, and I've been a manipulator too and every time I perform an act of manipulation myself, I close down another piece of my soul." To get this deep into Scott's sense of himself and the road he had travelled naturally required him to pour it out alone, a genuinely solo record of his aspirations and disappointments, of his joy and his angst, an autobiographical recounting of his artistic and spiritual rites of passage.

In the booklet to accompany the CD there is an exuberant photograph, by Jeff Mitchell, of Scott on the shore at Findhorn, leaping into the air, arms and legs outstretched, a visual statement of arrival at a sense of comfort and togetherness that he had found within the Findhorn community. He recounted it all on 'Long Way to the Light', a song that described his journey onward from the disappointments of *Room to Roam*. However defensive he would remain of that album, the fact is that here he talks about the end of his Irish adventure leading him back to performing in the style that he felt he worked best in, playing electric guitar and assuming the leadership of a band. That his relocation to America accomplished the first of these and failed miserably to provide the second is in itself noted with a wry shrug, 'if you want to give God a laugh/tell him your plans.'

Scott goes on to relate his American sojourn, his developing interest in the recuperative powers of meditation, the necessity in his life to take things one step at a time and achieve a sense of balance and perspective, his need to find something 'healing'. It seems like a metaphor for a search for redemptive calm in his existence. He talks about his discovery of the writings of Eileen Caddy and the way that they drove him to visit Findhorn. His return to his Celtic roots ('I knelt and kissed the tarmac'), his attempt to continue his life in America and the way that he realised that part of his time was over. And, put that way, the listener can get someway to understanding the restlessness that Scott had failed to shake-off in New York and come to think of that period as being a mirage of what Scott had been looking for.

It most surely was a 'Long Way to the Light'. That it was found in the peace and tranquillity of the furthest reaches of his homeland and not in the hustle and bustle of the place that had occupied Scott's dreams for much of his life was the most poignant discovery that could be made.

In this prodigal return, *Bring 'Em All In* surveyed much of the landscape of Scotland that had impressed itself upon Scott over the years, or that was integral to his early life and upbringing. He revisited the island of Iona, looking for its peace to ingrain within him and 'heal my black heart'. He was once again in Edinburgh, no love lost for the place, wandering down Princes Street and visualising himself a child holding his father's hand. Taking the number 23 bus to the Botanical Gardens or wandering down Forrest Road realising that this city, so old-world grand and dominated by its all-seeing Castle, was no longer a place where he wanted to be—his old school where he now found himself unwilling or unable to enter. And travelling out of Waverly Station, feeling cleansed by waking up and finding himself in Queen Street, Glasgow. "In the song I don't specifically want to blow down the castle," he confessed to Brock Davis, "but I am using at as a symbol for something. When I go back [to Edinburgh] I meet with a lot of unfinished emotional business." Aside from the deep and lasting impact of the disappearance of his father there was also "my old school... the teachers who picked on me... or when I had fights with other boys. Everybody's got stuff in their childhood that puts a pinprick in the present day. It's like I want to heal those things."

There was also a backward glance at his time in Dublin, fascinating in its reflective nature, wherein the entire story of Mike Scott's relationship with Ireland—the heritage, the adventure and the people is laid bare and a defining line drawn under it. Again he was pondering on the good and the bad, seeing it all as a time that had passed (the continual delineation of everything related to his Irish years as 'ghosts'). There is a reflective recollection of his relationship with Irene, and his associations with Thistlethwaite and Wickham, but in terms where all three are cast into the song as ciphers and not as people who can be explicitly named. Perhaps the avoidance of conferring or acknowledging identity made the reference once removed. So there could only be the 'her' who is remembered in a first night of passion, and there was the ghosts of the fiddle and the saxophone, dismissed as a sound that could not return and wrapped-up in the context of friendships 'curdled and sour'.

The other songs of *Bring 'Em All In* were immersed in his growing relationships, with the community at Findhorn and with his own perception of God. They are all distinctive in their openness, an uncomplicated joy in new associations. "I was living in the Findhorn community," he recalled, explaining the background to 'Wonderful Disguise'. "[I] started to see divinity in people's faces, in their eyes. I told a more experienced community friend and she said, 'You are seeing God in all his wonderful disguises.' I knew in my heart she was right." Another time, he attributed some of the song's sentiments as deriving from comments made by Mother Teresa about the life she had made amongst the lepers of Calcutta. "She described the lepers as Christ in some of his more distressing disguises. The song is coming from that place, of thinking that everyone is a sort of disguise for Christ or for universal spirit. The song is describing a day in the life of the narrator, who is seeing this in everyone he meets." This opening up of his religious thinking coloured the confessional tone of those songs on the album and addresses this directly. On 'What Do You Want Me To Do?' there is a admittance of becoming mired in the life he was living, an honesty that expressed personal exasperation in what he perceived to be his own faults—pride, prevarication, perhaps rejection of friendships—and a need to change the 'whole man'. The title encapsulates his emotional cry. Stephen Hunt, writing an impressive overview of Scott's output, noted it as being "quite simply, a prayer" and went on to describe "an honesty, vulnerability, open-heartedness and courage that utterly defeats any residual sneering or mockery amongst his listeners."

There is the zest and fervour of 'I Know She's in the Building', which he talked about as being "a specific kind of love song, written in the first flame and flush of real passionate love. The song's set in a residential college somewhere in the far North of Scotland! In the bleak of mid-winter—the snow is swirling and there's a storm… but inside the college it's hot! Two of the inmates have just fallen in love—and one of them is me." It's a deeper and more enduring coda for 'A Man Is In Love'. But it had a deeper resonance as he explained at the Greenbelt Festival in Northampton (28th August 1994). "I've been living at the Findhorn Foundation for about eight months. And while I was there I fell in love with someone who was also living there. [Interjection from the crowd, 'I thought you were married'. Scott, terse: 'I *used* to be married']. There's about seventy or eighty people living in this build-ing and at times I was so in love with this girl that I felt the building just couldn't contain it. I could tell when she was in the building and when she was out of the building… just *tell*, you know? Intuition or something." Janette Campbell, later to be Janette Campbell Scott, his *soul-mate*, the rock upon which he could build up a sense of who Mike Scott could be; at last a meaningful relationship removed from the music business. Janette was a 'Group Facilitator' at Findhorn and, as Scott recalled to Spencer Bright, he found it difficult to find the right way to approach her. "Someone advised me to put a notice on the board and say [I'd] like to speak to her. So I did and we went down to the local pub in Forres and I declared myself to her." Bright noted that Janette took a little convincing, with Scott adding, "It kind of happened quickly once it happened."

But if there is an overriding feeling throughout the album it is of a man who had found himself on the wrong track, who was burdened with feelings of being unfulfilled and seeking another personal revolu-tion. Most strikingly there was a constant referring to the 'Light'. So, although this was most succinctly a metaphor for his connection with God and the well being he found in his relationship with Janette, there was also the sense of having come through dark days and reaching out to the light at the end of the tunnel. He explained this some years later to Jon Wilde in *Uncut* magazine as being akin to discovering an internal need that had been hidden previously. "I found my centre and my school. I guess I was looking for what I would have called spiritual fulfilment, without really knowing what that would feel like. At Findhorn, God came down from my head and into my heart." This whole period could be seen as being representative of everything that had driven Scott's wanderings. It was as though his whole journey was wrapped-up in a search for stability that he had not known in his childhood with the disappearance of his father. That he had deliberately avoided in his musical associations, that had created the circumstances in which he would seek to lead a band of a line-up so fluid that it was rarely anchored in anything other than Scott's need to find different places and expressions. Findhorn was not just coming home, it was finding a home. Though he would return to London as a base for sometime in the 1990s (he presages this in 'She is so Beautiful' with an acknowledgement that 'my road is before me'), Findhorn has actually been his geographical anchor ever since his move back from New York.

The intensity of the spiritual aspects of *Bring 'Em All In* could have easily led to the record being filed away as simply a born-again New Age indulgence. But the often-painful autobiographical strands juxtaposed with the sense of quiet contentment in finding a soul mate took it away from being simply an extension of the religious satisfaction of, say, 'Glastonbury Song'. Rejecting comparisons of *Bring 'Em All In* with Dylan's *Slow Train Coming*, Stephen Hunt was moved to declare that "Whereas Dylan preached, Scott speaks his truth." Scott would see this within himself also, describing how in his early career he was "free with my passions. Then I went through a period in the late eighties when, probably to protect myself I shutdown on the outside a bit and became more guarded on what I'd allow myself to sing. It's a psychological thing that happens to a lot of artists, they come out at the start innocent and natural, then they have a bit of success and a bit of criticism and that twin cocktail can send them back into themselves—and I'm no exception. It's self-consciousness and it took me a while to master it so that I can now let the passion flow again." This release of emotion, though, wasn't about lecturing or hectoring. It was rather that "as I got older, I started making more measured comments," as he said in 2003. "I believe it's important to put the qualities of peace and love in my music. It's the easiest thing in the world to write a song for Presidents and Prime Ministers to tell them what you think."

Of *Bring 'Em All In*, Stephen Hunt went on to claim that "few artists manage to produce an album that is genuinely ageless and time-
less… Nick Drake, Neil Young, Joni Mitchell and Dylan all employed
the same basic guitars, piano and harmonica…" And whilst he heard
an "almost too-literal musical chronicle of his post-Waterboys scarper
from the mad streets of New York to the sailing boats of Findhorn,"
Rob Beattie described the work as "typically emotional and astute
songs." Unfortunately the perception of Mike Scott was shifting in
the music press and Beattie's gentle berating of his heart-on-sleeve
born-again redefinition was moderate in tone compared to some that
wrote about him. "Leave us alone, man, sod off back to your castle
and take your stupid cap with you," wrote one critic appraising the
single issued from the LP, the worthy and trenchant 'Building the City
of Light'. Hearing simply a "retread of 'The Whole of the Moon', the
reviewer attacked Scott as being a "clapped-put, half-arsed, deluded,
would-be Celtic mystic." It's fair to say that by being prepared to
describe the enlightenment that he perceived himself to have discovered, and by dint of being capable at communicating it, he was setting
himself up as a target in the mainstream. Asked by Maura McCay
whether 'Building the City of Light' was at least in part a reference
to his Findhorn experiences he enthused, "Very much, yeah. I would
think of Findhorn as part of a network of lights around the world.
One of many."

Despite *Bring 'Em All In* being rooted in the reflection and tranquillity of Findhorn, it gave some hints and clues that his tenure within
the community there was in his own mind a temporary arrangement.
'Building the City of Light' (placed last on the album) played out to a
coda that once again reminded the listener of Mike Scott's inherently
transient nature—'all may change in the blink of an eye'. The album
was released in September 1995, with Scott signing a new contract
with Chrysalis Records. By this time he'd moved on again and for
the first time in a decade was resident in London,[53] though he also
maintained a house, perhaps a bolt-hole, in Scotland. Doing, in this,

53   He and Janette moved down to London in 1995, renting a property in Kew where Janette trained as a therapist
    whilst he continued to develop his solo career.

exactly what he suggested in 'Building the City of Light', using both his head and his heart and striking an appropriate balance between needing to be close to the music business action and keeping a place where he could retreat and re-establish his spiritual equilibrium.

He'd already re-established himself as a live performer. Those two low-key shows in New York during November 1992 had been the last appearances he would make on stage for eighteen months. When he re-emerged it was in the comfort and ease of his Findhorn surroundings, playing a solo show at Universal Hall on 6th May 1994, following this up in June with two more sets there. They eased him into a new concept, of himself as a wandering minstrel, being able to open up his repertoire on the road in an acoustic environment rather than having to rely on band rehearsals and the flotsam and jetsam of maintaining a group. Without this hubris, he was able to explore both his extensive collection of songs and develop his new work unhindered and unburdened.

The early 1994 shows demonstrated just how long it had been since Scott had played live—here for the first time in a live environment were 'Glastonbury Song', 'Spiritual City' and 'Wonders of Lewis' from *Dream Harder*. But they also revealed how much new work was bubbling out of Scott—not only was much of *Bring 'Em All In* being brought out for examination and exploration, but many songs that would make up his second solo album *Still Burning* also fermented away. At the same time, his standing and reputation was receiving renewed attention—most publicly at Glastonbury where at the 1994 festival he appeared on the pyramid stage as a guest of Ian McNabb and Crazy Horse.

Ian McNabb had made his name during the Big Music-era with The Icicle Works through their two major hits 'Birds Fly (Whisper to a Scream)' and the glorious 'Love is a Wonderful Colour'. Scott had encountered McNabb only once—after a concert in 1986, also attended by Ian McCulloch of Echo & The Bunnymen. Scott recalled meeting McNabb and liking him but had no further contact with him until receiving, out of the blue, a letter asking Scott to perform with him at Glastonbury. "I went down to play with [him], and he treated me so great it was like suddenly I had a new friend from nowhere. Fantastic." Their first meeting had clearly made an impression on both of them and caused McNabb to take a strong interest in Scott's work. "I knew his life had been a bit weird since *Dream Harder*, and I just wanted to give him a big musical hug," McNabb reflected. They had a lot in common, from being only children to possessing that drive that propelled them into leading their own bands.

Both the positive energy and the spirituality inherent in Scott's *Dream Harder* songs had inspired McNabb who described the record as "the right thing for me to hear at that time in my life." In particular, the reference to Crazy Horse in 'Glastonbury Song', though it was a metaphorical Native American allusion, turned McNabb's thoughts to Neil Young's backing band. He'd recorded with them in California during the autumn of 1993,[54] and hearing their name in Scott's opus occasioned McNabb to ask them to play with him at the 1994 festival, though none of them (McNabb included) had played there before. Because of the karma or serendipity it seemed *right* that McNabb should invite that Glastonbury-veteran Scott as well.

A simple introduction: "I'd like to bring on a friend of ours, Mr. Mike Scott—*The* Waterboy!" Unrehearsed they played a quite bizarre part heavy guitar rock, part raggle-taggle version of 'Glastonbury Song' at such a pace that Scott barely managed to keep up with his vocals. His delivery, though, of 'a long last look at *CRAZY HORSE*' was exuberant and clearly demonstrated his joy at that moment. By the time they'd reached the end and were ready for stab at 'Preparing to Fly' they were almost flying themselves—magic moments. There is, though, a legend around the gig that maintains that Scott asked for 'Glastonbury Song' to be played "majestically" and 'Preparing to Fly' to be delivered at a "decent pace" and got exactly the opposite. Whatever the truth of this particular anecdote, it was a demonstrative acknowledgement of his stature, with Scott (and Anthony Thistlethwaite) later playing on McNabb's solo album *A Party Political Broadcast On Behalf Of The Emotional Party*. What came out of these cross-fertilisations was a strong creative friendship between two musicians both

54 The weeklong association bore fruit, contributing half of McNabb's Mercury Prize nominated 1994 album *Head Like A Rock*.

noted for the personal, confessional, tone of their song writing and their willingness to mix full-on rock music with stripped-down, bare, intensity. Kindred spirits, really.

Festivals were, of course, a comfortable way for Scott to play himself into his new persona. Aside from those at Universal Hall and his guest slot at Glastonbury, the summer of 1994 also saw him bring his one-man show to Northampton's Greenbelt Festival for a fine, confident performance before setting out on his first solo tour in November. What was noticeable was the ease with which he made the transition from band leader to being the single focal point, drawing his audience in with an intimate warmth, chatting, explaining and at times almost the raconteur. Roddy Lorimer had observed the significance of intimacy during his time with The Waterboys and his comments hold true for the situation that Scott had arrived at. "Anymore than about three thousand people don't exist, you can't intellectually get a hold on that amount of people, you can't see any individual faces. Whereas when you do a small gig you are actually so aware of everybody around you, the expressions on their faces and that's part of the buzz of the whole thing."

He continued in this mode through 1995, lining up one of his busiest performing years (though he has never been a notably prolific live artist). Playing British and European dates through the early part of the year, showing up again in his beloved Ireland in April and establishing a tradition by again appearing at Universal Hall in the Spring. A set on the acoustic stage at Glastonbury in June was followed by shows at the WOMAD world music festivals in Pamplona, Spain on 29th July and Morecambe on 2nd September. He managed to slot in Belgium's Festivale Botanique on 16th September and a trip across to New York to play the Merkin Theatre on the 18th before returning to play a substantial European tour, kicking off in Redcar on 14th October and lasting until Hamburg on 30th November.

Jamie Conway, reviewing Scott's gig at the Pavilion Theatre, Glasgow (15th October) claimed that this latest reinvention demonstrated that his "constant questing has merely betrayed his flickering belief in his own talent." Here was another music journalist lining up a pot shot.

"Scott has wandered from place to place, never quite smart enough to realise happiness lies within rather than somewhere over the event horizon, another sucker for religious conversion." In a review quite unbelievable in its vitriolic aggressiveness towards the path that Scott had taken, Conway challenged him to "ceaselessly test and question... those dark, swollen hours when doubt corrodes the soul." Seasoned Mike Scott observers would be forgiven for wondering if that wasn't what he'd been doing all along.

Curiously though, earlier in the year Andrew Mueller favourably reviewed Scott's date at London's Hackney Empire (24th January) and added that "someone tells me [Scott's] been hitting the bible a bit harder during the provincial dates, but the Almighty is, by and large, not asked to jam this evening."[55] Successfully identifying the conundrum that faces Scott's listeners, that his songs vary between "mawkish and magical, godstruck and godawful," Mueller noted that "Scott is equally capable of taking you places you never dreamed existed and places you'd never dreamed of going."

If critics were becoming increasingly disconnected with what they perceived as bible-thumping introspection, the new songs that were being liberally peppered through-out the set were surely proving anathema. Material that was being thought through for *Bring 'Em All In* had clear religious resonance—'What Do You Want Me To Do?', 'Wonderful Disguise', 'Long Way to the Light' and the title track itself all having spiritual allusions. And other new songs that were forthcoming during Scott's solo sojourn also took their emotional heart from the Findhorn-enhanced renewal of his relationship with God. 'Everlasting Arms', introduced at his set at Universal Hall on 11th June 1994 he acknowledged as being "in the Bible [as a phrase]" though he added that he considered "the Bible and that kind of organised Christianity has been responsible for so much bad stuff. I don't think they have a mortgage or a monopoly on all that spiritual stuff... you don't have to be a Christian or a Buddhist or something."[56]

55 Reviewed in *Melody Maker*.
56 Interviewed for *Vox* magazine.

Though the music of The Waterboys, in common with many of the Celtic rock bands of their era, had always had a distinctly spiritual lilt running through the background it isn't easy to follow the thought process of Mike Scott in his understanding of his religious inclinations. He doesn't tie easily into a Christian worldview by any stretch of the imagination and his meandering perception of his own inner belief-system doesn't give his followers a particularly strong handle on where his faith roots from.

Martin Day, author and long-time Waterboys' enthusiast, noted to me how he felt about his favourite era of the band. "*This is the Sea* is perhaps the most interesting Waterboys album for me, lyrically at least. The big theme seems to be the (inner) battle between 'human nature' and the spiritual/divine impulse. That's why there are so many songs that talk about *glimpses* of a bigger, more wonderful reality. The narrative voice moves from seeing this almost unattainable beauty in someone else ('The Whole of the Moon'), to seeing it in (some expression of) God ('Spirit'), to having attained it as some form of personal salvation, and thus encouraging others to follow in the same path (the title track). These songs in particular seem to capture something of St Paul. Romans 3 and 7 on the fallenness of human nature and the ongoing struggle with sin, 1 Corinthians 13 on the beautiful supremacy of love; and the black Gospel spirituals of the US (particularly the 'I hear there's a train' verse from 'This is the Sea'). No wonder (on my CD version at least) there's a picture of a unicorn at the bottom of this song, which was a medieval symbol of Christ."

Scott's religious convictions seem to be an amalgamation of influences and interests, mainstream and mystic, orthodox and nonconformist. "I've believed in God all my life," he explained to *Vox* magazine, "but I've never been into the Christian religion, really. I always found it very boring, grey. I think there's a lot in American Indian wisdom." To Allan Jones he noted, "I'm not interested in the church's idea of God. That's not God. The church gets all dogmatic and rigid. God's not like that." And to Matthew Magee (*The Sunday Business Post*) he added, "I don't belong to any religion, but I take a little bit here and a little bit there, whatever works and whatever makes sense to me."

You can take that as far back as the impressions that would be made on him by the great spiritualist writers like C. S. Lewis and George MacDonald, and the influence made by discovering Pan through the work of Kenneth Grahame. "I did this interview with a man from Glasgow who was writing for *The Trigger*," Scott once explained to an audience. "He was asking me 'what's this thing about Pan... why are you always writing about Pan? 'The Pan Within', 'The Return of Pan'." He even found a few mentions of Pan in some other songs that I wasn't even aware of. I found it very hard to explain what it was about but if you've ever read *The Wind in the Willows*, that fantastic book, there's a chapter called 'The Piper at the Gates of Dawn' with a description of Pan—that's who I mean when I write about Pan."

In the chapter, Rat and Mole in their river journey find what Rat describes as "the place of my song-dream, the place the music played to me... Here, in this holy place, here if anywhere, surely we shall find Him." Like the tantalising, one-step-ahead, quest for the Christ-substitute Aslan in *The Lion, The Witch & The Wardrobe*, the revealing of Pan ("an august Presence") when it comes is profoundly and symbolically spiritual.

> "Rat!" [Mole] found breath to whisper, shaking. "Are you afraid?"
> "Afraid?" murmured the Rat, his eyes shining with unutterable love. "Afraid!
>   Of Him? O, never, never! And yet—and yet—O, Mole, I am afraid!"

The use of the capital H (also employed by Lewis in his even more religiously analogous characterisation of Aslan) and the way in which the reaction of Mole and Rat is drawn ("he felt wonderfully at peace", "Mole felt a great Awe fall upon him") ties the scene into the Christian viewpoint and away from the Pagan. This is despite Grahame having displayed, like Scott, a significant interest in Paganism—an early collection of his writings being published as *The Pagan Papers* (1893), whilst *Dream Days* and *The Golden Age* contained stories inspired by his own unhappy childhood disconnected from his alcoholic father.

From an early age Scott was taking at least some of his impressions of the nature of God from the anthropomorphic idealism of Lewis and Grahame. "[Lewis] was my first great teacher—I read him when

I was growing up and he a huge a effect on me," he said. "The effect he has on me now is less, but I re-read him every few years and every now and then discover a new one I haven't read previously." In hindsight he saw the message of Lewis not in the way that Lewis would have intended, the writer having been a deeply devout Christian, but in terms of having read something that resonated truths regardless of the faith that had informed it. Though he attended Church as a youngster, the combination of what he quickly identified as inherent hypocrisy ("miserable people in their best clothes with flash cars outside") and ponderous services did little to endear organised religion to him. "I don't reject Christianity," he explained to Steve Stockman. "I grew up with the stories of the example and teaching of Jesus… but I am not a practising Christian." In his intimate and revealing interview with Stockman he rejected the concept of 'creed' and propounded what once again seemed a more paganistic view of the nature of things, seeing the idea of an encompassing wholeness, a 'One Life' as central to his philosophy. "This is perennial wisdom," he considered. There was also something of this within 'Wonderful Disguise'. "When I looked at people with an unconditional love, a love that's not expecting any return, and an acceptance of them, whoever they are, I saw them differently. I think at heart we're all one self."

As a way of reconciling the mortal existence to the concept of everlasting life and the power of love, he explained during a Radio One interview that he thought that death was a way of "[going] back to universal love. Everything I've loved in this world, or seen a shadow of in this world, is in the next one. I don't believe anyone dies, I believe we go on in another form. The soul probably won't feel like Mike Scott anymore… I think everyone goes back to some big spiritual melting-pot on the other side." The culmination of this seemed to be 'Everlasting Arms', a soft prayer of peaceful release addressed directly and simply, an uncomplicated summation of final need.

Scott's solo wanderings continued into 1996 with a low-key tour of Japan in January and another North American tour from 25th February to 23rd March. But they were to prove to be the tail end of this particular phase. At Minneapolis Fitzgerald Theatre (9th March 1996) he told his audience that, "I start recording a new a new album in May, and I'll have a little band behind me—bass, drums and a cunning lead guitar player. So perhaps, and it's my fervent wish, the next time I tread the boards for you in the Twin Cities I'll have a full-tilt rock'n'roll band." There were only to be two more solo performances—one at Alan McGee's Creation Records show at the London Subterranea, described on the official Waterboys website as a "short, sharp set" and a final gig in France on 18th April at the Bourges Festival.

He'd already cut demos for what would become his second solo album, *Still Burning*, taking some advice from McGee and reinventing himself as 'Mike Scott—Rock Star' from the burn of his electric guitar playing to the shades and open-necked shirt of the album cover. McGee had a hand in the production of *Still Burning*, making suggestions on the running order and assisting with the final mixing—"he would come round to my house and advise me," Scott recalled. As Scott's current relationship with Chrysalis Records had soured almost before the ink was dry on the contract, his friendship with McGee left him optimistic for a berth with Creation Records. "I had got the impression that Alan was going to sign me and then he changed his mind," he told Peter Bate. "We didn't fall out but we didn't stay friends."

Many of the songs selected for the album had already become familiar live numbers, culled from several dozen songs that Scott worked through during his acoustic shows where songs would appear in the set, get dropped and then re-examined or forgotten as the case might be. "There [were] probably another 15 or 20 songs written during the same period," he noted to Brock Davis. "I write one song and it's okay and I keep it in a file but then I write another song on the same subject and it's much better and that's the one I go with." He'd got into the habit of writing in what he described as his "music room," a sanctuary which he maintained purely for writing, "That in itself creates an atmosphere… All my books of songs and blank sheets of paper and various tools that I use are all in that room." He'd started to write exclusively on the guitar, instead of a mixture of piano and guitar as he had done during The Waterboys. From the recent tours there was 'Strawberry Man' and 'Everlasting Arms', which hailed from his original one-man shows at Universal Hall in 1994. 'Rare, Precious and Gone', introduced in December 1994, 'Love Anyway' which he'd started to experiment with during March 1995. 'My Dark Side', first played in Belgium in September 1995.

To work them up into a full band orchestration he again relied on the production skills of Niko Bolas and together they went about putting together a band of session musicians. Not just any session musicians—they gathered up a highly regarded collection of players. Chris Bruce, who'd contributed to *Dream Harder* in New York and whose versatility Scott particularly admired. "Whatever we did I never had to explain how I wanted it done. He'd listen to what I was doing and automatically concoct something that fitted," Scott explained to Dominic Hilton. Jim Keltner who'd drummed on John Lennon's *Imagine* album and John Hiatt's *Bring the Family* and, though it's a horrible cliché, whose résumé reads like a *Who's Who* of contemporary music. Welsh bass-wizard Pino Palladino, former member of Jools Holland & The Millionaires and of Paul Young & The Royal Family, bassist on Gary Numan's *I Assassin* and the man who filled John Entwistle's shoes in June 2002 when 'The Ox' died on the eve of The Who's USA tour.

Together with guest appearances from, amongst others, the Kick Horns and Ian McNabb they produced an album of fresh and contemporary rock'n'roll, warm and orchestral, commercial and upbeat. The sessions were time constrained, Scott aiming to record the album over a period of three weeks and in the end settling for ten days with the full band. "Me and Niko just followed our noses," he explained to Dominic Hilton. "I've learned from that that I don't work so well as a co-producer, I like to follow my own trail without having to ask anyone what they think." The promptness of the recordings fitted in with his own plans for the LP, wanting to set down his latest songs before he could have the chance to loose interest in them. Unusually, then, arriving in the studio straight after touring and not making his usual retreat to write and rework his latest material.

Released in September 1997 *Still Burning* was the final throw of the dice with Chrysalis Records. It was far from being a mainstream success even though its combination of veering toward grunge fuzz-guitars along with Scott's melodramatic vocal deliveries put it squarely into the territory being principally occupied by Paul Weller on the one hand and Oasis on the other. Indeed, *Still Burning* enjoyed a lot in common with Weller's 'Changing Man' and his *Stanley Road* album of 1995 with Scott's reinvention as 'Mike Scott—Rock Star' being firmly in the mould of Weller's brand of self-examining 'Dad Rock'.

Reviewing the album for *Vox*, Barry Lazell considered *Still Burning* as having songs that were "terminally over-arranged," citing the album's first single 'Love Anyway' as his prime example. "The track's orchestrated to the point of where the ranks of desperately sawing fiddle players eventually kick everything else into touch and just carry on for a couple of minutes by themselves" he noted. Paul Du Noyer, conversely, praised the same song for "the panoramic sweep we heard in early Waterboys anthems," and praised Scott for remaining "the ardent braveheart, the yearning romantic, whose every song is a leap of faith."

It kicks off with 'Questions', a typical slice of Scott's studied biographical introspection which talks of his musical changes and of how in another time he 'left the music behind' just when it got loudest. He's asking what things mean and what lurks around life's corners, and, mostly importantly 'how well have I loved', and as it brings his current relationship into focus it breathes out on a note of success and stability—'we know who we are'. 'My Dark Side' is a confessional and raw explanation of a complex personality, with an immediate counterpoint in 'Open' which is sparse in musical metre but has an infectious depth of optimism. By far the longest track, 'Love Anyway' is actually one of those Scott tracks that are so infuriating simply because they mix the abstract and the obscure with a majestic and sweeping melody that is so hard to get out of your head. 'We are Jonah' on *A Rock in the Weary Land* is the ultimate example, but 'Love Anyway' runs it a close second and though it wasn't successful as a single it had all the hallmarks of a good promotional choice—feel good and radio friendly. 'Dark Man Of My Dreams' covers, once again, Scott's missing relationship with his errant father, 'Rare, Precious and Gone' is soulful MOR material and was culled as the follow-up single to 'Love Anyway' to no greater mainstream recognition.

For all its flaws—and they range from Scott's drawn-out and over-pronounced diction to a tendency to cod-introspection that can characterise some of his lyrics—*Still Burning* was a definite stab at aligning the Mike Scott name in the mainstream. In the same way that the natural place for *Bring 'Em All In* amongst the Scott canon was as a quiet, reflective moment, *Still Burning* was its commercially minded sibling. It had the hooks, the tempo and the catches to have really propelled Scott back into the public arena—instead it lingers in the back catalogue as the forgotten end of his solo career, somewhat neglected and overlooked. How much Scott was actually committed to this regeneration into "Mike Scott—Rock Star" is, as always with him, open to debate. Certainly he very soon seemed to distance himself from the record and its presentation, noting his unhappiness with the photographic imagery of the cover and claiming himself uncomfortable with the way in which he was being bracketed into the archetypal 1990s rock figure. "I think the real challenge for me is to be myself" he told Hilton. "Not try to look like someone else, pitch my stuff somewhere else. It's enough to be Mike Scott and it's a challenge to stand on that and not compromise myself."

"As far as I know Mike," commented German *uberfan* Michael Mönsters on The Waterboys yahoo discussion list, "he's not likely to do things he isn't comfortable with when it comes to sound and atmosphere. I think [the production] was pretty much what he thought was appropriate for the songs. Probably an attempt as well to make a "breakthrough" in terms of getting publicity and airplay and thus establishing the name 'Mike Scott'. Niko Bolas did a pretty good job if you like polished, powerful, mainstream arrangements."

But it wasn't a financially successful work. No matter how much The Waterboys *was* Mike Scott, the audience for his music didn't seem to quite buy the equation in reverse and he later talked about having lost all of his money on *Still Burning* and through that having to sell his house.

Having released a rock'n'roll album backed by session musicians, Scott was in the same position as at the end of the production of *Dream Harder* in wanting to play the songs in a live situation but not having a touring band assembled. The *Still Burning* studio band performed live only once, at an EMI conference on 6th September 1996 playing 'Dark Man of my Dreams' and the first ever live rendition of 'Questions' whilst the album was given its final mix-down by Scott and Alan McGee at the end of the year.

Fast forward on to the spring of 1997 and there was a need to be able get out on the road and promote *Still Burning* when it was released. Playing out there with a full band for the first time since the demise of The Waterboys, find Mike Scott was in the unusual position of needing to recruit not yet another drummer but actually a bass player. He'd filled the other key positions—James Hallawell who'd contributed to *Still Burning* on the Hammond organ was again recruited. Dublin-born Gavin 'Fingers' Ralston, who was making a name for himself in Ireland as a guitarist, and drummer Jeremy Stacey, were also on-board. Auditions came and went but there was still nobody to fill the bass playing role, though former Deacon Blue bassist Ewen Vernal was under consideration.

By the time of the promotional video there was still nobody to even *mime* the bass part. Ian McNabb, for the sake of comradeship and without payment, took the role. And, in jamming with the band that Scott had assembled, he proved himself such an obvious asset to the touring group that, even though he wasn't actually a bass player, there was a clamour from the musicians to have McNabb come on-board. Scott chose to overlook the tensions that having another proven bandleader in his group might create.

Scott was initially nervous about even asking McNabb to play bass for fear he might be insulted? Or be too costly? As it happened McNabb saw Mike Scott as the Bob Dylan of his generation and agreed do the tour. Neither of them found it easy, one was conscious of the additional talent that he had brought in and the other knowing that despite naturally looking for the spotlight, he would have to defer to the other—but it worked.

Scott now had a foil every bit as strong as a Wallinger, a Thistlethwaite or a Wickham—someone on whom he could lean on if he needed advice or needed to sound off an idea. They didn't get along all of the time, being very different people of course—McNabb got to see the difficulties that others had experienced in working with Mike Scott—the demanding, complicated personality, the impatience or lack of tolerance. Being more laid-back and easier going, McNabb said openly and honestly: "There is a tension."

So, with a five-piece band, ready and able to rock, Scott was eager for some interaction after years of being a wandering minstrel dependent only on his voice and a guitar. Not yet at the point where could view any full band as being The Waterboys, he described to Erica Yamashita, during a tour of Japan, how different it is "… because of the personalities… Because they are not The Waterboys, they have different roles… [a] different relationship to me. They are all very strong personalities, and I welcome that."

The *Still Burning* live band (billed as 'The New Band') hit the road on 11th August 1997 with a compact set that was drawn predominately from Scott's two solo albums. In touring with a full band that was not designated as being an incarnation of The Waterboys it seemed as though he'd at the same time elected to distance himself from that era of his career and keep the material at arm's length. Of The Waterboys canon only 'Glastonbury Song' and appropriately 'Preparing to Fly' (both essentially from a Scott solo album by any other name), 'Be My Enemy' and 'Medicine Bow' made the set list of the opening night in Southend. By the time the band reached a five-night residency at London's Garage venue (14th—19th August 1997) they'd added 'Has Anybody Here Seen Hank?' but remained tightly focused on the new material with very minimal variance in the set.

For any long-time fans thinking that they'd seen the heaviest rock that Mike Scott was likely to produce during the 1990 gigs the Garage shows were an eye-opening, ear-splitting "noisefest" (as one internet poster put it). The New Band was hard rocking and energetic though certainly not to every enthusiast's taste—being variously described as having "lacking a something," having "no concession to musicality" or "subtlety," and being "Thrash metal" and "far too loud." Existing recordings reveal an extremely raw and gritty sound—introducing 'I Know She's in the Building' Scott would claim that "We're going to vamp it up, you've never heard it like this before." Like others from this era, particularly the way that 'Dark Man of my Dreams' descends into Heavy Metal jamming, the grinding aggressiveness of the playing is unexpected and at times very jarring but it's certainly possible also to identify Scott running away with this new found approach. "When I'm on stage and play guitar solo, [McNabb's] out there and I go wooarh…! He's really revving me up. It's fantastic," he told Yamashita. To the audience at the Garage he claimed, rather disingenuously, that "This is the best band I've ever had—and I hope you agree!"

"Two years of touring alone with his acoustic guitar have taken their toll, and now it's payback time" wrote Peter Bate of The New Band's show at Wolverhampton's Wulfrun Hall identifying "frenetic Scouse Ian McNabb on bass" and claiming "sometimes the bluster is excessive… but mostly it works." They continued through 1997, playing at European festivals with Zak Starkey replacing Stacey on drums and then back in the UK with Starkey in turn replaced by Scottish session drummer Geoff Dugmore who'd worked with artists as diverse as Rod Stewart and Killing Joke.

The New Band, in hindsight, was an interesting tributary of The Waterboys—distinct because of their focus on Scott's solo material and because unlike The Waterboys they were a specifically recruited collection of musicians rather than having the organically developed nature of Scott's most famous ensemble. As such they served a specific purpose in promoting his full-on rock recordings and re-energising him as a band member and leader. At the same time, as a group they had a built-in obsolescence, a limited life span that made them effectively redundant the following year when Scott would again be looking into his own past, rekindling old associations and friendships. The time was coming when he'd want to put the concept of "Mike Scott" back into its box and instead recreate and re-imagine The Waterboys.

10

WHATEVER NEEDS TO HAPPEN...

There are few more curious moments during a Mike Scott gig than a couple that occurred at the Milton Keynes Stables on 25th November 1999. The show introduced both a new musical partner, keyboard player Richard Naiff, and ran through material from the sessions for *A Rock in the Weary Land* ('Crown', 'Dumbing Down the World', 'Malediction', 'The Wind in the Wires'). In a rather testy manner he also managed to launch a few broadsides at varying targets that had clearly been getting under his skin. "The key note of my new songs is War," he noted, though as might be expected, the tone was principally of personal, one-on-one battles.

In particular, Scott savaged a critical write-up the Findhorn Foundation had received from a journalist who "writes for *Loaded* or GQ magazine, I can't tell the difference between them any more. He took a trip up to the Findhorn Community where I used to live and he did one of the programmes there, not telling anyone that he was researching an article. He wrote the article and put the place down and I figured, 'I'm going to write a song about this guy.' So I thought to myself, 'what kind of music will I give him', and I thought '*Kindergarten* music', and the name of the song is 'Martin Decent.'" What followed was a nursery-rhyme tirade against someone who Scott saw as a 'turncoat' telling 'a few little lillywhite lies.' The song was also played at Findhorn's Universal Hall in June 2001: when he'd lined-up a target Scott would prove unwilling to let it too far out of his sights. His distrust of journalists, alluded to in his lyrics as far back as 'Old England is Dying' had already produced 'Dumbing Down the World'. He later described that song as arising from being "on an aeroplane, reading *The Independent*, and there was an article by a man who edits one of those dreadful men's magazines... which take men back to pre-puberty. He was justifying it and I thought, 'You're dumbing down the world, mate, and I'm going to number you in a song.'"

"I moved house recently, into a house that's got a really big attic," noted Scott on introducing 'Calling Back My Spirit From You'. "For the first time since maybe the mid-80s I was able to get all my boxes and belongings in one place because I moved house a lot of times and every time I move half of what I've got goes into boxes and doesn't come out again. I got into this attic and got all my boxes from all the various storage places around the world and I started going through them. It was a fantastic experience because I'd open a box and it'd be a time capsule. It'd be The Waterboys tour 1986, the tour itinerary or my tour souvenirs like a map of Jerusalem or the hotel brochure, and it was a great experience. But also, amongst all the good stuff, I found there was a few people that I had unfinished business with, a few things that I had to work out... one in particular. So I did, and while it was happening, by this strange law that I don't understand, it wrote itself into a song." The song described something, an injustice or a perceived slight that had burned inside for a long time and which Scott had decided it was time to address—'calling back what is my own'. There was no indication of the identity of this mysterious offender but the lyrics, perhaps, presaged a return to the use of The Waterboys' name the following year.

"Mike is hitting some high spots again," wrote Waterboys' fan Tim Rafferty of the Milton Keynes gig, "though his mind is very much on the dark side of the world. He always did have a vitriolic streak and has raged against his foes many times." Not many times, though, had he gone out of his way to display the amount of hostility that he found it necessary to let out at this show.

What was a little strange about this public outpouring was that Scott was in the process of renewing and re-establishing old friendships. The New Band had made their final appearance together on Channel 5's *Jack Doherty Show* during February 1998 and his solo-era in hindsight effectively closed out the next month with the expiration of his contract with Chrysalis Records. Following on from this Scott had begun work on demos for another solo album whilst also looking backwards at his Waterboys associations. With Anto and Trevor Hutchinson he appeared on the Irish television programme *Sibin* in May 1998 to play 'Killing my Heart'. Back in the UK the following month Anto, along with Ian McNabb and Dave Ruffy, joined him in London for gigs at the Mean Fiddler on 5th June and the Fleadh Festival on the following day. In fact, the only solo Mike Scott concert for the year was a short set at the Northampton Greenbelt Festival on 19th August. Other shows across Europe were ad-hoc affairs, an appearance at the prestigious Montreaux Jazz Festival, where Preston Hayman on percussion augmented Scott's one-man guitar, piano and vocals style. The Cactus Festival in Belgium saw McNabb and Ruffy again, along with Scott's old friend from the Hothouse Flowers, Liam Ó Maonlaí (and Scott getting back to his Beatles' fixation with an encore of 'Why Don't We Do It In the Road?'). And in his home-from-home, Galway, for the 1998 Arts Festival there was the first all-Waterboys gig in many a long year when his solo-spot ended with an encore of 'Honky Tonkin', 'Fisherman's Blues' and 'Death is not the End' featuring Anto's mandolin and sax and Steve Wickham's fiddle. Scant wonder that rumours started to circulate of a full-blown Waterboys reunion, given fuel by EMI (owners of the Chrysalis Records catalogue) releasing a retrospective album spanning the length and breadth of Scott's career from *The Waterboys* onwards.

The Whole of the Moon—the Music of Mike Scott and The Waterboys, released in September 1998, ran through the obvious track selections but in doing so had something to offer both the casual listener and the die-hard fans. The version of 'A Girl Called Johnny' was taken from an aborted live album that was to have been released of The Waterboys' gig at the Hollywood Palace, Los Angeles from 13th December 1984. Mostly notably there was a previously unreleased recording of 'Higher in Time' that had been cut in Dublin during February 1991, at the very tail-end of Scott's partnership with Anto Thistlethwaite. It hailed from the moments when just the two of them were working through material in a last throw of the dice for the original Waterboys lineage. Though it's subtitled on the album as the 'real version', its home-studio aura gives it a thin and weedy sound far removed from its majestic counterpart from Windmill Lane which was included on *Too Close to Heaven*. But it's interesting none the less for the glimpse of the two of them working up material, presumably intent on hunting down a new record deal. Originally recorded in 1985 for a BBC radio session it's another song with a co-write credit for Thistlethwaite, though on this occasion he wasn't simply adding a bridge or a few bars. "On 'Higher in Time' I actually did write the music. We were in Brewery Road, John Henry's rehearsal studio in 1985 where he had some space that we used occasionally. I was playing the piano, playing some chords I got—a sequence that was in my head. Mike had some lyrics but, as far as I know, he hadn't thought about making a tune for them. So he started singing them over what I was playing and it worked and suddenly we had a song. We did a rather good version of it for a radio session with Karl. Actually we did a couple of good things for that, things that we never recorded again, or not until much later."

In a review for *Q* headed up "His heart was in the right place. His songs were often somewhere else," Mark Blake assessed the legacy of The Waterboys and contrasted it with Scott's more recent solo recordings. "Scott off-loads flowery sonnets with scant regard for the sniggers they might provoke," he noted of 'What Do You Want Me To Do?' and 'She is so Beautiful'. In fact, Blake saw this as a major part of Scott's make-up all along but announced a preference for the days when his "lyrical excesses were given free rein, but were bolted to a music that embraced rock, folk and a sort of post-punk pop." Post-*Fisherman's Blues*, Scott's outpourings were effectively dismissed as having traded "pounding melodrama and Celtic introspection for too much whimsy." A little kinder to his more recent offerings was *Record Collector*. It published a review that, whilst praising the omission of anything from "the self-indulgent *Room to Roam*, with its lumbering odes to the simple life," at least conceded that the "sweetly melodic 'Love Anyway' shows that the knack for the 'Big Music' is still there." Still, there was the consistent theme amongst critics that, "*This is the Sea* and before equals good", "*Fisherman's Blues* equals acceptable" and dismissed *Room to Roam* and beyond as "Bad" or at least as "off-track and somewhat worthy of a smirk." To work his way back into the arena of acceptability and recognition he was going to have to look outside of himself for his themes and re-embrace the wall of sound and the big landscapes of his early work.

Where Scott would find his new themes, and yet still remain true to himself as a writer of conscience and as a sharp observer of human frailties, weaknesses and temptations was once again in his surroundings. At the same time, he rediscovered something of the Big Music in the unlikeliest of places—the music scene at the turn of the century. Ian Gittins, writing in *Q* magazine, described Scott's first offering of the new millennium, *A Rock in the Weary Land*, as a "distorted and claustrophobic yet supremely articulate attempt to capture the pressures of modern urban living." It was, indeed, Scott's most accurate delineation of his surroundings since *Room to Roam* which, whatever its multiple faults, at least caught an atmosphere and was a telling conversion to vinyl of the surroundings, people and history that Scott had found himself in. So the same with *A Rock in the Weary Land*, one of Scott's more neglected works and yet certainly containing some of his greatest triumphs.

Unlike the hurried burst of activity that produced *Still Burning*, the recording of *A Rock in the Weary Land* took place across the whole of 1999 with just a handful of live appearances scattered through the calendar. Most significantly, Scott hooked up with Steve Wickham to play a set at the Hawkswell Theatre in Sligo, Ireland comprised of new songs and, naturally, a selection of *Fisherman's Blues* and *Room to Roam* numbers. There was the concert with Richard Naiff at Milton Keynes, a solo appearance in Norway, and, as it would transpire, poignantly, there was a short set at a benefit concert for the victims of the violence in Kosovo staged at the Swindon Oasis. He'd been persuaded to take part in this last show by long-time Waterboys drummer Kevin Wilkinson, who, along with Anto, made a guest appearance for 'Killing my Heart' and 'Medicine Bow'.

The Swindon show was played on 30th May 1999. Just six weeks later, on 17th July, Kevin Wilkinson took his own life at his home in Baydon, Wiltshire. He was forty-one and left his wife and three children. The cause of his extreme action was later identified by the coroner as having derived from a state of deep depression caused by marital problems and stress. Since leaving The Waterboys, and aside from his success with China Crisis, he'd enjoyed spells with Squeeze and The Proclaimers and, at the time of his death, had recently been drumming for 80s pop star Howard Jones. Announcing the news on Jones's website, David Stopps, manager for Howard Jones, said simply that he "one of the highest quality people and drummers imaginable. In the musical community and beyond, Kevin was very highly regarded and had many loyal friends." Glen Tilbrook and Chris Difford of Squeeze issued a statement to express their great shock. "In slipping the surly bonds of Earth, Kevin will always be remembered with love, laughter and affection by us all," they said. Anto, who thinks of Kevin with clear fondness and respect, recalled how "on the early [Waterboys] tours, I'd share a room with Kevin. I got on very well with him—we were two people who really didn't want to make things more complicated than they needed to be. We were very simple—we just wanted to play, get it right and then go and have a drink.""

There are lots of reasons why *A Rock in the Weary Land* is atypical, if, of course, you can discern a "typical" Mike Scott record in any case. One of the most significant is in the way that, for once, the contemporary music scene became as big an inspiration for the record as the surroundings and the people with whom Scott was interacting at the time. "After *Still Burning* I started checking out records like [Radiohead's] *OK Computer* and realised that every single sound had been sculpted and I thought, 'I don't do that with my records any more,'" he explained. He was absorbing the new breed of rock bands,

also citing The Chemical Brothers and Beck as being champions of
what was now technologically possible in the studio. His working
methods were once again exacting ("I made it to my own highest
standards") recording and re-recording take after take in search of
the perfect capture. Scott actually saw this affinity with the music
of Radiohead and their contemporaries as harking back to his own
roots, telling Richard Skanse in *Rolling Stone* how he "realised that
they had seen every instrument on the album as an opportunity to
explore sonically. I remembered a time when I used to do that, and I
decided to do it again." Like a kid in a sweet shop, he roamed London's
music stores, seeking whatever he could use to try-out new sounds
and new ways to treat, sculpt and redesign the music he would generate. "I developed almost a whole culture of own new sounds that I was
dying to try out," he explained to Skanse. "I still kept my eye on the
songs, the performances and the arrangements but I added the sonic
exploration." In an interview in Norway he predicted an album that
would be "more of a sonic record, with much more electronic guitar,
more noise, more sound effects. The past three records were very 'song'
based... [I'll] keep that but also discover different sounds." There was
a definite strategy in moving away from his recent work, which he
now viewed as being too conservative and unchallenging as he noted
to Chris Short. "There is no experimentation on [*Still Burning*]. It had
less Mike Scott and less Waterboys feel on that record than on any of
the others I've ever made." And to Dominic Hilton he confessed that,
"I didn't really listen to anybody other than myself when I made *Still
Burning*. I failed to explore the new trends in modern music, which
I think is probably a failing of the record. I was in my own creative
vacuum completely."

To assist him in this new voyage of discovery he recruited synthesiser specialist Thighpaulsandra (b. Tim Lewis), an exponent of
improvised electronic music who took his influences from the 1970s
krautrock scene—Can, Tangerine Dream, Neu!, Kraftwerk and their
ilk. His own lineage was of classical music, his mother Dorothy being
an opera singer and his father a conductor. As a matter of course he
learned the French horn, the piano and the church organ, whilst he

was also a member of the choir of Cathedral School in Llandaff and at Christ College, Brecon. "I developed an interest in contemporary classical music from an early age... Berio and Stockhausen" he recalled. "I loved Bach and a lot of 'classic' rock and pop [but] I always tried to experiment, be more unusual in my writing." Before enrolling in Scott's latest musical twist, he'd worked with Julian Cope on *Autogeddon* and *Interpreter*, some of Cope's most experimental albums as both musician and recording engineer, and on the slightly more pop-influenced *20 Mothers*. In 1997 he became a member of Spiritualized and the next year joined the cross-genre avant-garde Coil. If Scott's foils had traditionally been either musicians whose own influences and tastes reflected his own (Thistlethwaite, Wallinger) or those who could revolutionise the index of possibilities for his music (Wickham), then in linking-up with Thighpaulsandra, Scott was most emphatically looking again for new ways of expressing his music. "I gave a lot of direction to what the two of us did," Scott explained to Chris Short. "But he brought a wide palette of sounds, all these fabulous sounds that he has, and he knows exactly how to use them. He was able to give me something I couldn't have brought to the record."

Describing his association with Scott, Thighps noted that it had been set-up by Scott's manager Philip Tennant, explaining that, "Mike was a Cope fan and had enjoyed my synthesiser and Mellotron work with Julian. It was a great experience, [Mike] is a perfectionist and we share a similar sense of humour and interest in German history."[57] Thighps was not only in-tune musically with the darkly contemporary and industrial electronic noise that Scott had been absorbing in his reconnection with the mainstream but also had the same worldview when it came to the manner in which society was developing at the end of the millennium. Interviewed by David Keenan about his membership of Coil for Keenan's book *England's Hidden Reverse* (SAF Publishing, 2003) he described how he found travelling in the UK a problem because of his need to avoid the "two centres of evil, London and Leeds."

57 Interviewed in connection with his album *I, Thighpaulsandra* www.callnetuk.com/home/compulsion/album1.htm

"I have very little respect for the conventions of society and tradition," he told Keenan, describing the "poisoned semen of consumerism" and talking of "the herd mentality of large parts of society and the bleak choices offered by governments and media." He might just as easily have been delineating the themes and concerns of Scott's latest opus.

Scott's return to London from the sanctity and peace of Findhorn had opened his eyes to the pressures and demands of modern city life. "It seemed like a madhouse," he explained. "A place full of chaos, full of distortion, where the gods are celebrity and advertising… I wanted to make a record that was a shorthand for my emotional response at finding myself back in London." To David Peschek he expanded on the gritty, angry, tone of the record: "The album is really my adventures in London, or modern culture, as opposed to the west of Ireland. I was on the island of Iona and someone said, 'When are you going back to the real world?' I said 'This is the real world.' The modern world is the world of illusion, of distortion." Scott took the conversation and wrapped it up into an infuriated exchange in the lyrics of the opening track 'Let It Happen'. "Like a soldier who can't find the front, I wandered through the weary land," he grimaces in the album's sleeve notes and, indeed, 'Let It Happen' has this very texture. It has Scott, hands buried deep in greatcoat pockets, slight figure hunched inside for warmth, wandering the 'lights of London', despairing in the dumb, mindless depths that the city had sunk into. But it also reflected some of the positive attributes that he'd brought back to London from Findhorn, as he noted to Dee McLaughlin: "Whatever needs to happen, then let it happen is an affirmation I learned when I lived in the Findhorn community… whether it is something comfortable or not."

"This is the sound of Scott emerging from hibernation, casting his eye across Britain on the cusp of a new century and venting his sorrow and spleen," commented Peschek, "excessive, ludicrous—no make that brazen, unapologetic." As to the band who, on 'Let It Happen' were described as playing 'endless, mindless'? "The band playing the hooligan's lament in 'Let it Happen' was Oasis," Scott told Geoff Olson.

'Let It Happen' sets the pitch and the metre of the album, from its exaggerated wailing synthesisers, almost Space Rock in their weird predominance, to its overarching electric guitars and its grim tone wrapped around Scott's own proud determination. 'I'm still here, I'm still breathing,' he notes at one point in the song, whilst on 'Crown' he talks about having and losing money, the close relationship between euphoric success and the 'hard lessons' that come with it. In the title song, itself a marriage of slow-beat electric guitars and the gospel music that Scott had loved for many years there is an overwhelming sense of depression and lack of motivation—the 'power' that he'd often used as a metaphor for his own creative abilities taken away. "I wanted to catch [the] grotesqueness of late 20th century British culture and life," he told Short. "The boorishness of so much of it. I wanted to get that in the sound of the record, not just in the context of the songs. Hence the distortion and the darkness."

This feeling of despondency rarely lifts throughout the record. 'Is She Conscious?' is a recall of the fateful night of 31st August 1997 and the death of the Princess of Wales in a Paris car crash. Never specifically referring to her in person ("I don't even want to say her name") but comparing her with the fabled beauty of the Queen of Sheba (who "could have shined her shoes" the lyrics claim) it's still an uneasy piece of work. It has some rather unpleasant undertones, notably towards the unnamed Princess's ex-husband who is described as being as ugly as she was beautiful. Despite being a full-band affair it's totally centred around Scott's doom-laden piano, practically a funeral-march in miniature, that plays on the initial reports of the accident when it was for a time believed that the Princess had not been fatally injured but may have had escaped without major harm.

'Dumbing Down the World' is Scott, as noted, raging at the mediocrity that surrounded him, despairing of the myriad ways in which the culture of life had become less intelligent, less sincere, more downmarket and lowest dominator. He described it as being "in honour of them that would reverse our evolution and dumb us all down," and claimed that he'd "turned the drums backward on this song" with the intention of making it sound like it was "recorded in hell." For 'His Word is not his Bond' he used a sample taken from a recording of a gospel ('The Liar'[58]) by Isaiah Shelton noting that he "liked the way it sets up my song on the same subject."

But there are some positive outlooks through the record and so to portray it exclusively as a morose 'State of the Nation' study for the new millennium doesn't precisely nail the character of the album. 'Crown', whilst it might aurally represent some of the record's more plodding moments, does have some optimism that life's education can lead to greater and better things, even if—as with his previous lifting of the C.S. Lewis *Last Battle* next-world idealism—it might be found beyond Earthly horizons. "It's another idea from gospel music" he claimed, "that the Earth isn't our true home, when we die we cross over to God's country... when we get there, we will wear a crown. That speaks to me." And 'We are Jonah' is a radio-friendly, up-tempo slice of psychedelic whimsy with its quite bizarre meeting between film star Montgomery Clift, Jonah and the Whale and the song's narrator. But across the album is a windswept darkness and despair, not an internal angst that his listeners might have come to expect, but an external grimness. That almost certainly derived from, or at least was informed by, the contrast of the tranquillity of Findhorn (one of the charges levelled against the Foundation by its critics is its apparent rejection of the concept of evil) and the overbearing greyness and futility of city living.

David Peschek, reviewing the album sympathetically for *Mojo*, noted the long path that had led Mike Scott to *A Rock in the Weary Land*, from "patchily convincing raggle-taggle folk rock" through to "the sparse Dylanisms of his unfairly over looked solo work." In fact, it might be tempting to see the album in the context of a post-Waterboys Mike Scott trilogy. In this respect then there would be the intimate and personal *Bring 'Em All In* being the work of an artist in emotional and geographical retreat. The vibrant upbeat pop of *Still Burning* would be an enthusiastic revisiting of cherished musical landscapes and *A Rock in the Weary Land* the downbeat coda to this revisiting of the modern world. But Scott chose to release the album as a Waterboys record,

58   Available on a compilation of preaching and congregational singing released by Document Records in 2005 featuring Revs E D Campbell, Isaiah Shelton and C F Thornton.

entering the new century with the name that he'd buried almost a decade previously.

"These are songs that are defiantly the product of a real live pumping heart," enthused Peter Kane despite describing 'Crown' and 'We are Jonah' as "pratfalls" and dredging up the by now hoary old cliché of Scott previously having "hung a sharp left and turned into a card-carrying folkie." Still, Kane, praising the "bold and blustery" nature of the album heard "epic intent that gamely goes its own way" and conceded "there are times when the vaulting ambition really does pay off." In that, Kane had nailed the aspect of *A Rock in the Weary Land* that made the critics, who'd largely cold-shouldered the introspective and confessional solo albums, sit up and take notice of the grand scheme of Scott's latest creation. Richard Skanse, in *Rolling Stone*, considered the work "big, bold, brash and beautiful." In the *NME* praise was made of "a welcome reminder of an almost forgotten talent," going some way to justifying the readopting of The Waterboys by-line as a profile raising tactic. However the review paints a picture of a patchy work that varies from songs that are described as "magnificent" and that "dwarf anything attempted by the class of 2000" to the "hollow bombast of 'We are Jonah' and the sludgy 'Dumbing Down the World.'"

Controversial, though, was the decision to place the album into the market place as being by "The Waterboys"; the first time the name had been fired in anger since the release of *Dream Harder.* "There is a commercial aspect to it," Scott noted to Peter Bate. "I re-adopted the name before I approached RCA. It's important to me not in terms of sales but that the maximum number of people hear it… important for me that The Waterboys are in contention." Or, asked at one point what the difference between Mike Scott and The Waterboys was, he simply answered that The Waterboys "has a three times bigger audience."

Nobody told Anto Thistlethwaite, drafted in to play on three tracks for the album, that this would be The Waterboys however. "I played on *A Rock in the Weary Land* in a very small way. [Mike] phoned me up and asked me to play on the recording but I thought it was a Mike Scott album. I didn't know it was The Waterboys, didn't know that was going on. If someone had said to me, 'Look, Anto…' but I played on the record thinking it was a Mike Scott record and then found out later it was to be released as The Waterboys..." He'd had similar feelings the last time that a Waterboys' album had emerged. "The *Dream Harder* album? I thought that was... my dad would have said, 'That's a poor do.' I thought it was a bit crap, going out as The Waterboys. If you're in pursuit of excellence then you should say, 'OK, it's finished,' and I think that's what Mike should have done because he's always strived for excellence. I think for him to suddenly decide, 'Oh, it's The Waterboys again,' and go out with a bunch of people that are nothing to do with The Waterboys is less than excellent. What we did in 1982 was excellent, and 1983 was excellent, 1985 excellent, what he did in 2001 wasn't excellent. He said to me at one point that, 'I should have called the *Dream Harder* record a solo release, I was wrong'—so if he was right to say that... You can see that it's a way of saying 'It's my name, I'll use it, I'll do whatever I want.' But I don't think it's great."

"The most band-like albums we ever made were *Fisherman's Blues* and *Room to Roam*," would be Scott's counter-argument, in *Rolling Stone*. "With all the other albums, I was the guy with the record deal and the guy driving it, however much it looked like a band." He'd announced the decision to the faithful late in March 2001 through an established Waterboys Internet forum, saying that the move was a result of wanting to work "on a larger scale." Although he explained that "being Mike Scott was a necessary phase for me," noting particularly the benefits he felt had derived from having a more intimate relationship with his audiences, it was time for him to "once again be the leader of the world's great Aquarian band." He went on to describe the sound of *A Rock in the Weary Land* as being "electric guitar/keyboards sonic rock, noting that he saw no place in the touring band that he was attempting to assemble in time for that year's Glastonbury Festival for Steve Wickham or Anto Thistlethwaite. "This isn't fiddle/sax/mandolin music," he said whilst promising that "both will be back... when the music swings around in their direction again."

That Scott was using the Internet, particularly the Delphi forums, to communicate directly with his fan base was a development that, in and of itself, was part of the mystique and intrigue with which he liked to tantalise his followers. Similar, of course, in its own way to his cryptic commentary at Milton Keynes which could not have done anything other than provoke speculation and conclusions jumping amongst the audience. Like many bands, the second half of the 1990s had seen a major crossover onto electronic communication and away from the printed fanzine as a method for dispersal of news and views amongst their fans. In particular, Nicole Moreau, described by current official Waterboys webmaster Michael Mönsters, as "the mother of all Waterboys-internet fans," and who claims that "most things in The Waterboys-internet-universe wouldn't have happened without Nicole," started a site called *In A Pagan Place*.

"Affiliated with that site I ran a mailing list," recalled Nicole on The Waterboys Yahoo discussion list. "At the time there was no Waterboys' sites and there was no e-mail lists. My unwritten rules for the mailing list was to be nice, and keep personal information on the band outside of it. One day Mike and his tour manager found my site and began e-mailing me bits of information. Mike once signed my guestbook thanking me for the site and was kind. Eventually Mike and his manager parted ways and I stopped receiving communications from them. Life changes, I moved on and eventually let the site go by the wayside. Years later I had the wonderful opportunity of actually meeting Mike Scott. I mentioned to him that he had once e-mailed me and I really appreciated it, I reminded him of the name of the site, and he remembered it and me."

On-line Waterboys fandom grew organically with the development and increase in easy access of the Internet. The Delphi forum was joined by what eventually became the Yahoo *Waterpeople* list, a wide-ranging discussion group, which itself was later joined by Phil Ord's more arts-and-philosophy focused *Waterboys* mailing list. Michael Mönsters organised a distribution network for non-profit trading of Scott's music, now retired, and Sean Miller started a long-running Waterboys website *Waterboysfans*. Along with Tim Rafferty, Miller generated some official interest in this activity by handing Mike Scott a collection of printouts from the Internet at the Milton Keynes gig, and this precipitated Scott's own involvement with this electronic community.

He made his first appearance on the Delphi forum over the millennium New Year, posting under the name of 'Wingfeet', though signing
off with his own[59]. This was in response to some comments made over
the ownership of the piano parts on 'The Pan Within' and their having
been attributed to Karl Wallinger during an on-line discussion. He
noted that as he was browsing the forum "for one time only I wish to
set things straight." Listing many of Wallinger's outstanding contributions to The Waterboys, Scott none-the-less was determined to claim
this particular playing as being his own. "It is annoying when people
think someone else did something I did," he firmly stated. Though at
the time he announced that this would be his one and only posting
to the forum he was soon back again to confirm the completion of
A Rock in the Weary Land and continued posting intermittently for
some time, also adopting the identity of 'Tresmegistus'.

Most of his Internet postings were corrections of perceptions of specific songs or contributions, but he also acknowledged that interaction
with his Internet followers made one significant contribution to his creative thinking. An overwhelmingly positive response from the forum for
the song 'The Wind in the Wires', which was amongst the new songs pre-
miered at Milton Keynes made him re-evaluate a piece that by his own
admission he hadn't considered to be particularly promising. "I got myself
into the studio fast and recorded it," he explained to Dee McLaughlin.

The new-found fascination with contemporary rock music was, however, to be as short-lived as his enthusiasm for participating directly
with his fan-base on the Internet. Once he'd written of how at the
point when his music had become "loudest" he'd "left it behind." It was
to prove the same with his foray into experiment and electronics.

He'd been playing these new songs during the later part of the
1990s and took them on the road with a full Waterboys band with
Richard Naiff becoming a permanent member (though he continued
to work with Ian McNabb and with former Stranglers front man Paul
Roberts in different projects). He recalled Jeremy Stacey to drum-

---

59 The veracity of the posting was questioned for some time, with the positive identification of 'Wingfeet' as Mike
Scott being made by his manager, Philip Tennant. Scott actually seemed to relish the sowing of doubt as to
whether the postings were indeed made by him, telling *Virginmega.com* that "I went on as an invented character for
a few weeks. I left them some clues and eventually they figured it out, but that was a lot of fun."

ming duties and brought with him studio session-player Livingstone Brown on bass. Adam Sweeting, viewing the band at the Cambridge Corn Exchange (17th October 2000) for *The Guardian* saw Mike Scott "less like the Celtic minstrel of yore and more like a man ready to fill arenas and kick some ass."

Sweeting heard 'A Rock in the Weary Land' as a "heavy metal avalanche... swaggering like a squadron of tanks," and thought 'Let It Happen' was "a dramatic maelstrom of swirling keyboards and pile-driver percussion." Ian Gittins, attendant at the Munchen Brewery in Stockholm (4th December) for *Q* magazine found Scott "focused, driven, a captivating figure [spilling] out accusatory fables of modern waste and decay... Mike Scott's campaign is intensely personal." And David Peschek, at the band's Irish homecoming at the Olympia in Dublin (13th December) noted how the session players—"who aren't, however good they are, The Waterboys"—had "gelled significantly since the autumn shows" and saw Scott as "the anti-Thom Yorke: unafraid of grand gestures." Scott himself seemed pumped up, ready to take on the decadence and coarseness he saw everywhere in London and almost ready to revisit those old challenges of making The Waterboys a big band in all senses. "It's fantastic to be playing every night and feel the music following through me" he told the *Daily Telegraph*. "All I can do is keep making records as great as I can under my rightful name and then proving myself on stage."

At Dublin, though, the whole thing started to turn again—not on a six-pence in the way that the Big Music had given way to the Raggle-Taggle adventure but perhaps for some of the same reasons. Scott's liaison with Steve Wickham down in Sligo at the start of the year had caused all sorts of press speculation that a *Fisherman's Blues* reunion was on the cards. It wasn't, but Wickham's joining of the band in Dublin to play that album's title song and what Peschek called a "pulverising" 'Be My Enemy' set up that old triangle, the past love meeting up with the new. That would start a gradual but audible move away from the electronic hurricane where Steve would be out of place, to a gentler reinterpretation of the material, with Mike Scott again looking back at his own history and pulling out songs that would once more suit the "fellow that fiddles."

Wickham wouldn't rejoin immediately—though the following night his appearance was not just for a couple of numbers at the end of the set but a more expansive role contributing to 'Sweet Thing', 'Savage Earth Heart', 'The Pan Within' and 'This is the Sea' amongst others. He also arrived at Ulster Hall, Belfast on 14th December to play 'Happy Birthday' to Mike Scott during the first encore and to stay-on through to the end of the show's second bow.

Scott would actually carry-on through the early part of 2001 with a similar set and approach to the previous year, though with another session band, which included his old friend Ian McNabb and the second Watergirl to tread the boards with him, bass player Jo Wadeson. But by the time The Waterboys were ready to make their return to the USA in March and April 2001 they'd re-acquired not only the services of drummer Jay Dee Dougherty on a temporary basis, but those of Steve Wickham on a permanent one. With the then up-and-coming Black Rebel Motorcycle Club opening for them, Scott was reportedly in ebullient mood but the set-lists show him gradually easing-out the material from the new album and working back in Windmill Lane songs. More of a pointer to where he was going next could be found back in England, at The 'F' Word, Maidstone (13th April 2001) and the following day at the Gosforth and Fareham Festival. There, The Waterboys would be Scott, Wickham and Naiff, establishing the core 'Trio' that would be the foundation upon which all future incarnations of the band have been built to date.

The Waterboys would remain a shifting ensemble through the next year or so, by the autumn dates in 2001, Dougherty was again enlisted and Jo Wadeson continued on bass. But the overall feel of the band was becoming increasingly focused on the great musicianship of the key trio and the way that they grew in confidence together. It wasn't the return to the raggle-taggle Irish way of playing, it was something new again—a quiet, increasingly spiritual, sense of ease that was working through the music and wiping away the dour depression of *A Rock in the Weary Land*. In a sense, it was almost a bottling of that sense of calm and of the right path well trodden that Findhorn had brought into Scott's life and it turned the music around again.

11

THIS LIGHT IS FOR THE WORLD

If *Bring 'Em All In* was Mike Scott's most intensely personal recording then *Universal Hall*, the second album by the 'reformed' Waterboys, should be considered as his most spiritually intimate moments. Once again a sense of place had informed his outlook and buried its atmosphere deep into the fabric of his writing and composing. There'd been another sharp turn on Scott's journey taken, but this time (and now only time can tell) perhaps brought his travels full circle and rounded out his philosophical and emotional quests.

For a start, Mike and Janette had washed their hands of the London that he'd so sharply delineated in *A Rock in the Weary Land* and had made their way back to full time residency in Findhorn. And, in amongst his talk of reclaiming energy and power, itself a healing process based on a coming to terms with the past, he'd sought out and found his father. What he found was something that sharply contrasted with his own angst over his father's departure so many years previously—that his father hadn't followed the career ups and downs of his mercurial offspring, wasn't aware of Mike Scott's abilities and reputation, didn't know of his success. None of that particularly mattered. Scott Senior had of his own volition, and regardless of the stresses and strains of his relationships, taken himself out of the life of his wife and son. By seeking him out and confronting him in both a physical and an emotional sense, Scott was, in his own words, creating for himself a "choice in the matter." "I just had to turn up and be myself," he explained to Alastair McKay in *The Scotsman*. "I found out where he lived and went and visited him one Saturday afternoon. He was surprised, but I think he figured that this day would come. We've had a nice gentle relationship since, being in touch with each other. He came to see my show when I played near where he lived." In all of Scott's wanderings and seeking, twists and turns, this surely must have been the most complete circle that he'd managed to draw for himself. That the lyricist of 'Father' and 'Dark Man of my Dreams' could come away from the centre point of these shadowy and Cimmerian reflections and find something in the outcome that he could describe with a comfortable ease suggests one shoreline finally reached. Approached by *Uncut* magazine to contribute to a 2003 Springsteen 'covers' CD, Scott, curiously, chose 'Independence Day'[60], a world-weary monologue autobiographical in context. Springsteen's biographer Christopher Sandford described the song as "an Oedpial blast—all the better for being muttered—at [Springsteen's father] Doug." 'Independence Day' is rooted in Springsteen's long and bitter feud with his father and is introduced, as Phil Sutcliffe once put it, "with both of them too worn-out to row anymore, like a couple of characters in a Eugene O'Neil play... hurt, weary grace." In a poignant description that might well sum up what Scott might have seen in the song, Sutcliffe wrote that, "the real breakthrough into awareness... comes at the end when Springsteen sees that he and his father really are of one flesh, pieces of the same jigsaw, victims." Of Springsteen's original, Scott simply noted "It doesn't get any better than this."

And so, settled back into Findhorn's contemplative aura, he brought Steve Wickham and Richard Naiff to the tiny little studio at Universal Hall in early 2003 and began the process of assembling another predominately acoustic collection of songs. His stated intention at the

---

60 Originally written and recorded for *Darkness On The Edge Of Town* but eventually released on *The River*. The Waterboys' version of this song, recorded during the making of *Universal Hall*, appeared on the second volume of *Born To Run 2003*, cover-mounted with *Uncut*. It's a blowsy, overblown rendition that really doesn't add anything to the original. The Waterboys also included 'Independence Day' in their live set during 2006.

start of 2003 was to produce something "bright, light-filled, sparse, airy and beautiful." Songs that would exhibit a state of mind that was now emotionally centred, mellow and reflective and which would rejoice in the healing and wholeness that he'd found within himself. Perhaps at last reaching that point that Wickham had identified as so necessary way back at the end of their original adventure together, that internal requirement to be "emotionally well fed." He'd taken to attending the 6.30am meditative hour at Findhorn, silent and cleansing time that inspired him to produce new songs of spiritual sanctuary and comradeship. "'This Light is for the World', 'Silent Fellowship', 'Ain't No Words for the Way I'm Feeling' and 'Every Breath' came out of those experiences," he revealed to Sally Peterson in an interview for *Caduceus*. His intention was to create "songs that articulate—to the best of my ability—the vision that drives, challenges, sustains and transforms me." Or, if we can echo the words of Eileen Caddy, songs that opened up and brought out of him "the small, still, voice within."

"I definitely think there's a place for spiritually-charged music today," Scott told *Chicago Innerview*, once again confirming that this had continually infused his music. "Not necessarily as up front as it is on [*Universal Hall*], but it's always been there. This is a particularly intimate record." To Sally Peterson he additionally noted how, "There is a strength in vulnerability itself. I've learned at Findhorn that the greatest protection in intimate circumstances is to show oneself and be vulnerable. It's only when one hides oneself that there's any need for protection."

Universal Hall wasn't going to prove to be a universally accepted and loved piece of work, and in any case the range of material presented under The Waterboys banner was by now such a diverse canon that producing an album that would appeal to all wings couldn't be achieved. And, of course, Scott has never been in the business of satisfying his listeners instead of taking his next creative step. "I play what I want, and happily that often coincides with what the fans want to hear," he said. "But if it doesn't, that's tough luck."

In this instance he would release a collection that was by turns immediate and accessible and then dense and impenetrable. The same person that might have enthused about the upbeat tempo of 'Always Dancing, Never Getting Tired' and the strident optimism of 'This Light is for the World' could have found themselves lost in the mantra of 'EBOL', the Zen-like repetitive enunciation of the meditative still-point. The minimalist structure, simple phrases identified as being akin to the concept of Taize Chants, might have worked in the quiet reflection of Universal Hall itself, but released out into the wider domain the freedom from lyrical complexity wouldn't necessarily translate. "I'm trying to get under the defences of the intellect with some of these songs," he explained to Sally Peterson. "I'm using one or two lines repeated over and over, like an affirmation or a mantra. This repetition means that the listener has to suspend the intellectual faculties if they are going to stay with the song." And to Steve Stockman[61] he commented that "Taize chants are very popular in Findhorn so I'm used to the idea that a few short lines of words, carefully chosen and repeated aloud or inwardly, can have a powerful inspirational effect." He saw this development in his writings as being an organic process that, once started upon, needed to be followed to its conclusion. "When my songs started coming in this minimal form, with only 2 or 3 lines, the challenge was to allow them to be so, and not to be tempted to flesh them out into a 'normal' structure. I resisted the temptation!"

There is, of course, a danger in taking the sentiments of Scott's work in too literal a sense, and that is true even of the minimalist chanting of *Universal Hall*. Of his meditative musings in 'The Christ in You', he revealed that any reading of this lyric in a Christian sense would be flawed. "I don't think Christians have a monopoly on the word 'Christ'. A lot of different traditions use it," he commented. "In my understanding, and I'm still learning, it's the living presence of God."

What he'd actually created was essentially something that taken away from its New Age roots and discussed in a rock music context would have been derided as a that anathema of music journalists, the 'concept album'. *Universal Hall* is as rooted to its sense of place as that other perplexing juxtaposition of place and tradition, *Room to Roam*. It's a

61   *Rhythms of Redemption.*

survey of Findhorn as much as it is a summation of personal wellbeing and peace. So 'This Light is for the World' champions the ideals and values that Scott had embraced on his first visit a decade before. 'Silent Fellowship' is another mantra of meditation directly related to his experiences and way of life, held-up by the musicianship of his colleagues. "I don't have to live like Mike or be part of the Findhorn Foundation, but I definitely think I have to understand my friend," Wickham told Peter Murphy during Murphy's own visit to Findhorn. "I have to understand where he's at. And I do. To a certain extent."

"I generally make 'em wherever I find myself but on occasion I have made a decision in advance to write and record in the West of Ireland, or to record *Universal Hall* in Findhorn," Scott told Steve Stockman. "I am always inspired by the places I live and by what I feel and see around me. This inevitably flows into the music and the albums." This inspiration that he found in his surroundings lead him back as well to his grandmother who hailed from the island of Mull and who he'd brought into mind when he wrote about Mull's neighbour, the island of Iona, in 'Peace of Iona'. The song has an easy and repetitive phrasing that makes it akin to a Celtic Blessing. Back again to the sleeve-notes for the remastered *This is the Sea* and here was a composition that, despite Wickham's eerie, melancholic fiddle winding its way through and describing solitude and thoughtful isolation, was focused around Scott's intoning voice. "I was familiar with the idea that Iona is Scotland's sacred island—a special place set apart," he told Steve Stockman. "When I eventually visited it I found the spiritual peace and presence there and loved it." Thousands of others have made the same pilgrimage to Iona[62]. Saint Columba founded a Celtic monastery there in 563, a Benedictine abbey existed there in the Middle Ages and today the Iona Community promotes its message of "justice peace and the integrity of creation." As in 'Wonders of Lewis', Scott had found something within his Celtic heritage that promoted a sense of oneness and well being. "I think about giving my music a sense of healing and peace," he said. "What I always want to hear in music, and hear so rarely, is a sense of the spiritual. Peter Gabriel had it... and Kate Bush."

---

62 The Labour Party leader John Smith was, with special dispensation, buried on Iona after his untimely death in 1994—the island is also the final resting place of several Scottish Kings.

He'd also captured this out on the West Coast of Ireland, a feeling of identity and belonging that he described in 'I've Lived Here Before', and which Liam Ó Maonlaí of the Hothouse Flowers had set to music. "It's a song with a lyric written when I first visited the Aran Islands, three storm-lashed rocks off the coast of County Galway," he'd relate to his audiences. "The first time I went there the place was familiar to me in ways that I couldn't explain or understand." But even though this collection of songs (not all new, 'Peace of Iona' and 'I've Lived Here Before' both originated in the early 1990s) were largely concerned with place—whether geographic or spiritual—the title track was a litany, a summing up of passions and loves. MacDonald, Lewis, and particularly Helprin and his *Winter's Tale* appeared again in Scott's writings, this time also talking of sacrificing of power to achieve renewal rather than reclaiming power from those who'd crossed him or held him back.

Infuriating some of his long-time followers, who yearned for the angry young man of the Big Music, he'd reached a mellow feeling, perhaps artistically complacent and satisfied, from which he'd write that 'All is very, very well.' It was the sort of accomplishment that played better out in the wide world, amongst the critics and reviewers than perhaps it did with Scott's devotees. "*Universal Hall* rewards repeated inspection," considered Paul McNamee in the *NME*. "A minor classic built around little more than pianos and fiddles and his own rasping, raking voice. On every Waterboys album there is one truly great song. Here it's the title track, about brave leaps into the unknown. You should follow." David Peschek, in *The Guardian*, wrote of "an impressively brave collection of songs from one of music's last true mavericks" and heard "immensely moving… simplicity."

"It can be difficult to communicate knowledge of a higher order without coming across as a hamfisted tubthumper or some kind of hippie," Peschek added. "There was always an otherness, a wild magic, in Mike Scott's dream of the Big Music, and here it finds its simplest and most explicit expression." Another critic heard Scott sliding "gracefully into middle age" and making "his most straight-forward, direct album."

12

THAT WAS THE RIVER

There are times were you could be forgiven for wanting an artist to walk away from a body of work saying, "Here, take this, this is complete and done. It tells you all you need to know and it delivers all I have to say." Of course, this rarely happens in any walk of life. Politicians wait for that moment when every career has to end in failure. Sportsmen reach for that final season, that last glorious hurrah that will inevitably be not a golden lap of honour but a pale reflection of former glories. And for musicians, songwriters, there's always that next contracted album or that comeback tour that diminishes rather than enhances. No one ends on the high point, nobody sees that the work is done.

I'm not trying to suggest or imply that Mike Scott has completed his work or his journey taken its final twist or turn, though the strength of *Universal Hall* was in its sense of completion and resolution. And though a second retirement of The Waterboys' name appears to be on his radar, it doesn't seem to be imminent. "I'd say The Waterboys have got another six or seven years," he told the *Galway Advertiser* back in 2004. "I really respect the way Bob Dylan, Van Morrison, and Neil Young grow old gracefully. They are the three shining examples of not trying to be younger than they are… happy to be curmudgeons inhabiting their music. I would hope we would be like that."

There's always been the touch for the curmudgeon ingrained in Mike Scott, of course. The sense that I get of him, not only through talking to his admirers and his detractors but from Scott himself over the years in his published or recorded interviews, is that he is a somewhat difficult and single-minded individual. That hasn't totally gone away as he's grown older and wiser. There is still the element of the control-freak at concerts, demanding quiet and quite happy to berate his audience at times if they don't behave in the way that best suits the way in which he wants to perform. At a show in Rotterdam in October 2004, by eyewitness accounts a good performance being well received, The Waterboys made a silent retreat from the stage only five numbers into their second set, with another four songs left on the set list, not to return. One Internet poster recalled some "not so friendly banter between Mike and a Scottish member of the audience right at the start," and some "inappropriate shouts and singing during songs." On other occasions though, Scott might gently chide the attendees for being "a quiet audience." His patronage of up-and-coming musicians is well-documented and impressive. But again in 2004 there was a flip side to the coin, one performer at a festival in Florence recalling being "really disappointed in seeing Mike preventing the other bands playing on the same stage as him. Forcing the other bands to play acoustic because after his soundcheck no one [could] use the stage." Matthew Magee, who has interviewed Scott on several occasions, described him in an article for the *Sunday Business Post* in February 2006 as a "tense, brittle man who comes out fighting every criticism, slight or critical injustice" but now finds him "calmer, gentler, softer than in years past."

Though he has confounded his critics and astonished his followers on a regular basis, he seems, at the time of writing, to have settled into a creative lull. Post *Universal Hall*, his modest amount of new work has not specifically been of the same-ilk, but it hasn't indicated any major change of tack either. 'Strange Arrangement', a haunting and pensive song of mistakes made and the wrong path trod—perhaps a confessional monologue from man to maker ('the invisible captain' who 'must be laughing out loud'). 'Crash Of Angel Wings', a vaguely Bowie-tinged, slightly 70s, eastern flavoured romantic mystique. The self-deprecating but under-worked 'Dunderheid' (a Scottish slang expression for a 'person of unsound mind') which Scott, at a Dublin show, introduced as dedicated to the sports journalist Eamon Dunphy, entertainer Graham Norton, and himself. At the time of writing, 'Crash of Angel Wings' was listed as intended for the next Waterboys album, which the band commenced work on in September 2006.

If he walked away right now he would leave for examination and comprehension one of the most fascinating and articulate studies of artistic and emotional development ever created in the rock music world. Findhorn gave it meaning and definition; *Universal Hall* completed the circle. "I look at my life and I see that there are different keynotes at different times," he explained to Sally Peterson. "There are different values that I'm working with, or different mountains that I'm climbing." Fran Breen noted to me how he saw it in very basic terms, not difficult to reconcile or understand. "Mike is a very spiritual person; he keeps in contact with his inner self, which is a good thing. I think that's his quest in life, to be totally 'One with Thee'. To me, it's very simple in itself. Sometimes we can try and package it and make it complicated and it's not—it's a really simple thing."

He's successfully stood outside of the music business, if success is measured not in commercial clichés of units sold or chart positions achieved but if it is taken in terms of the respect and affection bestowed by colleagues and peers. They're a tightly knit group, Scott's friends, and though starting on my project with a good heart and the right intentions I find them closing ranks and stonewalling. But it's a great pleasure to find that the ones who do want to talk do so with respect and warmth, even if sometimes it is mixed with a little bit of frustration and exasperation. Partly it seems to be a genuine admiration of talent and ability and sometimes it seems to have something of the wait for the clarion call to arms in it—the time when Scott's inspiration will once again require the saxophone, or maybe the tin whistle, perhaps the accordion. "Come on down and be a Waterboy again."

Part of it is Scott's particular way of pulling together component parts, mixing and matching until he's found something that seems to him to be *right*. Early in his career he explained it as being not about ambition, but about "hearing two sounds and putting them together to make something new."

"He has an idea of what he wants and if it goes beyond that, then that's the icing on the cake," suggests Fran Breen. "But at the same time he might tell you that he wants this and this and this, but he's waiting for the spark more than anything else. There's no point in having all the parts if you haven't got the spark."

"I got a chance to play with Mike and Steve and Richard recently, they played on the island [where I live], doing a benefit for the Hall which I thought was very good of them," says Colin Blakey. "They played 'A Man is in Love' and 'Room to Roam' and it was lovely. We played about five numbers together and it was great fun, really good craic. Mike was trying to persuade me to come down and do a couple of gigs later on in Edinburgh and Dundee but there were other things I was trying to do myself and it wasn't possible—but, you never know what the future holds. Once a Waterboy, always a Waterboy! It was a very big thing and I'm very proud that made I made my contribution, the bits I got to do. Like, Mike would say, 'Here's a song, would you arrange it' and so I got to arrange 'A Man Is In Love', a chance to tell people what to do, fantastic. I learnt so much by getting to do stuff like that." Blakey has taken that education and produced his own infusion of traditional Celtic music in his band Orchestra Macaroon, mixing piano, double bass horns and bagpipes to produce an internationally flavoured instrumental sound. "It's a vehicle for the presentation of my compositions, based around a five-piece band, four of whom, including my partner Phil [We Free Kings' Philippa Bull] are on the island where I live. I write from the basis of a traditional groove, or a groove that I've heard on the radio, or from Brazil or West Africa. I'll come up with a bass line which emerges as counterpoint to the groove, and on the basis of that I might find a chord sequence. And at the very end, the icing on the cake, the decoration, is the melody, the tune. And because I'm ok at writing melody I can make it sound like the tune came first and the whole thing fits together in an organic kind of way that surprises people. It puts a smile on people's faces." Orchestra Macaroon released their debut CD *Breakfast in Balquhidder* in 2004, a light-hearted, up-tempo recording which bears the legend, "Warning: This product may contain traces of bagpipes." The ever-reliable Steve Wickham was called upon to provide his violin, continuing the camaraderie that has always seemed a part of his own association with the ever-changing Waterboys ensemble.

Maintaining her place in Waterboys lore, Sharon Shannon made a guest appearance with Scott and Wickham in November 2004, at shows in Ennis, Athlone and Waterford, temporarily replacing Richard Naiff, who was unavailable through illness, and bringing The Waterboys back around to the reels and jigs of the late 80s. Dusted down and brought into the set were 'The Windy Windy Road' (a *Room to Roam* out-take), 'The Raggle-Taggle Gypsies'—and 'Song For The Life', which made the selection for Scott's appraisal of the contemporary 'live' Waterboys *Karma To Burn*.[63]

Now playing together again, this time as the rhythm section of the Saw Doctors, Anto Thistlethwaite and Fran Breen joined the current Waterboys for a Saw Doctors/Waterboys double-header in Galway on 7th May 2005. Some attendees were disappointed to see Anto in the background on bass rather than up-front with his saxophone and speculated that perhaps here was a relationship that had become strained over the years, with some good cause. Although Anto himself would confess to finding Scott's expectations for the show perhaps a little high for what was essentially an ad-hoc outing, there was also an overriding sense of wanting the show to be *exceptional*. "For me it was very important and very special, I wanted to do a good job and get it right—I hadn't played 'Pan Within' for fifteen years or something so I was concentrating very hard." And it was special, too, for Fran Breen: "It was great to see Mike again—he wore us all out during sound check! We were doing one number and Steve went into 'The Whole of the Moon' on the fiddle... 'Not today!' [Mimes Mike Scott

63   Released on Puck Records in 2005, *Karma To Burn* was culled from various live performances in 2003/4 including the acoustic Scott/Wickham/Naiff line-up and the glued-on electric band featuring Carlos Hercules and Steve Walters.

shaking his head]." The show ended with an almighty jam session, a
flashback to the unruly, anarchic days of Scott's Irish adventure, a fif-
teen-minute rendition of 'On My Way To Heaven' and a ten-minute
version of 'And A Bang On The Ear'. Joining in were Leo Moran, early
Saw Doctors bass player John 'Turps' Burke, and Sharon Shannon
who'd been playing in Sligo earlier in the evening and had come along
for the finale. "To me, he's always looking," ponders Fran Breen. "On
reflection, thinking back to the Galway gig, he's still doing it. But he's
also looking back on some of his stuff; with the volume of work he's
done over the years there must be some little gems that he's overlooked
the first time, so he's going back as well."

It is not every Waterboys fan's cup of tea, this sense that "all is very,
very well," and this stage that Scott has reached. Amongst his followers there is a natural hankering for the Big Music of the early band or
the expansive exploration of country, rock, folk and traditional sounds
that characterises *Fisherman's Blues*. The acoustic strings and piano
approach that swept away the sonic rock of *A Rock in the Weary Land*
before that particular era had become fully formed has now been the
focal point of The Waterboys for half a decade. And, at the time of
writing, it shows absolutely no sign of giving way to any new style or
change of direction.

   To a large extent that takes us back to the idea that no matter how
focused and single-minded a band leader is, there needs to be the
interaction with the other musicians to bring out the tone of the band
at any one time. Here it seems to have successfully become a three-way
thing, with Richard Naiff's classical training and Wickham's mercurial wizardry (now he's sprightly and inspirational, next he's become
melancholy and mournful) underpinning Scott's ethereal lyrics. They
can achieve a lot, these three together, and to add that additional electric energy there's a space, a freedom, in the songs that means that
every so often they can mix things up by bringing in rhythm section
and playing a full band set. That's become the modus operandi over
the past few years. They don't play extensive tours, probably in defer-
ence to Wickham's preference to not be away from home for more
than a month at a time, but they do look for the unusual setting or

opportunities to bring their music to environments that complement what and how they play.

Findhorn's Universal Hall is one such place, visited now it seems on an annual basis. This is not always as the acoustic trio, the participation of the band members is varied and fluid. Scott and Richard Naiff, for instance, performed as a duo there in March 2005 at the 'Universal Voices' conference, a festival dedicated to 'the spirit of creativity and joy.' Introducing the performance, Findhorn's Peter Vallance talked about Scott as being "very much a contemporary bard, following on in that ancient tradition." Then there was a two-night residency in the superb acoustics of London's Bloomsbury Theatre during April 2004. Here, reviewing the show for *The Independent*, Gavin Martin described Scott as "idiosyncratic… but a fearless adventurer capable of catching the big one." Referencing a moment when Scott chose to read from a book of 12th Century Persian poetry, Martin was captivated with his power to create a show of quiet introspection peppered with rock music sensibility and still not lose sight of the traditional muse that he'd followed for so long. "Scott's love of esoteric mysticism isn't a problem—where else will you find a rock star who can combine a Madame Blavatsky séance with Patti Smith-style pagan polemic and still have time for a jig and a reel before reaching the finishing-post?" Few others could achieve that peculiar blend of quirky, unexpected performance art, a reverence for the past and a commercial accessibility.

Mike Scott has had a lot of chances to become a really big star and one way or another passed them all over. During his Big Music days he watched similar bands reach much greater heights than The Waterboys ever did. As Peter Paphides noted in *Word* (reviewing the 2004 release of the remastered *This is the Sea*), if you'd surveyed the field of runners and contenders in the mid-80s, "you'd have been hard pressed to predict an eventual winner out of Bono, Ian McCulloch and Mike Scott. Pondering Bono's gaucheness and Mac's arrogance, you could have done a lot worse than plump for Scott." Simple Minds, another Celtic rock group with measurably less ingenuity and spark, reached stadium rock status and, of course, there is the stratospheric success of U2, the biggest band on the planet. In the days of Scott's quirky Irish adventure, with a major record company behind him and giving him his head, he had an opportunity to explore and develop unhindered by deadlines and product demands. Through his time in New York the music press feted him; he was much sought after by labels and held-up by Geffen Records as a star of international standing. For this he reluctantly embraced some of the requirements of rock stardom (promotional videos, *Top of the Pops*) but then determined that a live band couldn't be put together and retreated into relative obscurity as a solo artist and Findhorn resident.

"I wanted to do music that turned me on," he explained simply.[64] "I think I can compete with anyone in my generation, but I don't feel the need to commercially." Perhaps that stemmed out of the feelings he got from the initial burst of success in the early 1980s that led him to feel awkward with the concept of celebrity. "At the time a lot of people were predicting 'we're going to do this' and 'we're going to do this.' But predictions are hypotheses. I never listen to anyone who is trying to foretell the future."

Of course, it would have taken a fortune-teller of quite extraordinary ability to foresee Scott's journey. That's why the question is so pertinent right through the story of The Waterboys. "Where have you been, Mike Scott?" It's interesting to contrast some of the artists that Scott has been involved with, with the body of work that Scott himself has produced. His early support for the Saw Doctors and the way that the two bands have to a degree cross-pollinated is such a case in point. 'N17', their Scott-produced first single is totally wrapped up in the importance of their roots and the sense of home. Most of their best work since has also been firmly centred in community and family, very much like the strongest recordings of a musician that Scott and the Saw Doctors would look to as an inspiration, Bruce Springsteen.

Scott, on the other hand, has made his creative mark in writing and playing music that has a strong sense of geography and tradition within the fabric of its sound but lyrically looks within the songwriter rather than outwards at the world at large. So though he's used his words at times to comment on what he sees around him ('Let It Happen', 'Dumbing Down', 'Old England'), what he has really wanted to commu-

64 Patrick Corcoran, Chicago Innerview.

nicate is internal strength ('Sustain', 'This Light is for the World', 'Spirit'). He's looked out into the world and, in trying to see 'The Whole of the Moon', received glimpses of better ones. As Mark Helprin would have put it, 'I have been to another world, and I have come back.'

The great joy in following the meandering river of The Waterboys, tracing its source and tributaries, is in seeing the journey completed and understanding that someone can pull together the varied strands of life and find something through it that really *means* something. It doesn't have to be so tangible that, in and of itself, it is accessible and meaningful to the listener in the same way that it has been to the traveller himself. The enviable skill of Mike Scott though is that, outside of some of his excesses, he has the ability to draw in his listener and create a mood that explains at least a little of how something has affected or inspired him—'Silent Fellowship' is a fine example. In terms of that great dramatic plot line of hard times and good times, anger, loss and redemption, the story of The Waterboys really covers the whole range of emotions. And in the end it leaves its followers and listeners perhaps a little bemused but also perhaps enlightened, certainly inspired and enriched. That's not a bad path to have trodden really.

❧ ❧ ❧

Just before this book went to press, Mike Scott signed The Waterboys to a major label, W14/Universal Records, and announced the imminent release of his next studio album, *Book of Lightning*. Although at the time of writing it was still a couple of months away from its planned release date of 2nd April 2007, it was becoming clear that the tide had ebbed out on the bare acoustic style of *Universal Hall* and washed in again on full band electric rock.

The new album contains contributions from that old stager of Waterboys line-ups, Roddy Lorimer, and the musician whose electronic zeal stood *A Rock in the Weary Land* aside from the Waterboys and Mike Scott albums that surrounded it, Thighpaulsandra. And with other long-time Scott compatriots Chris Bruce and Jeremy Stacey joining new collaborators Brady Blade, Mark Smith and Leo Abrahams that sense of 'once a Waterboy, always a Waterboy' still rings true.

In support, the core trio of Scott, Wickham and Naiff revealed an extensive British and European tour through March, April and May, with a showcase, and status affirming, stopover at the Royal Albert Hall planned for 11th May 2007.

Book of Lightning doesn't have the musical revolution that *Fisherman's Blues* displayed after *This is the Sea*, or the experimentalism that characterised *A Rock in the Weary Land* in comparison to Scott's solo albums. Much of the material is already familiar, having been worked through in set-lists over recent years: 'Crash of Angel Wings', 'Strange Arrangement', 'Everybody Takes A Tumble'—and a version of 'Sustain' laid down in Vancouver by Scott and the Canadian group Great Aunt Ida. Additionally, having made its first, unexpected, appearance on the remastered *Fisherman's Blues*, 'You in the Sky' is now consolidated into the Waterboys canon by its second outing.

The newer material revisits much of Scott's traditional themes and metaphors and has a vaguely psychedelic sixties flavour, though not to the degree that the band's new logo and the visual packaging would suggest. The epic 'She Tried to Hold Me' takes in old relationships, their constraints and chains. 'It's Gonna Rain', like much of the lyrical work here, employs the favoured lexicography of heavy weather, storms on the horizon and overhead; and elsewhere he returns to the running journey of the river. So it's Scott's customary ground, delivered with his increasingly exaggerated and overblown diction, but it's also a positive statement that, after 2003's introverted and thoughtful *Universal Hall*, he's ready to take a profile-boosting step with accessible, mature, rock music.

Mike Scott has not exactly taken another of his sharp lefts or immediate right turns. *Book of Lightning* has change, but also continuity and development—though it's interesting to hear Wickham and Naiff becoming a little more marginal to some of the arrangements. But there is the sense, as suggested by Fran Breen after his appearance with the Waterboys a couple of years previously, that here is Scott looking backwards and forwards. His meandering journey has rounded another bend in the river, but the flow is strong and the Strange Boat is still running true.

THE WATERBOYS INTERNET LINKS

There is a wide range of Internet websites and discussion groups dedicated to the Waterboys and these are just a selection of the many places to visit. Unlike some on-line fandom, it's noticeable that Waterboys sites are a haven of tranquillity, reasoned debate and welcoming contributors so visit with confidence and good heart! With such a number of past and current members it has not been possible to compile a definitive guide but most of these sites have onward links to the wider Waterboys ranks.

Official Waterboys

Official Waterboys website (www.mikescottwaterboys.com). An impressive resource that not only has biographical data and the most up-to-date Waterboys news, but also contains a fine collection of touring history and other articles.

Official Waterboys Myspace page (www.myspace.com/mikescottwaterboys). Overseen by long-time Waterboys fan Paige O'Neill, this site also contains current news and is the home of Mike Scott's always intelligent and thought-provoking blog.

Discussion Groups and Forums

The members of Waterpeople (http://launch.groups.yahoo.com/group/waterpeople), a Yahoo discussion group for all things Waterboys related, are a friendly community that manage to avoid the flame wars and personal attacks that spoil or devalue so many mailing lists. Noticeably absent of postings for several months, but still noted because of its past collection of excellent musical and philosophical debates is Phil Ord's Yahoo list the Waterboys (http://launch.groups.

yahoo.com/group/theWaterboys/). I've also browsed the Waterboys
Delphi Forum (http://forums.delphiforums.com/waterboys), which
looks to be a fine source of Waterboys debate and interaction. Recently
resurrected and, as I understand it, looking for new contributors is
Sean Miller's unofficial Waterboys Fans website (www.waterboysfans.
com).

Current & Past Waterboys

Steve Wickham maintains a surprisingly diverse presence on the
Internet, from his Myspace page (www.myspace.com/stevewickham)
to an official website (www.stevewickham.ie) and pages for his Sligo
based No Crows band (www.nocrows.net and also with a Myspace
page www.myspace.com/nocrows).

Anthony Thistlethwaite and Fran Breen currently play with the Saw
Doctors (www.sawdoctors.com). Trevor Hutchinson is a long time
member of Lunasa (www.lunasa.ie). Both of these band's websites
include news, articles and galleries.

Roddy Lorimer (www.kickhorns.com). Biographical information,
photographs and details on how to acquire the services of the Kick
Horns for session work.

Colin Blakey (www.orchestramacaroon.com). Includes information
on purchasing Breakfast in Balquhidder, Orchestra Macaroon's highly
recommended infectious and quirky roots music fusion CD.

Karl Wallinger (www.worldparty.net). Extensive resource with news,
discussion forum and Karl's occasional blog.

Ian McNabb (www.ianmcnabb.com). The Gentleman Adventurer.

I also came across a small tribute site for Kevin Wilkinson complete with text and photographs (www.geocities.com/SunsetStrip/
Towers/3059/kevintribute.htm).

INDEX

saf publishing

www.safpublishing.co.uk
info@safpublishing.co.uk